HOLDING THE LINE

Compulsory arbitration
and national
employer co-ordination
in Australia

HOLDING THE LINE

Compulsory arbitration and national employer co-ordination in Australia

David H. Plowman

School of Industrial Relations and Organizational Behaviour
University of New South Wales

CAMBRIDGE UNIVERSITY PRESS
Cambridge
New York Port Chester Melbourne Sydney

CAMBRIDGE UNIVERSITY PRESS
Cambridge, New York, Melbourne, Madrid, Cape Town, Singapore,
São Paulo, Delhi, Dubai, Tokyo

Cambridge University Press
The Edinburgh Building, Cambridge CB2 8RU, UK

Published in the United States of America by Cambridge University Press, New York

www.cambridge.org
Information on this title: www.cambridge.org/9780521125963

First published 1989
This digitally printed version 2009

A catalogue record for this publication is available from the British Library

National Library of Australia Cataloguing in Publication data
Plowman, D.H. (David H.).
Holding the line, compulsory arbitration and national employer co-ordination in Australia
Bibliography
1. Australian Council of Employers' Federations — History. 2. Arbitration, Industrial — Australia — History. 3. Industrial relations — Australia — History. I. Title.
331.89′143′0994

Library of Congress Cataloguing in Publication data
Plowman, D. H.
Holding the line: compulsory arbitration and national employer co-ordination in Australia / David H. Plowman.
p. cm.
By-product of thesis (Ph. D.) — Flinders University of South Australia.
Bibliography: p.
1. Australian Council of Employers' Federation — History.
2. Arbitration, Industrial — Australia — History. 3. Industrial relations — Australia — History. I. Title.
HD5630.AGP56 1988
331.89'143'0994—dc 19

ISBN 978-0-521-36085-2 Hardback
ISBN 978-0-521-12596-3 Paperback

CONTENTS

TABLES AND FIGURES

TABLES

FIGURES

ABBREVIATIONS

ACAC	Australian Conciliation and Arbitration Commission
ACCA	Associated Chambers of Commerce of Australia
ACEF	Australian Council of Employers' Federations
ACM	Australian Chamber of Manufactures
ACMA	Associated Chambers of Manufactures of Australia
ACOLA	Automatic Cost of Living Adjustments
ACSPA	Australian Council of Salaried and Professional Associations
ACTU	Australian Council of Trade Unions
AMIA	Australian Metal Industries Association
AMMA	Australian Mines and Metals Association
AR (NSW)	Arbitration Reports (NSW Industrial Commission)
AWGC	Australian Woolgrowers' and Graziers' Council
BCA	Business Council of Australia
BWSC	Basic Wage Steering Committee
BWWP	Basic Wage Working Party
C and AA	*Conciliation and Arbitration Act*
CAGEO	Council of Australian Government Employee Organisations
CAI	Confederation of Australian Industry
CAR	*Commonwealth Arbitration Reports*
CCC	Consultative and Co-ordinating Committee
CCCA	Commonwealth Court of Conciliation and Arbitration
CCEA	Central Council of Employers of Australia
CEO	Central Employers' Organisation
CIS	Central Industrial Secretariat
CLR	*Commonwealth Law Reports*
CMNSW	Chamber of Manufactures of NSW
CSOA	Commonwealth Steamship Owners' Association
CWAI	Confederation of Western Australian Industry
DEIR	Department of Employment and Industrial Relations
DL and NS	Department of Labour and National Service
EATD	Engineering and Allied Trades Division (of the VCM)
EFNSW	Employers' Federation of NSW
ER	*Employers' Review* (Journal of EFNSW)
FCCM	Federation Council of the Chambers of Manufactures
FEAWA	Federated Employers' Assurance of Western Australia
GFCA	Graziers' Federal Council of Australia
ICE	Interstate Conference of Employers

List of abbreviations

IRC	Industrial Relations Council
MATFA	Meat and Allied Trades Federation of Australia
MLAC	Ministry of Labour Advisory Council
MTEA	Metal Trades Employers' Association
MTIA	Metal Trades Industry Association
NEA	National Employers' Associations
NEIC	National Employers' Industrial Committee (to 1977); National Employers' Industrial Council (after 1977)
NEPC	National Employers' Policy Committee
NETIC	National Employers' Trade and Industry Council
NFF	National Farmers' Federation
NLAC	National Labour Advisory Council
NTEF	National Territory Employers' Federation
NTIC	National Trade and Industry Council
NSW IG	*New South Wales Industrial Gazette*
PATEFA	Printing and Allied Trades Employers' Federation of Australia
P & CC	Policy and Consultative Committee
QCI	Queensland Confederation of Industry
QEF	Queensland Employers' Federation
SACM	South Australian Chamber of Manufactures
SAEF	South Australian Employers' Federation
TEF	Tasmanian Employers' Federation
TLC	Trades and Labour Council
VCM	Victorian Chamber of Manufactures
VEF	Victorian Employers' Federation
VEU	Victorian Employers' Union
WACM	Western Australian Chamber of Manufactures
WAEF	Western Australian Employers' Federation
WEB	Women's Employment Board

List of abbreviations

IRC	Industrial Relations Council
MATFA	[illegible] Federation of [illegible]
[illegible]	[illegible]
MTEA	Metal Trades Employers Association
MTIA	Metal Trades Industry Association
[illegible]	[illegible] Employers' Association
NTIC	National [illegible]
	[illegible]
NPPC	[illegible]
NELIC	National Employers' [illegible]
NFF	National Farmers' Federation
NLAC	National Labour Advisory Council
NTEF	[illegible] Employers' [illegible]
[illegible]	National Textile Industry Council
NSWCA	New South Wales [illegible]
PATEFA	Printing and Allied Trades Employers' [illegible]
PCC	[illegible] Consultative Committee
[illegible]	[illegible]
[illegible]	[illegible]
[illegible]	South Australian [illegible]
[illegible]	South Australian Employers' [illegible]
[illegible]	[illegible]
[illegible]	[illegible]
[illegible]	[illegible]
VEF	Victorian Employers' Federation
[illegible]	[illegible]
WAEF	[illegible]
[illegible]	[illegible]
[illegible]	[illegible]

ACKNOWLEDGEMENTS

This history of national employer association co-ordination is a by-product of my PhD thesis submitted to the Flinders University of South Australia. I thank the many people who helped me in the writing of that thesis. Professor K. Hancock, my supervisor, was generous in his time and efforts notwithstanding his onerous responsibilities as Vice-Chancellor of Flinders University. During the course of the study he headed the Committee of Review into Australian Industrial Relations Law and Systems. Even with this added responsibility, he still made time available to me and diligently attended to my needs. I thank him for his enthusiastic guidance and patience in what was a long joint venture. I am also indebted to the staff of a number of libraries, in particular those of the University of New South Wales, the Flinders University, the Mitchell Library, the Employers' Federation of New South Wales, the Confederation of Western Australian Industry and the Australian Chamber of Manufactures. A number of organisations made their records available to me. These included the Confederation of Australian Industry; the Employers' Federations of New South Wales, Victoria and South Australia; the Australian Chamber of Manufactures; the Confederation of Western Australian Industry and the Wool Selling Brokers Employers' Federation. A number of employer association officials and ex-officials who were key actors in national co-ordination developments in the post-war period generously shared their experiences with me and answered questions. To these organisations, officials and former officials I acknowledge my gratitude. I am also indebted to my colleagues in the Department of Industrial Relations at the University of New South Wales for their continued interest and encouragement. Mr W. Hotchkiss, a former member of the Department, kindly proofread the manuscript and gave a number of helpful suggestions. Mrs M. Pressley patiently edited the manuscript and assisted in making it more readable. Last, but by no means least, I thank my wife and children for their continued support and long-suffering patience.

INTRODUCTION

This study examines the factors that have led to employer associations forming co-ordinating machinery and the rationale for the particular form of combination used at different points in time. Historically, three factors have been important in stimulating inter-association co-ordinating mechanisms. The first has been the need to counteract union activities. This factor was of prime importance in the first decade reviewed in this study. The second factor was the opposition of many employers to the imposition of compulsory arbitration and the need for effective political lobbying machinery to oppose arbitration legislation. Unity on this score was hampered by manufacturers' support for protection, even 'New Protection' with its implied acceptance of arbitration. Following the introduction of arbitration and legislation enabling unions to aggregate claims and mount 'test cases', employers found it necessary to co-ordinate their approach in such cases to ensure their submissions were not at cross-purposes with each other. This third factor continues to provide for a symbiotic relationship between national employers and arbitration machinery.

Over the years national employer co-ordinating machinery has been numerous and varied. It has included the Federal Council of Employers (1889); the Employers' Defence Association of Australasia (1890); the Central Council of Employers of Australia (1904); the Committee of Control re Basic Wage (1924); the Committee of Control re Basic Wage and Working Hours (1926); the Interstate Conference of Employers (1930); the Consultative and Co-Ordinating Committee (1940); the Basic Wage Steering Committee (1947); the Policy and Consultative Committee (1950); the Basic Wage Working Party (1956); the National Employers' Associations [sic] with its policy and industrial committees — the National Employers' Policy Committee and the National Employers' Industrial Committee (1961); the National Employers' Consultative Committee (1970); the Central Industrial Secretariat (1972); and the Confederation of Australian Industry (1977).

Up to 1958 the machinery was *ad hoc* and developments were spasmodic and discontinuous. After 1958 developments were more continuous and in the same general direction. Some bodies were given a wide ambit and a large degree of discretion, others were considerably restricted in their scope and authority. Some co-ordinating mechanisms were short-lived, others had a degree of longevity. The Co-Ordinating and Consultative Committee of 1940, for example, handled only one basic wage case. The National Employers' Associations, on the other hand, continued in existence for nearly 20 years before its functions were taken over by the Confederation of Australian Industry (CAI) in 1978. The formation of the Confederation was the culmination of confederation attempts dating back to the 1920s.

The Confederation came into being in December 1977 by the merging of the Australian Council of Employers' Federations (ACEF) and the Associated Chambers of Manufactures of Australia (ACMA). Both these inter-industry umbrella organisations featured significantly in all the post-1904 national co-ordination machinery, and collectively had a controlling influence over such machinery. Thus the historical evolution of either the ACEF or the ACMA (or both) would have provided an appropriate underpinning for this study. Because the period under review is a long one, and because each organisation consisted of autonomous state affiliates, it was decided that the study would be more manageable if it focused primarily on one organisation.

For a number of reasons the ACEF was considered the more appropriate organisation for the purposes of this study. In the first instance, under its original name, the Central Council of Employers of Australia, it was founded as the prototype national co-ordinating body. A second reason relates to the industrial relations focus of this study. The ACEF was exclusively an industrial relations organisation. The ACMA, on the other hand, was primarily a trade (or more precisely a protectionist) organisation. Though it featured prominently in national industrial relations proceedings, its primary interests concerned trade and protection. A third reason is the lack of research undertaken into the ACEF and its affiliates — the state employers federations. Matthews (1971) is the only major study to include an examination of employers' federations. That study of the political activities of employer organisations examines the activities of the predecessors of both the ACEF and ACMA and their state affiliates in Victoria and New South Wales in the period to 1939. By way of contrast there have been a number of studies of the national and state Chambers of Manufactures. These include Chamber of Manufactures of NSW (1985), Coleman and Miles (1969), Dobson (1979), Hall (1971), Hainesworth (1971),

Matthews (1971), Parnaby (1951), and Parsons (1972). A final reason for selecting the ACEF is the fact that from its inception it was the initiator of most co-ordination attempts and from the mid-1920s to 1960 made frequent attempts at bringing into being a Confederation. In this respect it differed from the ACMA, which, until the 1960s, took an independent and aloof attitude to national employer activities and frustrated Confederation developments. After 1960, ACEF became the linchpin of any Confederation moves because of its dominant national industrial relations role. Its Executive Director (Mr G. Polites) increasingly came to oversee national employer activities. He was a member of the National Labour Consultative Council, a tripartite body that was an important forum for discussing industrial legislation at ministerial level. He also had a controlling influence over the national employer co-ordination machinery. Thus he was the Convenor of the National Employers' Industrial Committee, which had charge of national test cases on behalf of employers in general. In addition, he was Secretary of the National Employers' Policy Committee, the National Employers' Associations, and the National Employers' Consultative Committee. He was also the Director of the Central Industrial Secretariat, the joint industrial relations unit of the ACEF and ACMA. Mr Polites also became the first Director General of the National Employers' Industrial Council, the industrial relations wing of the CAI.

Though the ACEF and its affiliates are the major foci for this study, ACMA developments and its input into industrial relations and national employer co-ordination have not been ignored. For most of the period under review the Victorian Chamber of Manufactures undertook the ACMA's industrial relations work. This chamber was also an integral part of employers' test-case machinery and for many years provided the Convenor for the industrial committees that had charge of the day-to-day conduct of employers' submissions at national cases. The VCM's records have been used extensively in this study.

The study is arranged in chronological order with the time period of each chapter determined by important developments affecting national employer co-ordination. Chapter 1 reviews the formative period from the strikes of the 1890s to 1906. During this period three parliaments legislated for compulsory arbitration and the previously largely transient employer associations were forced to organise on a more permanent basis. The activities of these associations were largely directed at frustrating the operations of industrial tribunals and at limiting their scope and operations.

The appointment in 1907 of Mr Justice Higgins, a man enthused with extending the realms of the 'new province for law and order', marked a new epoch in tribunal regulation. Higgins' activities, together with High Court decisions in the period from 1913, increased the scope of federal arbitration far beyond that considered by employers to be constitutionally permissible. Employer associations devoted much of their resources to preventing the expansion of the federal tribunal system. The year in which Higgins tendered his resignation (1920) marks the end of the second period (Chapter 2).

The third chapter covers the period 1921 to 1929. The earlier year was one of marked recession, the later of marked depression. By 1921 unions had been successful in enlarging the scope of the federal arbitration system without having to abandon their awards secured through the state systems. The unions' treatment of federal and state industrial tribunals as competing or rival shops came to dominate the concerns of employer associations and parliaments. In 1926, the High Court's decision in Cowburn's case enabled a high degree of compartmentalisation between jurisdictions for those employers opting for the federal system. This was not the tribunal system that interested most state-bound associations, and problems of dual arbitration remained. It was on this issue that the Bruce Government lost office in 1929. It was in this period that the Central Council of Employers of Australia first sought the establishment of a Confederation of Employers, a reflection of the increased scope of federal arbitration.

The period of depression and recovery is treated in Chapter 4. This chapter ends in 1939, the year in which war with Germany was declared. The depression resulted in a concerted and unified approach by employer associations for a reduction in the basic wage. In 1930 some 24 organisations and companies met as the Conference of Employers' Organisations and formed a Committee of industrial officers to handle basic wage and hours cases. This Committee, or similar committees, operated on an *ad hoc* basis as needed until 1958. The rapid economic recovery after 1934 was accompanied by an amazing transformation in employer associations' approach to federal arbitration. By then the Court of Conciliation and Arbitration was recognised as the major tribunal in setting minimum wage standards. More importantly, by 1937 most national associations had come to support this and to urge that it also provide national standards in respect of hours of work. By 1937 federal arbitration was considered a more benign standard setter than New South Wales Labor Governments or market forces in a period of high employment.

The centripetal forces of federal arbitration were accentuated during the war period in which the defence powers of the Constitution enabled the Commonwealth to legislate in a range of areas normally outside its competence. The war period was also one that reinforced employers' support for federal arbitration since it offered one method of attempting to counteract the executive action of Commonwealth Labor Governments. In such a context, the conciliation and arbitration system, which associations had strenuously opposed for over three decades, became the cornerstone of their industrial relations policies and strategies. With the ending of war hostilities and the resumption of basic wage cases, an Interstate Conference of Employers formed the Basic Wage Steering Committee in 1947. This *ad hoc* Committee handled such cases for the next decade. These developments are reviewed in Chapter 5.

Labor lost office in December 1949 and remained in Opposition for the next 23 years. The period of Coalition rule is broken into two chapters: the periods 1950–59 (Chapter 6), and 1960–72 (Chapter 7). Both were periods of general economic buoyancy in which unions placed heavy demands on the federal arbitration system. In the 1950s, the ACEF increased its efforts at forming a Confederation that would co-ordinate the increasing number of national test cases. The abolition of 'Automatic Quarterly Cost of Living Adjustments' in 1953 accentuated the role of such test cases. Further, the use of economic indicators and other measures to adjust the basic wage according to national economic capacity to pay forced unions and employers to expend greater resources on such cases. On the employer side, this necessitated the elimination of the dissipation of finances through the separate representation of different employer groups at test cases. In 1956, a meeting of national employer organisations formed the Policy and Consultative Committee to direct basic wage cases. The preparation of cases was left to the Basic Wage Working Party, the renamed Steering Committee formed in the 1940s. In 1958, both these bodies were constituted on a permanent basis.

By the 1960s employers were confronted with frequent, and varied, national test cases. These came to include not only annual basic wage cases, but also Metal Trades Margins cases (which were in the nature of general reviews) annual leave, standard hours and long-service-leave cases. In addition employers mounted their own Total Wage case, which sought to remove the bifurcated wages system. They were successful on this score in 1967. Shortly afterwards the ACTU mounted two important test cases in relation to equal pay of the sexes. Under these pressures the *ad hoc* co-ordinating machinery established in the 1940s and refined in the 1950s proved inadequate. In 1961, 40 national organisations met and brought into being the National Employers' Associations (NEA). This rather loosely knit organisation, the first co-ordinating machinery to have a formal constitution, assumed control of the Policy and Consultative Committee and the Basic Wage Working Party, which were now designated the National Employers' Policy Committee and the National Employers' Industrial Committee respectively.

Industrial developments in the metal trades, whose award had become the linchpin and benchmark for national arbitration, resulted in a high degree of in-fighting between national associations in the late 1960s. The Metal Trades Industry Association was formed at the expense of the ACMA's major affiliate, the VCM. The ACMA's industrial outlook increasingly came to parallel that of the ACEF. In 1972 these two organisations merged their industrial relations functions to form the Central Industrial Secretariat. This proved to be the first step towards total merger and the formation of the Confederation of Australian Industry. The post-1972 developments form the substance of Chapter 8.

The final chapter synthesises and analyses the major features of the organisational developments during the hundred year period reviewed.

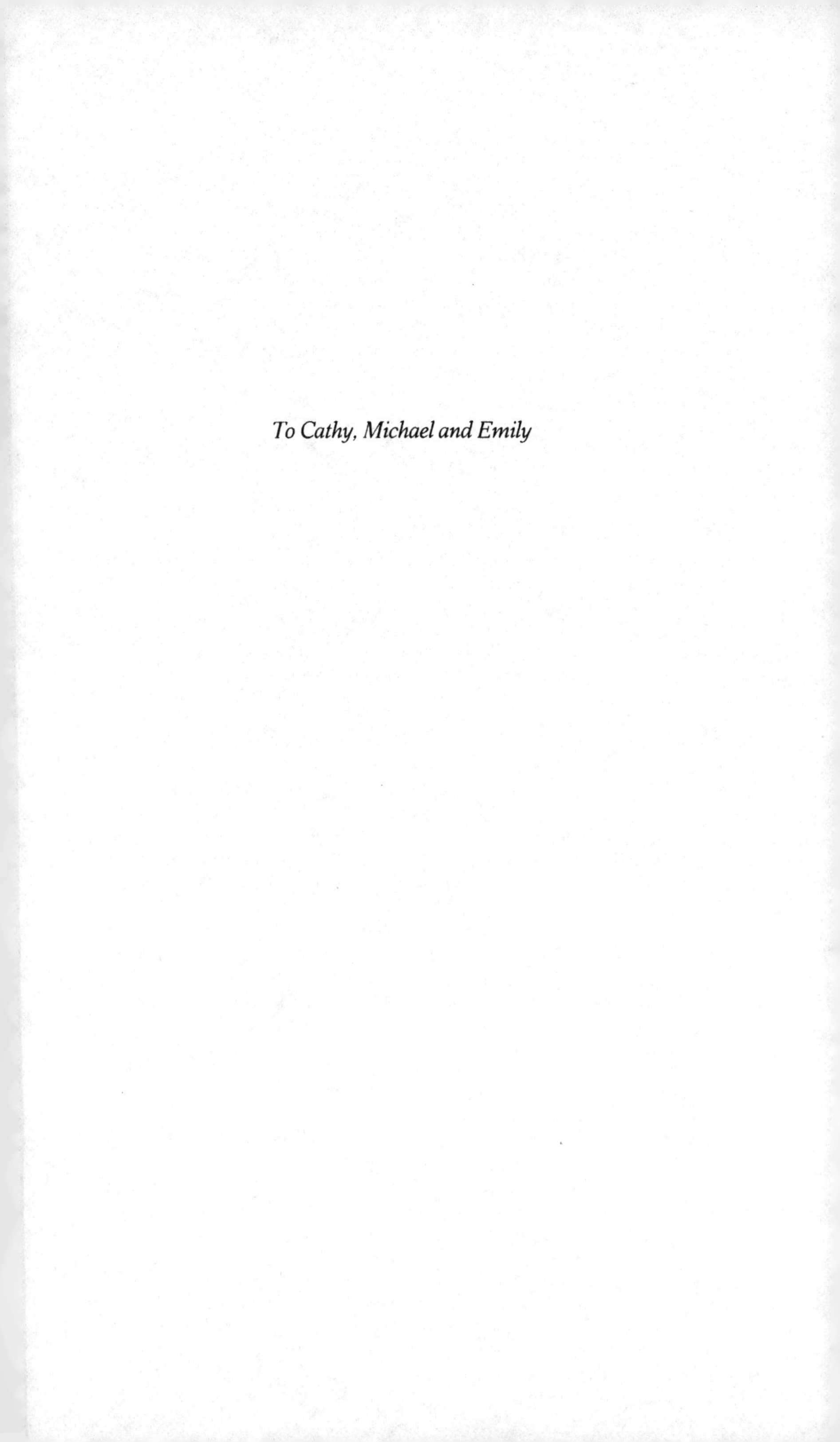

To Cathy, Michael and Emily

1

INDUSTRIAL LEGISLATION AND THE RISE OF PERMANENT EMPLOYER ASSOCIATIONS 1890–1906

Employers devote resources to, and submit to the authority of, their associations only out of necessity. Historically, the need to form a countervailing force against unions has necessitated employer cohesion. The nature and longevity of that cohesion has, in turn, been influenced by the nature of the union challenge and the ability of unions to sustain that challenge. Where employees, because of legal, financial or economic circumstances, have been able to form only ephemeral organisations, employer organisations have also tended to be transient. Where longer lasting and more effective unions have come into being the relevant employers have had to organise with greater effectiveness. The first part of this chapter argues that the history of employer organisations until the Great Strikes of the 1890s was one in which such organisations existed only as long as the need to confront the challenges of unions existed. With the employer victories in that decade, and with the ensuing union decline, employer organisations also tended to succumb to financial and organisational decay.

Industrial legislation following the Great Strikes forced employers to form more permanent organisations to combat that legislation. This was particularly true of legislation providing for the enactment of compulsory arbitration. The nature of this legislation is reviewed in the second part of the chapter.

The third section reviews the organisational responses to the industrial legislation, with particular emphasis on the formation of state-bound employer federations and the Central Council of Employers of Australia. This section also outlines the divisions between manufacturers and other employers over tariff protection and the formation of separate manufacturers' organisations.

In combating industrial legislation, employers used both parliamentary and industrial means. These activities are discussed in the penultimate and final sections of the chapter respectively. It is argued that by 1906, the year in which the *Excise Tariff Act* passed into law as the second major plank in the New Protection, the three arbitration systems then established were largely ineffective and on the defensive as the result of employer hostility.

Temporary associations

On 2 September 1890, at the height of the maritime strike, nearly 700 'employers and commercial men' met in Sydney under the auspices of the New South Wales Employers' Union and the Steamship Owners' Association of Australasia 'to consider the crisis brought about by the action of the combined maritime bodies and the Shearers' Union' (New South Wales Employers' Union 1890:3). The enthusiastic gathering unanimously supported four resolutions: one condemning 'the system of boycotting now practised by the representatives of Trades Unionism' (ibid:26–7) and the others directed at better combinations of employers at the state and national levels. Motions were adopted urging all employers to join the Employers' Union. Other motions called for the establishment of an intercolonial organisation for 'mutual defence and protection':

> That the time has arrived when it is absolutely necessary for all employers of labour, capitalists, and others directly and indirectly interested, to form themselves into an association for mutual defence and protection. (ibid:10)

And:

> That this meeting approve the formation of an Employers' Defence Association of Australasia, and that the following gentlemen be requested to form themselves into a committee to draft a scheme and report to a subsequent meeting, and invite co-operation in all the colonies. (ibid:15)

A 22-member committee representative of a wide range of business and commercial interests was appointed to 'draft the scheme'. Despite the enthusiasm displayed at the meeting, however, the results were no better than those of the Conference of Employers, which had met in Melbourne 10 months previously to establish the Federal Council of Employers (Coghlan

1918:1840). There is no evidence to suggest that the 22-member committee ever met and no national body that combined commercial, manufacturing and primary industry employer groups came into being for another 70 years. Not only was the Mutual Defence Association the victim of vacillating employer interest and apathy occasioned by prevailing circumstances, so too was the Employers' Union itself. It appears to have gone out of existence soon after 1891. Like most employer associations formed up to this time it proved transient. Employer associations arose, or trade associations diversified to meet the challenge of trade unions, dispersed once the challenge had been confronted, and reappeared in any subsequent wave of union militancy (Ford et al. 1980: 222–5). Thus union successes in the 1870s and 1880s, and in particular the successful strikes of the Operative Bootmakers' Union in Melbourne in 1884, brought about the formation of the Victorian Employers' Union:

> The 1884 strike was a traumatic experience for many employers. Capital, unorganised, divided and poorly led, was no match for organised labour. What manufacturing group could defeat an alliance which had been able to distribute [$1400] per week in strike pay for thirteen weeks? It was clear that employers were going to have to organise on a permanent basis if only as a defence against their employees. Out of the defeat of 1884 was born the Victorian Employers' Union and a whole new range of trade associations. (Parsons 1972:25)

The Victorian Employers' Union, on which its New South Wales counterpart was modelled, was formed in March 1885. In the words of W. E. Murphy, Secretary of the Melbourne Trades Hall Council, this Union represented 'a combination of capitalists from all branches of commerce, manufactures, and general industries formed to wipe out the indignities and repay with interest the score attendant on the 1884 strike' (Norton 1888:179–80).

In the ensuing struggles of the 1890s unions found themselves no match for organised employers, especially when assisted by the agencies of the State and by economic circumstances. The employer counter-federation that challenged the union federation, however, was not the product of any national mutual defence organisation as proposed by the New South Wales Employers' Union. The Pan-Australian Conference of Employers, which met in Sydney only a week after the meeting organised by the Employers' Union, was composed primarily of representatives of two federal bodies — the Steamship Owners' Association and the newly constituted Federated Pastoralists' Union of Australia. Other industries were 'sparsely represented' (Coghlan 1918:1596). Because of the ownership links between shipping and coal mining, the latter was also strongly represented (Gollan 1963:71–84, 117–9).

It was this trilogy of select employer groups whose own interests were under immediate challenge that affirmed 'the right of freedom of contract between employers and men, their determination to oppose the use of force and boycotting, and their intention to retain labour engaged during the strike' (Coghlan 1918:1595).

To some members of the employer combine (and to many subsequent historians) the labour struggles of 1890 to 1894 represented a trial of strength in which elimination of the union movement, rather than its taming, was the major consideration. This was particularly so of the shipping interests, influenced by Bruce Smith of the shipping firm W. A. Smith and Co., a moving spirit behind the Victorian Employers' Union (VEU), its first President, and the architect of its confrontationist policy against the Iron Workers' Assistants' Union and the Melbourne Trades Hall in 1886 (Parsons 1972:26–7). Smith was the author of 'Trades Unionism in Victoria; or Who Shall be Master? A Note of Warning to Employers', published in the *Victorian Review* and subsequently in pamphlet form by the VEU. In this, Smith derided any notion of commonality of interests or mutual dependency between capital and labour, and was opposed to any conciliation or appeasement. As this view won employer support, a natural development was deep class antagonism between masters and their employees. Smith's class sentiments were echoed by Jesse Gregson of the Australian Agricultural Company, credited as being the mastermind behind the shipowners' and mine-owners' successful anti-strike strategy (Ross 1970:67–91; Gollan 1963:68–94).

With the demise of the unions many employer associations also lost their impetus. The Newcastle Coal Owners' Mutual Protective Association, which had figured prominently in Gregson's anti-union strategy, dissolved in 1893. The New South Wales Employers' Union, and subsequently the VEU, also disappeared.[1] Nothing came of the proposal to establish a national mutual defence association. The less ambitious development of the New South Wales Mutual Defence Association was also short-lived.[2] While economic conditions made for impermanent or ineffective trade unions, so too they made for ephemeral employer associations.

The industrial legislation of the 1890s and early 1900s, which afforded unions continuous existence and avenues of securing improved working conditions by means other than their own strength, also necessitated the establishment of permanent industrial employer associations. The legislation brought into being two types of tribunals: wages boards whose function was to establish minimum wages; and conciliation and arbitration courts which, in addition to establishing minimum wages, were also required to prevent and settle industrial disputes.

Western Australia (1900) and New South Wales (1901) opted for compulsory arbitration and the other states for wages boards.[3] The Constitutional Conferences (1890–1896), which led up to Federation (1901), witnessed strong divisions over the national legislature's industrial powers. The final outcome was to vest the Commonwealth with limited powers directed towards arbitration. These Constitutional Conferences also witnessed sharp differences concerning the issue of tariff protection. The Commonwealth's industrial program served to unite employers; the fiscal question to divide.

Industrial legislation

The period leading up to Federation was one in which much imitative industrial legislation was enacted. This legislation related principally to Factory Acts, Mines Acts and Shops Acts. Stimuli to the Victorian imitation of English legislation were a series of articles in *The Age* in 1882, and the Royal Commission into the working of the *Factory Act* 1873. This Act had been modelled on the English Act of 1867. The question of home-work, which became synonymous with 'sweating', became a major focus of the Commission, whose report was followed by the *Factory Act* of 1885 and subsequent revisions in 1893 and 1896.

In this early legislation, which in one form or another was imitated by other colonies, two important elements that were to influence subsequent industrial legislation are discernible — notions of the 'New Protection' and its racial overtones. It is significant that it was *The Age*, a leading advocate of protection, which also advocated factory legislation. Victorian manufacturing employers had benefited from a protective tariff and were advocating a system of national protection. They were chagrined

> to find unscrupulous employers enjoying the benefit of a high protection yet carrying on their business with an entire disregard of sanitation and the elementary rights of their work people, and thus early identifying in the public mind the principle of protection to manufactures with the systematic oppression and exploitation of the employed. (Coghlan 1918:2096)

Restrictions against Chinese labour and enterprises provided for in the legislation were not dictated by an interest in their well-being but rather to prevent unrestrained competition with white labour.

Though employers were not enamoured of the various Factory and Shops Acts, and in many cases attempted to obstruct their passage and subsequent amendments in parliament, the fact that such legislation was marked 'neither by originality nor intelligence but was in fact the offspring of factory legislation in the United Kingdom' (ibid:2096) helped in it being accepted. So too did the fact that, though similar in principle to the Acts in force in the United Kingdom, they were 'much more limited in their scope and much more tender on the rights of property' (Wise 1909:294). It was easier for liberal governments to secure legislation considered necessary in England 'than it would have been to have secured independent and, from the Australian standpoint, more necessary legislation' (Coghlan 1918:2097). Thus wages boards, conciliation and voluntary arbitration did not offend against Anglophile sentiments. It was not until legislation for the settlement of industrial disputes by way of compulsory arbitration was enacted that more original action was taken by the Australian parliaments. A major criticism of this innovative legislation was that it breached British standards of justice and 'fair play'.[4]

The movement towards tripartite systems of conflict resolution was a long-term result of the industrial upheavals of the 1890s. 'It cannot be said', wrote Coghlan, 'that the Australian public disapproved of the strike as a weapon before it had made acquaintance of it on a large scale' (1918: 2100). This public sympathy for state regulation of industrial disputes was supported by liberal politicians, as well as by members of the newly formed Labor Parties. Strike losses had converted the labour movement from a 'vague and hesitating' stance towards arbitration to one of firm commitment. Employers, on the other hand, though they had supported arbitration in their pre-strike insecurity, now completely rejected arbitration and its implied assault on the freedom of contract: 'What we maintained in that self-denying struggle is now threatened to be taken away by legislation. The legislation . . . will strike directly on the fundamental principle of freedom of contract' (CCEA Minutes of 1905 Convention: 110–12).

Able to ward off advances from unions for the inclusion of arbitration clauses in contracts, employers devoted resources to ensuring that unacceptable legislation did not impose arbitration on them. Their ability to frustrate voluntary arbitration, however, strengthened the movement towards compulsory arbitration.

In 1890 the NSW Parliament appointed a Royal Commission to inquire into the question of strikes. The Commission reported in May 1891 and recommended the establishment of a State Board of Conciliation and Arbitration. Disputes not settled by the parties ought, in the first instance, to be referred to a Board of Conciliation. If the Board failed in its task of conciliation then a Court of Arbitration would be constituted from its members and would give a decision (Report of Royal Commission on Strikes 1891:34). The Commission considered public suasion a major instrument for ensuring the Board's success, claiming that 'public opinion would be adverse to those who, except for very good cause shown, refused to avail themselves of its good offices' (ibid:28).

The outcome of the Report was the Trades Disputes Conciliation and Arbitration Act, 1892. This Act provided for the voluntary reference of disputes to an Arbitration Board. The Act was ineffectual. 'In spite of energetic work on the part of officials, it soon appeared that public opinion was not as strong and cohesive as had been hopefully supposed, or else there was ever an infinity of admirable reasons for refusing the good offices of the Board' (Coghlan 1918:2104). Though unions sought to refer the Broken Hill lockout (1892) and the Shearers' strike (1894) to the Board, employers refused.

By 1894 South Australian employers had succeeded in emasculating the first Bill introduced into an Australian parliament providing for compulsory arbitration and in turning it into a voluntary arbitration Act. The Bill, introduced by Charles Kingston, provided for the regulation of labour relations by way of a Bureau of Labour. Under the direction and control of this Bureau, Boards of Conciliation were to be appointed whose composition and functions were similar to those of the wages boards subsequently introduced by Victoria. In addition there was to be a State Board, which was to have powers to inquire into any industrial dispute referred to it by the Minister of Labour or by agreement of the parties concerned. The Board would be enabled to compel the attendances of witnesses. Though providing for voluntary arbitration, the principle of compulsion was 'deeply rooted in the Bill' (ibid:2104). It became the 'sport of three sessions of parliament' and was thwarted by the introduction of an opposing Bill by Chaffey Baker on behalf of the Federated Employers' Council. When finally accepted by the Legislative Council in 1894, the legislation provided for voluntary arbitration alone.

Voluntary arbitration proved no more effective in South Australia than in New South Wales. Employers now considered they had less to fear from strikes than their opponents. Convinced of their ability to defeat labour they saw any reference to arbitration as a hindrance to complete triumph. For unions the need for outside avenues for arresting their organisational decline and the loss of employment conditions became more pressing. State arbitration provided one such avenue. By the end of 1900 compulsory arbitration Bills had been introduced in all mainland parliaments [5], and the newly adopted Constitution was permissive of similar measures being introduced at the national level. The possibility of such legislation, with its potential to alter existing power relations and to challenge the hard-won freedom of contract, goaded employers to coalesce in opposition. The nature of the challenge was to require permanent rather than transient combination.

THE ORGANISATIONAL RESPONSE

Employers' federations and the Central Council of Employers of Australia

In direct response to the challenge of compulsory arbitration employers' federations were created in Victoria (1901) and New South Wales (1903) and the moribund Queensland Federated Employers' Union and the South Australian Federated Council of Employers reconstituted as federations (1904 and 1907 respectively). The Western Australian Labor Government's enactment of the *Industrial Arbitration Act, 1912*, which enlarged the scope of the previously unobtrusive Arbitration Court, resulted in the formation of a federation in that state in 1913.

The establishment of the Victorian Employers' Federation (VEF) has been described in detail by Matthews (1971). This federation arose in direct response to the Arbitration Bill of 1901 introduced by the Labor leader W. A. Trenwirth. It was intended as a predominantly extra-parliamentary political organisation, which would leave the VEU to attend to the industrial needs of employers. By 1903, however, the more virile VEF had subsumed the functions of the VEU and the latter went out of existence. In its first two decades of operations the VEF expended much energy in keeping compulsory arbitration off the Victorian statute books, in opposing giving permanency to the wages boards system that had been introduced on a trial basis, and in co-ordinating employers' opposition to the national Conciliation and Arbitration Bill.

The Employers' Federation of NSW (EFNSW) was inaugurated at a 'largely attended meeting of about 120 gentlemen representing various branches of industry' in May 1903 (SMH 15/5/03:6). Henry Hudson, manager of the Clyde Engineering Company and former president of the New South Wales Employers' Union, was the organiser of the meeting. He was an influential member of the Iron Trades Employers' Association and claimed that since the formation of that body 'they had been considering the advisability of calling the employers together for the purpose of establishing a federation' (ibid). He was supported by J. P. Wright, who claimed that 'the time had arrived when employers of labour of all descriptions should band themselves together to confer on the prospect that was immediately before them'. On all sides they could witness the growing tendency by governments to 'make the State the employers of certain classes in the community'. Industrial Acts had been passed, the effect of which 'had been to cause undue interference and great loss and trouble to employers'. The Arbitration Act had stimulated the formation of unions in every industry. 'Some of the decisions of the Court', said Wright, 'had been extraordinary, and he did not know what the ultimate effect would be'. He successfully moved:

> That a federation of employers of all descriptions, representing commercial, manufacturing, and trading interests be formed with the following objects:
> (a) To protect the interests of employers from undue aggression and excessive interference by the State or Commonwealth Governments.
> (b) To watch legislation affecting employers, and to propose measures in the same direction.
> (c) To adopt whatever procedures may be considered advisable in the interests of employers and the welfare of the state and Commonwealth generally.
> (d) To take such other steps as may be deemed expedient or necessary to protect the interests of the federation. (ibid)[6]

A committee drawn from 15 associations was elected to draft a constitution. This was adopted in June 1903 when a full-time Secretary was also appointed.[7]

The new federation received support from its Victorian counterpart and together they sought to establish a national organisation to oppose the Arbitration Bill introduced into the Commonwealth Parliament in July 1903. In February 1904 delegates from the Victorian, South Australian, Queensland and New South Wales Federations, together with representatives of the Western Australian Chamber of Mines, met in Sydney to determine on a method of fighting this Bill.

> As an immediate defensive step the conference agreed to address a remonstrance to the Commonwealth Parliament against the Bill on the grounds that it was uncalled for, that it would prove unworkable, that it was unconstitutional, and that it was an encroachment upon the rights of the States and a breach of faith with the intentions of the founders of the Commonwealth. (Matthews 1971:42)

The conference was also decided to accept a VEF motion to establish a Central Council of Employers of Australia (CCEA). This was to be constituted to 'take up matters of urgency' and to 'exercise a vigilant watch upon all that is passing through the legislature'. The objectives enshrined in the CCEA constitution replicated, at a national level, those of the EFNSW.

The federations, and at the national level the CCEA, attempted to co-ordinate the industrial and political activities of the trade associations. Because of the divisions over tariffs, the Chamber of Manufactures of New South Wales (NSWCM) distanced itself from the EFNSW, which was largely influenced by the anti-protectionist Sydney Chamber of Commerce (SCC *Annual Report* 1903:42). Though the Constitutional Conference and the *Tariff Act* 1902 set the Commonwealth on a protectionist course the levels of tariffs imposed, and the range of commodities protected, were still areas of dissension. In Victoria, where employers were less divided on the fiscal question, the Victorian Chamber of Manufactures (VCM) was a prime mover in the formation of the VEF and a founding member. Increasing differences over protection, however, caused the VCM to disaffiliate in 1905. In the preceding year the chambers had formed their own peak council, the Federated Chambers of Manufactures of Australia, which was renamed the Associated Chambers of Manufactures of Australia (ACMA) in 1908. Employers, ever reluctant to accept the authority of any co-ordinating body, were confronted with two such bodies before the passage of the *Conciliation and Arbitration Act* 1904, which had been the major catalyst in bringing the CCEA into being.

The parliamentary front

Labor's prospects for securing compulsory arbitration legislation were most propitious in the Western Australian, New South Wales and Commonwealth Parliaments where it held some balance of power and was able to use this power to obtain concessions in return for support. In South Australia, Labor suffered from relatively poor parliamentary representation. In Queensland, it encountered a different problem. There its ability to elbow aside the other liberal groups and to take 'from the first the direct opposition benches, put out of possibility the fruitful method of "support for concession" pursued in the southern colonies. As a result, legislation to set up industrial courts made a slow start in Queensland' (Shann 1930:374).

In Victoria, the general weakness of the Labor Party, and the introduction of the wages boards system in 1896, which satisfied the desire for industrial justice of concerned liberals, reduced the prospects for compulsory arbitration in that state. The most important factor in disposing of W. A. Trenwirth's Arbitration Bill of 1901, however, was the control of the Legislative Council by conservatives and employers.[8] This Council was elected on a property franchise basis, which, at the turn of the century, deprived nearly half of those enrolled to vote for the Legislative Assembly from being able to do so for the Council (Matthews 1971:119). The

Legislative Council was not only able to prevent compulsory arbitration from going onto the statute books, but was also successful in having proponents of such legislation expend much time and energy in keeping the wages boards system (which was introduced only on an experimental basis) afloat. Permanency was finally afforded the system in 1906, in large measure to ensure that compulsory arbitration was not introduced.

Employer control over the Legislative Council enabled the VEF to devote much attention to the Arbitration Bill before the Commonwealth Parliament then located in Melbourne. The other centre of major anti-arbitration activities was in New South Wales where employers sought to frustrate the trial arbitration legislation of 1901. These activities were helped by the number of members of the Legislative Councils who belonged to employer organisations and who, as the Victorian experience demonstrates, could be effective in blocking legislation (CCEA Convention Minutes 1905:14 and 789; EFNSW *Annual Report 1904:5–6)*. In the Commonwealth Parliament there were a number of politicians with employer association links.[9] In addition, the presidency of the CCEA was held by politicians until 1926.[10] Where necessary, these and other politicians were supplied with lengthy memoranda prepared by the VEF. Petitions to parliament and deputations to the relevant Ministers became an established part of employer association activities. Amendments were sought in the lower Houses where it appeared outright rejection was unlikely. With the exception of the Senate, Upper Houses were used to reject legislation, or to seek such dilution as would nullify the intention of that legislation. Employers bitterly complained that the Labor-controlled Senate was not a 'real house of review' (*Liberty and Progress* April 1904:131).

Though these tactics were not without influence, in the final analysis arbitration was enacted on the basis of the 'numbers game'. Where Labor could extract concessions in return for support, legislation was enacted. Where support for concessions was not possible, arbitration stayed off the statute books.[11]

The industrial and legal offensive

By the end of 1904 four parliaments — the Victorian, Western Australian, New South Wales and Commonwealth — had legislated to establish industrial tribunals. Employer organisations acted to restrict the activities of these tribunals and to make them unworkable. In this they had initial success. Two of the tribunals remained largely inactive for the next decade or so, the others impermanent for much of that time.

The *Conciliation and Arbitration Act* passed into law in December 1904.

The Commonwealth Court of Conciliation and Arbitration (Arbitration Court) established under this Act had very slow beginnings. Mr Justice O'Connor of the High Court was appointed first President in 1905. In that year the Court heard only one case, that relating to the registration of the New South Wales Rail Traffic Employees' Association. The matter was referred to the High Court where employers obtained their first restriction on the Arbitration Court. The Act, in so far as it purported to determine industrial conditions of employees of a state, was declared *ultra vires*. In 1906 the Arbitration Court made two awards after employers unsuccessfully contested the Court's jurisdiction. Both awards related to the maritime industry.[12] The only other work by the Arbitration Court in that year was to issue certificates of exemption under the *Excise Tariff Act* 1906 to six employers. This excise tax was the second plank in the New Protection.

The Western Australian Industrial Court also proved relatively inactive until the *Industrial Arbitration Act* was amended in 1912. The original Act of 1900 proved a 'dead letter' and was repealed in 1902 when a new system was introduced. Frequent changes of the President (there were four appointments between 1902 and 1904) made for a slow start by the new Industrial Court. Once operational, the very limited interpretation of the Court's jurisdiction by the President reduced the Court to little more than a minimum wage-fixing tribunal. The Court adopted 'from the first a course in limiting the issues it would consider in an award to the fewest possible. Piecework, apprenticeships, the common rule, preference to unionists, and industrial regulation in general have not been allowed to take up the time of the Western Australian Court' (Clark 1905:130). Employers opposed the passage of the original Act and were less than co-operative with the operation of the new system (Dufty 1986). The gold-mining industry lobbied against state intervention. It helped to form the CCEA and continued to provide a Western Australian presence on that Council until it was replaced in 1914 by the newly formed Western Australian Employers' Federation (WAEF).

In Victoria the restricted role of the wages boards, and the fact that the Legislative Council could be relied on to protect management prerogatives from the intrusion of the boards, might have been expected to reduce employer hostility. In the main this was the case as many employers saw advantages in the establishment of a minimum wage that standardised wage cost throughout an industry and protected employers from 'unfair' competitors (Pember Reeves 1902:164). In some cases, however, action was undertaken to undermine the effectiveness of wages boards. One such action was simply to evade the provisions of the boards. Dependent employees were frequently induced to support employers' claims of paying the right wages when such was not the case (ibid:59-61). Another intimidatory practice was the victimisation of employee representatives on the boards. 'In more than one case', claimed Spence (1909:311), 'the whole of the members of the Board lost their positions shortly after an award was made'. Further, until 1906, employers successfully used appellate courts to circumscribe the boards. 'Very little was accomplished', in this initial phase, wrote Hammond (1914:128), 'since the Supreme Court had the effect of paralysing the determinations of the boards'. Such appellate procedures became an important part of employer attempts to frustrate the New South Wales and Commonwealth arbitral systems. The most dramatic action by employers to render the wages boards ineffective was in the fellmongering industry. When a wages board decision went against them they closed their establishments and dismissed their employees in protest. In some instances plant closures were made permanent by the plant being transferred to another state.[13] As a result of this experience the *Factories and Shops Continuation Act* 1902 provided that no determination could be gazetted unless it had been reached by at least two employers voting with the employees or vice versa. This provision effectively gave employers a veto right.

In Victoria a natural inhibitor to excessive employer activity against wages boards was the possibility of their replacement with compulsory arbitration. 'Employers', noted Hammond (1914:623), 'are unanimous in one negative conclusion, namely that wages boards are preferable to Arbitration Courts, but on nothing else'. In New South Wales employers undertook a major campaign to have the arbitration system replaced by a wages boards (trades boards) system. The introduction of the Trades Disputes Amendment Bill by the Wade (Conservative) Government in 1908, when the original Act was due to lapse, indicates that the campaign was successful.

The employer offensive in making the trial Industrial Arbitration Act, 1901 inoperative took several forms. Some firms threatened to relocate in other states, others not to proceed with planned investments in New South Wales (Clark 1905:85–7; Pember Reeves 1902:136–40). Employers sought to reduce the impact of awards by installing labour-saving machinery (Clark 1905:125; Gollan 1963:115), by replacing males with more poorly paid females (Clark 1905:175) and by resorting to sub-contracting (ibid:123). At the organisational level, they attempted to frustrate the arbitration system by refusing to register their associations; by establishing and having registered bogus unions; by deliberately lengthening procedures thereby choking the Industrial Court with work; and by frequently appealing against the Court's decisions to superior Courts more in sympathy with the employer viewpoint. Employers also used their parliamentary majority to frustrate the trial legislation to ensure that once the period of experimentation had been completed compulsory arbitration would be replaced.

A major difference between the wages boards system and that of arbitration was the latter's reliance on, and hence encouragement of, registered organisations of employers and employees. The absence of group representation would so increase the volume of work as to choke the system. The employer offensive aimed at eliminating the registration of employer organisations, subverting that of employee representation, and challenging the common-rule provisions that had been designed to save the Court from having to 'frequently travel over similar ground' (Black 1929:9). One of the EFNSW's first actions (an action replicated at the national level by the CCEA) was to direct affiliates not to seek industrial registration (CCEA Conference, 1905, p.17). This tactic was not particularly successful. Employers were, in the main, respondents to arbitration proceedings. Registration was critical for unions as award applicants, but a lack of registration did not prevent employers from being made respondents to awards. As these employers required their associations to negotiate on their behalf and to represent them in arbitral proceedings, employer associations were forced to play the role required of them by the system. Manufacturers were beyond the employers' federation's pale, and they registered.[14] Other groups were forced to register to protect their own interests against already registered groups as well as against the larger employers who were able to register in their own right.[15]

Though the registration of employer organisations was largely incidental to the system's functioning, that of unions was essential. 'Without unions', wrote the author of the Act, arbitration would be 'to play the play of "Hamlet" leaving out the part of Hamlet' (Wise 1909:314). One of the first effects of the Act according to the Labor proponent, Black (1929:26), was the 'creation of 46 new unions, representative of well nigh every industry in the land'. Evatt (1942:88) claims that in the first 2 years of the Act no fewer than 111 new unions were registered compared with 26 in the preceding 10 years.

Since the system depended on unions, one response was for employers to create and have registered bogus unions. Such unions were established in the trilogy of industries that countered the unions in the 1890s and at various times came to include the Non-Political Union (Fitzpatrick 1940:236), the Australian Agricultural Implement and Machine Employees' Association (McCarthy 1968:27), the Tramways Employees' Union (ibid:239), the Coastal Seamen's and Firemen's Union (Black 1929:26), the Independent Workers' Federation (Higgins 1921:17) and the Mechanical Shearer's Union (Spence 1909:141). The Non-Political Union was established at Broken Hill with management support. It took its name because its rules forbade financial support for the Labor Party. This union accepted a wage reduction on behalf of members and continued to work when other unions struck over the reduction. The existence of a bogus union of 'scabs' intensified the dispute. One of the conditions imposed on management for a return to work was the liquidation of the union. Concerning the Coastal Seamen's and Firemen's Union one member of the New South Wales Industrial Court reported: 'the union has never been a *bona fide* union at all. It never seems to have advanced a single claim on behalf of the employees' (Black 1929:26). H. B. Higgins (1921:17) notes of the Independent Workers' Federation that it was 'a body supported chiefly by employers' money and devised to frustrate the ordinary union'. The Mechanical Shearers' Union was important because of the economic significance of the wool-growing industry. In the view of the Royal Commission formed to investigate this union in 1902, it 'had been in all probability formed, officered, and financed by persons working in the interests of the pastoralists'. This union was subsequently deregistered.

'Capitalists are great believers in law and order', wrote Spence, 'so long as they can control its administration' (1909:91). The Industrial Arbitration Act permitted the use of legal representation, a provision objected to by unions. Employers made use of this provision both to slow down Court procedures as well as to raise unions' costs (Clark 1905:133–4). Once employers used legal representation, unions invariably found that they had to do the same. In 1905 V. Clark instanced the case of a union whose award had still be be dealt with 7 months after the dispute had been filed. At that stage there were still 48 cases ahead of its application. 'The government and employers rejoiced to see the Labour organisations tied up', wrote one union official, 'they could not strike under the Act and they could not get their grievances remedied except in some minor degree and in special cases' (Black 1929:11). Employers' success in having the common rule in relation to industrial agreements declared illegal further added to the Court's congestion (Clark 1905:138).

As well as the use of delaying tactics to limit the Court's output, the use of the appellate process to restrict the Court's scope became an established part of the employer strategy. This tactic was particularly effective since the legislation was 'avowedly experimental' (Wise 1909:144) and therefore subject to possible repeal. Employers' efforts to ensure that the Act would be repealed when the trial period ended in 1908 resulted in no legislative action to ensure that the Industrial Court was able to function as intended by the Industrial Arbitration Act. The 'Progressives' who passed the Act in 1901 lost office in 1904. The new government 'set out to kill the Act by inaction and refused for years to make any amendments which were required in consequences of unexpected legal decisions' (McCarthy 1968:190). 'It was inevitable', claimed the author of the Act, 'that the working of any novel measures should disclose mistakes and flaws' (Wise 1909:144). Wise noted that the New Zealand Act had been amended five times in the first 7 years of its existence. In the case of New South Wales, no such amendments were passed even though 'the legal decisions which defeated the purpose of the Act were plainly such as required to be corrected by amending legislation' (ibid). By not amending those portions of the Act found deficient or *ultra vires* the Conservatives hoped to reduce the enthusiasm for continuing legislation in 1908 when the Act was due to lapse.

The success of employers' parliamentary tactics was augmented by the appellate Courts' hostility towards the Industrial Court. 'The judges in the other Courts', wrote Spence (1909:308), 'seemed eager to get opportunities to declare the Act *ultra vires* on any pretext, and some of them did not hesitate to extend their functions by making speeches from the Bench condemning such legislation'. So severe were the limitations placed on the Industrial Court that its President considered the operation of the 1901 Act in no way served as a fair trial for the settlement of industrial disputes by arbitration:

> The barque of the *Industrial Arbitration Act* made a brave show with its sails and bunting at its launching . . . but since I took the helm the Act has been riddled, shelled, broken fore and aft, and reduced to a sinking hulk. No pilot could navigate such a craft. Do not say, however, that no ship can sail the seas because this one has been so badly built. When an Act is passed which really means what it seems to say, in which "industrial dispute" means industrial dispute; in which a dispute "arising between" certain persons does not mean a dispute which must arise between totally different persons; in which legal rights such as the right to strike and lockout are not taken away without anything being given in their place; then, and only then, can the principle of industrial arbitration be really tested, and if it breaks down, be fairly pronounced to have broken down. (1907 *AR* (NSW) 59)

As already noted, the Government was less disposed to give arbitration a 'fair trial'. Its 1907 election package included the replacement of arbitration with trades boards (Wise 1909:323-4; EFNSW *Annual Report* 1907:2). It appeared as if employers had been successful in their attempts to remove arbitration from the New South Wales statutes.

Summary and conclusion

Until the enactment of compulsory arbitration, employer associations tended to be transient, impermanent organisations. They were formed to meet particular challenges and became dormant once those challenges had been surmounted. The strikes of the 1890s, together with the accompanying recession, convinced employers of the ineffectiveness of the general strike as a union tactic and therefore weakened the growing movement towards the formation of a national employer body. Following the strikes employers were less enamoured of the prospects of arbitration, which they had previously espoused. On the other hand unions saw advantages in arbitration and when the voluntary systems were made ineffective by employer actions they sought the establishment of compulsory arbitration. The portents of such legislation brought employers together again. The nature of the challenge confronting employers caused them to form permanent associations. National organisations were formed to cope with national legislation. Because of the conflicting vested interests concerning the first, particularly in relation to tariffs, divisions in the employer ranks were quickly manifested. Employer organisations were active on the parliamentary and industrial arenas. On the first front, employers were successful in restricting tribunal legislation in three states and at the national level, and in preventing such legislation in the other states. Sympathetic appellate courts were also used to further reduce the effectiveness of the legislation. On the industrial front, employers used a number of tactics to frustrate the tribunal systems. Because of employer activities, by 1906 the federal tribunal was largely inactive, the Western Australian system unobtrusive, the Victorian system restricted and impermanent, and the New South Wales system about to be changed through legislation.

Notes

1 The New South Wales Employers' Union became defunct about 1894. Membership of the VEU fell after 1890 and in 1903 its functions were taken over by the Victorian Employers' Federation (formed in 1901).

2 The only documentary evidence of this association that the author could find was the Rules of the Association published in 1891. These provided for the insurance of employers against strike losses of up to ten times the amount contributed. In the case of 'test cases' against unions, the trustees could award compensation in excess of the above proportion (Employers' Defence Association of New South Wales 1891).

3 Queensland replaced wages boards with compulsory arbitration in 1912. In the same year, and notwithstanding the different philosophy underlying wages boards and compulsory

arbitration, South Australia followed the New South Wales (1908) experiment of combining wages boards with compulsory arbitration.

4 In August 1903 Bruce Smith told the Commonwealth Parliament that 'the spirit which has led to the introduction of the (arbitration) Bill is a retrograde one, and is opposed to the experience of the last century, during which individual liberty matured and became a living principle among Anglo-Saxon people' (*Commonwealth Parliamentary Debates* vol. 15, p. 3464). Compulsory arbitration was condemned at the 1905 Conference of the CCEA for *inter alia*, being 'an instrument of oppression . . . a great check to progress, and a violation of the very foundations of the principle of British Freedom'. The President of the Federated Master Builders of Australia reported at that organisation's eighth Convention (June 1904): 'I regard it [compulsory arbitration] as an undesirable departure from the principles of British freedom which are our boast and pride'. At its 1917 Convention the CCEA claimed that 'the federal act substituted for British jurisprudence the arbitrary will of one man'.

5 The respective dates are: South Australia 1890, Queensland 1894, New South Wales 1899, Victoria and Western Australia 1900.

6 When the constitution was adopted in June 1903 'pastoral' was added to the industries in the first paragraph.

7 The first secretary of the EFNSW was Mr Wedge-Horn, the part-time Secretary and Advocate for the Iron Trades Association.

8 For an account of earlier attempts to introduce compulsory arbitration in Victoria in the period 1888 to 1894 see Chan (1971).

9 These included Senator Walker, a member of the EFNSW; R Knox (MHR for Kooyong), a director of BHP, the Vice-President of the Associated Chambers of Commerce of Australia, and for many years a representative of the WAEF on the CCEA Executive Committee; Bruce Smith (Parkes) the founder and former President of the VEU; Patrick McMahon Glynn (Angus) who as a member of the SA Parliament had challenged Charles Kingston's arbitration Bill of 1890; G. Edwards (South Sydney) who, with Bruce Smith, was endorsed by the EFNSW; Senator Vardon (SA) who represented the SAEF at CCEA meetings; and J. Gibb (Flinders), A. Robinson (Wannon) and J. G. Wilson (Corangamite) who had been extended financial and propaganda support by the VEF in the federal elections (Matthews 1971:239; Dobson 1979:148; CCEA Conventions 1904–10).

10 These Presidents were: E. Smith (1904 to 1914) a Victorian MLC; G. Fairbairn (1914 to 1924) a Victorian Senator; and E. Drake-Brockman (1924 to 1926) a Senator from Western Australia.

11 For an account of parliamentary events in the state and Commonwealth Parliaments in relation to compulsory arbitration, see Plowman (1985)

12 The first award was for the Merchant Service Guild, the second for Marine Engineers.

13 An example of this was the brush factory, owned by Lord Jones and which employed 500 women. Rather than accept a wages board ruling he closed the factory and relocated in Tasmania. Ironically, that state introduced a wages board system in 1910.

14 The first union of employers registered in NSW was the Iron Trades Employers' Association (ITEA) even though at this time it was affiliated with the EFNSW, and Henry Hudson of the ITEA was President of the federation. Other manufacturers and large companies also sought registration.

15 The Arbitration Acts provided that a company that employed 100 or more employees could register in its own right as a union of employers.

2

THE HIGGINS ERA 1907–1920

The previous chapter reviewed legislative developments following the strikes of the 1890s. These developments, which included the enactment of compulsory arbitration by three parliaments and some form of minimum wage machinery in all the mainland states, caused employers to coalesce with the same intensity as did the strikes. Employer federations were formed at the state level and these confederated to form the Central Council of Employers of Australia (CCEA). Because of differences over New Protection — the coupling of arbitration with tariffs — manufacturers formed separate peak organisations at the state and national levels. Employer hostilities resulted in the federal arbitration system remaining circumscribed, the Western Australian system unobtrusive, and the New South Wales system being reduced to a 'sinking hulk'.

This chapter reviews employer and tribunal developments from 1907, the year in which the Harvester judgement attempted to give practical expression to the New Protection, to 1920, the year in which Prime Minister Hughes' *Industrial Peace Act* attempted to fragment the monolithic structure and operations of the federal industrial tribunal. The period was one in which Mr Justice Higgins was President of the Commonwealth Court of Conciliation and Arbitration (Arbitration Court). Appointed to the Presidency in 1907, he was re-appointed for a second 7-year term in 1914. He resigned in 1920 before the expiration of his second term in protest against the Hughes initiatives. His High Court judgements supported the expansion of the 'New Province of Law and Order' of which he was a major architect. His pioneering work in the new field of industrial arbitration — a field in which he had to 'learn the business, with no book of instructions, no teacher other than experience, no kindly light except from the pole star of justice' (Higgins 1922:v) — was to have a lasting impact on industrial relations in Australia.

The chapter is divided into two major parts. The first examines the industrial context and reviews the employers' High Court challenges against the New Protection and the Arbitration Court. Though by 1908 the legal trappings of New Protection were removed, after 1914 High Court challenges served to increase the scope of federal arbitration. The first part of the chapter also examines the employers' parliamentary initiatives for securing a more benign system of industrial regulation and their involvement in the curial functions of the system. The second part of the chapter has two components. The first examines the organisational developments within the Central Council, and the second, the Council's attempts to secure greater co-ordination among employer groups. Such co-ordination was made necessary by the expansion of federal jurisdiction and by the emergence of 'test' cases in the last year of the period under review.

Litigation

By 1907 New South Wales employers had successfully reduced the 'barque of arbitration' in that state to a 'sinking hulk' through successful Supreme Court and High Court appeals. It is not surprising, in view of the constitutional restrictions on the federal legislature's industrial powers, that employers also used the High Court to constrain the operations of the Arbitration Court. Such appeals were intended to force on that Court the limited role they perceived as being intended by the Constitution — the settling of rare industrial interstate disputes — rather than the more encompassing role associated with the New Protection. This New Protection entailed two major aspects: the protection of local manufacturers by tariffs, and the ensuring that the fruits of such protection were equitably distributed by way of arbitration. The *Conciliation and Arbitration Act* 1904 and the *Excise Tariff Act(s)* 1906 were augmented by other legislation that formed part of a consistent policy.[1] Employers challenged these and supportive Acts with such frequency that in the first 25 years of the Commonwealth the industrial power came to play 'a greater part in political history and legal controversy than the whole of the rest of the Constitution put together' (Garran 1958:464).

The most significant challenge to the New Protection followed the Harvester judgement (November 1907), in which Higgins J declared the 'fair and reasonable wage' that would satisfy the requirements of the *Excise*

Tariff Act and thus enable the issue of a certificate of exemption from the payment of the excise under that Act. In August 1907 CCEA carried a resolution condemning the New Protection in the following terms:

> THAT this Council strongly protests against the stated intention of the federal government to attempt to attain what is called 'The New Protection' by regulating wages, conditions of labour, and prices of goods, on the ground that the Commonwealth Parliament has no constitutional powers to deal with these matters, such measures as the *Excise Tariff Act* being plainly in contravention of section 55 of the Constitution. This Council also considers that the practice of such illegal enactments is misleading to the public, and wishes to point out that it has already involved, and must lead to further, almost endless litigation, thereby causing heavy expenditure to prove their invalidity. (CCEA Meeting, 10/8/07).[2]

Following the Harvester judgement the CCEA levied affiliates and raised a fighting fund of $10 000. In Rex v. Barger (March–June 1908), the High Court majority claimed that the Constitution had granted the Commonwealth power to levy excises in order to obtain revenue. The *Excise Tariff Act* had sought to regulate labour conditions and so was invalid (6 *CLR* 41). Attorney General Groom noted that 'this invalidation deprived the New Protection of its foundation, and left the Government without the means of carrying out its declared policy' (Groom 1941:70). Other High Court challenges resulted in other New Protection appendages such as the *Trades Mark Act* (i.e. Union Label) and *Australian Industries Preservation Act* being invalidated. By 1909 the New Protection was in tatters. The major piece of legislation still intact was the *Conciliation and Arbitration Act*, although already this had been restricted in relation to state employees.[3]. Over the next decade employers expended considerable time and resources to ensuring that the scope of this Act remained minimal.

The doctrine of implied prohibition or reserved state powers, namely that the Commonwealth powers should be narrowly construed since the general residue of powers was with the states, had underpinned the High Court's emasculation of the New Protection. It also served employers well in restricting the Arbitration Court since the majority of the High Court consistently gave narrow interpretations to the Arbitration Court's authority because industrial powers were seen as reserved to the states. This is evidenced in the Sawmillers' case of 1909 (8 *CLR* 465), which suggested that there could be no dispute capable of federal settlement if the matter were already regulated by state law.

This line of reasoning was furthered in the first of three Bootmakers' cases in March 1910 and in which the High Court declared that the Arbitration Court was not competent to make an award inconsistent with the terms of a state law that applied to the parties in dispute (10 *CLR* 266). In the second case (June-July 1910) employers made a direct attack on the federal arbitration system by contending that its compulsory features were unconstitutional in that they were inconsistent with the voluntarism implicit in the common law notion of the term 'arbitration'. The High Court dismissed this argument on the ground that compulsory arbitration was a feature of the industrial legislation in Australia when the Constitution was drafted (11 *CLR* 1). In the third case — the Whybrow case (September–October 1910) — it was held that 'the constitutional industrial power did not permit the investment of legislative authority' and so the Arbitration Court could not make a common rule (11 *CLR* 311). Section 38(f) of the Act, which purported to confer this power, was declared *ultra vires*. This decision was a severe block to exercising federal industrial authority because it made it well nigh impossible to co-ordinate industrial conditions in any industry throughout Australia. It also considerably lengthened proceedings 'because the President could not investigate one concern and apply his decision to all concerns of a like character, but had to examine each firm's case separately' (Lee 1980:21). This, employers hoped, would eliminate similar exercises to the Harvester case, which aimed at establishing fair and reasonable standards on the basis of 'test' cases. The decision further meant that non-unionists were beyond the reach of the Arbitration Court and their employers were not bound to observe award conditions with respect to them. This was considered by some as inducing employers to prefer non-unionists to unionists (Foenander 1952:55).

Employers continued their assault, now seeking restricted interpretations of the key terms in section 51 (xxxv) of the Constitution. In the Sawmillers' case and the second Bootmakers' case the majority held that disputes must be 'real and genuine and not fictitious and illusory'. In the first of these cases Griffith added that 'such a dispute is not created by a mere formal demand and formal refusal without more . . . Mere mischief-making cannot, therefore, by the expenditure of a few shillings in paper, ink and postage stamps create such an occasion' (8 *CLR* 488). This was a rejection of the 'paper dispute' and essentially meant that unions had to be strong enough to engage in 'real' disputation. In the same year as the Bootmaker cases, Higgins settled the Brisbane Tramways dispute, a dispute of sufficient bitterness to warrant the swearing in of citizen police (6 *CAR* 130). The award Higgins made was set aside by the High Court on the ground that no interstate dispute existed. The Court further held in a subsequent case that no dispute could exist over matters in which the parties had an agreement. Thus, the Arbitration Court could not be asked to substitute its norms for those existing between the parties before the federal authority was invoked (Musicians case, December 1912, 15 *CLR* 636).

The Fisher Labor Government attempted remedies by legislation and referenda to open up what Attorney General W. M. Hughes described as a 'forbidden . . . industrial Eden whose gates were jealously guarded by many angels with flaming swords' (Groom 1941:240). Section 31 of the original *Conciliation and Arbitration Act* had provided that 'no award or order of the [Arbitration] Court shall be challenged, appealed against, reviewed, quashed, or called into question in any other Court on any account whatever'. In the second Bootmakers' case it was held by the High Court that, notwithstanding this section of the Act, the High Court could issue prohibitions on Arbitration Court awards (11 *CLR* 1). In 1911 the Federal Government sought, by way of referendum, Commonwealth control over trade, commerce, financial corporations, employment and monopolies. The range of powers sought was sufficient to return a 'No' vote in all states. The Government then amended the Act and provided under section 31 for the removal of the High Court's power to issue prohibitions in respect of federal awards as had happened in the Brisbane Tramways dispute. The High Court declared this section of the Act invalid, thus reserving to itself the right of deciding whether the Arbitration Court was acting within its powers under both the Constitution and the Act (18 *CLR* 54). Rather haughtily the EFNSW's *Annual Report* for 1911–12 (p.9) noted:

> As foretold in our last report, the amendments to this most illusory of Acts have proved quite ineffective, and it is time that Federal Parliament as a whole recognised the inutility of the Act. Mr Justice Higgins has, in some of his more recent decisions, also in his references to the High Court for interpretations, demonstrated his appreciation of the many deficiencies of the Act. The recent judgement of the High Court, wherein it was shown that the work of some employees, such as Engine Drivers and Firemen, does not constitute an industry under the Act, opens up a new aspect of deficiency, which must impress even the Unions. The earlier High Court decisions, depriving the Federal Arbitration Court of the power to make a common rule, strikes at the roots of the latter Court's usefulness, and something must be done to mend this, or frankly abolish the Court on the ground of its failure to serve any good purpose.

A second referendum designed to give the Commonwealth control over industrial matters accompanied the elections of 1913. Labor lost both the referendum and office. By then, however, it had made appointments to the High Court, which, over the next decade, were to oversee the abandonment of the doctrine of reciprocal immunities, severely circumscribe the doctrine of prohibitions, and expand the empire of the 'new province for law and order'. Notwithstanding the defeat of the 1913 referendum, and Labor's short exit from power (it regained office 15 months later), 1913 marks the high-water mark of employer victories in the High Court. Within 4 years, the CCEA was to lament:

> you can understand our being particular about personnel of the Court, we do not want High Court Judges, and we have to clip the Act in such a way that they have not the power to do as they can at present: and the Act should be altered in such a way that the Judge [Higgins] cannot have the illimitable power of spreading the Act in one direction, and keeping it solid in the other. (CCEA Annual Conference 19/9/17:41)

In 1912 O'Connor J died in office and had to be replaced. In addition, the *Judiciary Act* 1912 increased the size of the Court to seven members. Labor's appointments, together with the Isaacs and Higgins JJ who had dissented in most previous High Court judgements concerning arbitration, tipped the scales in favour of the expansion of federal jurisdiction.[4] From 1913 on, employers' challenges brought about increasingly diminishing returns.

One of the first industrial results of the new High Court appointments was the acceptance of the 'paper' dispute as constituting a 'genuine' dispute. Just prior to the appointment of the new members, the majority of the Bench had reasserted 'that a process of written demand for improved working conditions and refusal thereof had not brought into existence a "dispute" within the meaning of section 51 (xxxv) of the Constitution'. In the Merchant Service Guild case (September 1913) the new Bench, this time with Griffith CJ and Barton J dissenting, held that a paper-created dispute could be sufficient to create a 'dispute' within the meaning of section 51 (xxxv) (15 *CLR* 586). This interpretation was reaffirmed in the Felt Hatters case (March 1914) over the strong dissent of Griffith, who urged that the purpose of section 51 (xxxv) was to 'prevent and settle real industrial disputes, and not to facilitate the creation of fictitious disputes' (16 *CLR* 586).

The 'paper dispute' made it easy for unions to gain federal awards. This is illustrated by the Builders' Labourers' case of 1914. The Builders' Labourers' Federation had served a log of claims on employers in a number of states. When the Arbitration Court sought to determine an award employers appealed to the High Court. Griffith CJ, supported by Barton J, held there was not an interstate dispute. In their view there were five different sets of disputants, with five different sets of disputes, which had merely been consolidated into one set of demands. 'If such a joint demand is sufficient', added the Chief Justice, 'it is plain that the whole subject matter of the regulation of any and every branch of industry can be taken out of the hands of the State and transferred to the Federal Arbitration Court' (18 *CLR* 88).

The majority held that there may be an interstate dispute even in a highly localised industry such as the building of houses. In their view a dispute acquired an interstate character if workers 'make common cause against their respective employers'. As Griffith foresaw, this decision 'made it possible for almost any avocation in Australia, by appropriate organisation, to get itself within the jurisdiction of the Commonwealth Arbitration Court' (Sawer 1956:126). Sawer adds: 'the doctrine was the logical development of the view finally established in the Merchant Service Guild case that disputes can be created by a 'paper' process; the dissent of the Senior Justices was a last despairing attempt to assert the primacy of the States in industrial regulation and the residual character of the power intended to be given to the Commonwealth by Section 51(xxxv)' (ibid). This decision opened the way for industries, such as tramways undertakings, which had been areas of previous High Court prohibitions, to come under awards of the Arbitration Court.

Realising the important implications of the builders' labourers' action, the CCEA communicated with all federations and with the Attorneys General concerning the threatened invasion of state rights. It also resolved that 'this Council is prepared on the usual terms and conditions to act for the federations interested in the Master Builders' action in law if in the opinion of Mr E. F. Mitchell it be considered one which can be fought successfully' (CCEA Meeting 4/2/14). Counsel was sent to London but the Privy Council ruled it was not competent to hear claims relating to constitutional questions unless the High Court first issued a certificate under section 74 of the Constitution. This the High Court would not do.

The expanded role of the Arbitration Court in the private sector was accompanied by High Court decisions that also increased its scope in the governmental and semi-governmental sectors. This was as the result of the rejection of another important doctrine that had guided the early members of the High Court, namely the doctrine of reciprocal immunities. This held that the Commonwealth could not interfere with state instrumentalities, nor the states with those of the Commonwealth. The whittling away of this doctrine of immunities began with the Broken Hill cases of 1911 and 1912 (16 *CLR* 508), which differentiated between the 'governmental' and 'trading' activities of state instrumentalities. The High Court held that the trading activities of these instrumentalities were not immune from Arbitration Court authority. This separation of state instrumentality activities into 'governmental' and 'non-governmental' activities was taken a step further in the Municipalities case (1919), when even the non-commercial activities of municipal councils were held to be within the authority of the Arbitration Court. The majority held (with Griffith and Barton dissenting) that municipal corporations 'that owe their creation to State laws are not, in the matter of the making, maintenance, control and lighting of streets, State Government instrumentalities' (26 *CLR* 508). The thrust of the majority decision was that the immunities doctrine extended only to state activities controlled by the 'central' or 'general' government of the states and not to bodies such as municipal council, which were 'substantially independent of the control of government'.

The reciprocal immunities doctrine was laid to rest in the following year in the Engineers' case (July–August 1920, 28 *CLR* 129) in which the Court held that 'a State, or a person representing a State, could be made a party to a dispute cognizable before the Commonwealth Court of Conciliation and Arbitration'. The practical effect of the Engineers' decision was to expand greatly the potential scope of federal awards. The decision made it possible for all state industrial activities to come under federal control. Railway unions successfully sought a federal award in 1930, a situation that had been denied in 1906.

These constitutional developments were not welcomed by employers, who, for the next decade or so, were to be confronted with a system of dual federal–state awards until a different test of 'inconsistency' was developed. Even before the doctrine of reciprocal immunities was laid to rest in 1920, employers were complaining that the industrial powers of the Constitution had been 'so strained that the difficulty is to know if there is any industry or trade beyond the jurisdiction of the Court and if there is anything more than a shadow left of the State Courts which are best able to deal with most disputes' (CCEA Annual Convention 20/9/17: 110). At the 1917 CCEA Convention, a Convention notable for the hostility displayed towards Higgins and petitions for his removal from the Arbitration Court, the need to secure the 'right' personnel on the High Court was put forward by Mr T. P. Berry, a Queensland representative. Berry claimed:

> It seems we are taking a wrong step in condemning the Judge when we ought to condemn ourselves for not having worked to see that a proper Judge was put there in the first instance. The United Federations might appoint a judicial committee to watch matters of this sort in future. I warn members that there are pitfalls ahead. We know that our respected Chief Justice is a very old man. The second Judge, Sir Edmund Barton, is also not a young man, and when these two Judges disappear, unless we are prepared to use our influence to get the right class of man on top, we may have all this trouble again in years to

> come. I think our proper policy should be to start out now to see that right action is taken by the powers that be in the appointments that are likely to be made. (ibid:177)

The Convention decided 'that the National Union be urged to take immediate steps to ensure that a suitable person was appointed Chief Justice in succession to Sir Samuel Griffith' (ibid:35). The Convention also supported a scheme presented by a parliamentary draft committee, which proposed establishing a tribunal consisting of three Judges — one High Court Judge and two from the state industrial courts — which would determine whether or not federal jurisdiction existed. If such jurisdiction were found to exist, the matter was then to be handled by an Interstate Wages Board (ibid.).

With the appointments of Knox CJ and Starke J in 1920, however, new areas continued to come under the potential control of the Arbitration Court, with Isaacs J claiming that 'while the basic meaning of "industrial disputes" . . . remains the same, the progress of industry itself, its advancing reliance on science and art, must bring more and more instances within the ambit of [the Arbitration Court]' (27 *CLR* 540). These new instances included establishments not engaging unionists (Burwood Cinema case, 35 *CLR* 528, thus negating one of the outcomes of the Whybrow case), and the banking industry and the insurance industries (33 *CLR* 517). It was not until the State School Teachers' case of 1929 that some brake was placed on the advance of the Court's authority (41 *CLR* 569).

By 1920 the frequent failure in test cases had robbed the CCEA of any enthusiasm for High Court challenges and had made the raising of the not inconsiderable amount of money required for such challenges more difficult. For example, in February 1919, the EFNSW requested a High Court challenge to the Federated Clothing Trades Award, which had intruded on several areas of 'management prerogative'. In view of the general importance of the subject matter, the Council recommended 'that affiliated Federations contribute on the pro-rata basis, payment of half the Counsel fees for undertaking a challenge' (CCEA Annual Conference 11/10/20:73). This recommendation was conditional on ACMA agreeing to bear half of the costs of the case and on condition that federations be required to contribute 'no more than [$150] if the case be won, and no more than [$300] if the case be lost'. This parsimonious approach may be contrasted with the earlier euphoric approach in which $10 000 'with more if needed' was voted to High Court challenges. In 1922 confidence in High Court appeals had so waned that the CCEA refused to vote any money or assistance to the EFNSW in the Burwood Cinema case, notwithstanding the great importance of that case to employers.[5] By then the CCEA and its affiliates had been forced to expend much of their financial and other resources in the tribunal systems they had unsuccessfully sought to eradicate.

The 'New Province'

The increasing number of employees coming under the awards of industrial tribunals (some 75 per cent of the workforce by the end of the Higgins era (Sells 1924:962)[6] and the growing range of industries coming under federal jurisdiction necessitated employer associations playing a representative role before tribunals. The extent of these representative activities is indicated by the creation of industrial departments by federations and chambers and, at the federal level, by the necessity of the CCEA, ACMA and the Associated Chambers of Commerce of Australia (ACCA) to co-ordinate major 'test' cases before the Arbitration Court rather than rely on the more remote methods of parliamentary lobbying and legal action. The Court's increased scope is indicated by its official records, the *Commonwealth Arbitration Reports*. In 1909, a year in which the Court's scope was severely circumscribed and restricted exclusively to the maritime and pastoral industries, only seven cases came before the Court. Employers were successful in having prohibitions applied to three of these cases. Higgins dismissed the Institute of Marine Engineers' application for the deregistration of the Society of Engineers and the latter's application for the former's deregistration. Two agreements were certified. In all, the Arbitration Court's proceedings for 1909 take up just over 100 pages of *Arbitration Reports*.

This rather low level of activity can be contrasted with that of 10 years later, the last year of full-time activity by Higgins.[7] By then some 96 federal awards and 570 federal agreements were in force, half the workforce was unionised and 80 per cent of unionists belonged to federally registered unions (*Labour Report* 14). The *Commonwealth Arbitration Reports* for 1919 take up over 1200 pages. Twelve new awards were made and some 79 awards varied. A further 35 agreements were certified. Twenty-four compulsory conferences were held and 25 'miscellaneous' items were dealt with. Only one case was dismissed on the grounds of jurisdictional incompetence.

This period was important for employers, not merely because of the increased activity of unions and industrial tribunals, but also because it was a formative period in which the latter articulated enduring principles and in which unions developed methods of making common cause by way of joint applications. Such applications were to become a feature of the New South Wales Living Wage cases from 1914 on, and in the other state arbitration systems subsequently. At the federal level they became evident with the major basic wage and standard hours cases from 1920 on. Such union activities invited a joint, co-ordinated employer response.

The Harvester case, which was to be an important bench-mark case throughout the whole period, is illustrative of the principles and procedures incorporated into Arbitration Court proceedings by Higgins. He undertook a painstaking inquiry of a representative firm with a view to extending his findings to other establishments. In this, Higgins early displayed two traits that were to be a hallmark of his approach: that of judicial inquiry and a penchant for uniformity. Both of these traits, particularly during a period of an expanding realm of the new 'province for law and order', stimulated the centripetal forces operating in the federal system and the resultant 'test case' syndrome. Other aspects of the Harvester case were to have long-term implications for the parties. The rate prescribed, $4.20 per 6-day working week, was about 27 per cent higher than the unskilled rates that generally prevailed (Palmer 1931:210). It confirmed employers in their opposition towards the federal system and, once its durability was proved, had a magnetic attraction for unions. The 'lowest wage' (after 1911 referred to by the Arbitration Court as the 'basic wage')was to be 'an irreducible sacrosanct minimum' reinforcing the alleged 'needs' basis of its determination. Yet several criteria were evidenced by the Harvester case. These included not only social welfare considerations (i.e. needs) but also the reputable employer, capacity to pay, and, in relation to the secondary wage of McKay employees, work value, comparative wage justice and an attraction wage to induce 'lads to take on apprenticeships'.

One might have expected these developments to result in the CCEA becoming actively immersed in Arbitration Court proceedings. Such was not the case for most of the period though other organisations, particularly the EFNSW and the VCM, were very active in the federal sphere. A major factor in this lack of involvement was the CCEA's intense activities on the judicial plane to force the Arbitration Court out of business. Another factor was the state orientation of both union and employer associations at this time and the CCEA's dependence on affiliates to refer matters, to approve and finance operations. For most of the period it had no full-time staff.[8] In 1908 the fund available to meet running expenses was set at only $400 per year. In the same year the rules of the organisation were amended and the major role ascribed was distinctively legal: 'to safeguard the interests of employers by opposing all prejudicial legislation in progress and by testing the validity of any acts which may be against the interests of employers, and to deal with any matters inimical to employers generally'. Not surprisingly, in view of this rather limited objective, the CCEA saw its role as frustrating, rather than working within, federal arbitration. Thus the CCEA took no part in arbitral proceedings concerning the Harvester case but used the case to initiate a High Court challenge. For most of the period the CCEA played a legislative watchdog and appellate role, leaving affiliates to monitor and attend to industrial activities. The fragmented or piece-meal nature of most federal tribunal work following the successful Harvester challenge facilitated this approach. As noted below, however, that situation changed in 1920.

The Central Council's High Court sorties against the New Protection have already been recounted. The *Conciliation and Arbitration Act* was the major piece of legislation not invalidated though employers had attempted this in the second Boot Workers' case (1910). Amendments to this Act were hawkishly scrutinised and frequently challenged in the High Court. In addition the CCEA was also active in trying to promote 'favourable' legislation.

The legislation most actively pursued was the enactment of an Anomalies Bill by state parliaments. With the advent of Labor administrations in Queensland and New South Wales, the federations in these states became concerned about their competitive disadvantage because of greater employment costs. They therefore pressed for industrial uniformity between the states. Rather than have such a system implemented by the Arbitration Court, it was proposed that state industrial uniformity be achieved by requiring each of the states to legislate uniform industrial laws. The Anomalies Bill was designed to achieve this.

The Bill envisaged uniform wages boards legislation in each state, and that where anomalies were found to exist between two or more wages boards, if those boards could not resolve the differences, then the matters were to be referred to a central state authority for adjudication. An interstate industrial tribunal that could only deal with those matters referred to it by the state industrial tribunals would be established. The notion of uniformity was somewhat vague:

> In exercising its powers under this part the interstate tribunal shall make allowances for the differences in the economic conditions in different parts of the Commonwealth, shall have due regard to the interests of producers, workers and consumers, and of the public generally. (EFNSW *Annual Report* 1914–15:9)

This impractical Bill was to consume CCEA activities from 1912 to 1917 by which time the Victorian Liberal Government had indicated its disapproval and the state Labor governments ignored it. In 1915 the CCEA was further involved in lobbying state Premiers to ensure they did not legislate to hand over industrial powers to the Commonwealth as promised in that year's Premiers' Conference.

Though seemingly seeking uniformity, employers were reluctant to grasp the most effective instrument for bringing it about — federal control. Three immediate factors influenced this ambivalence. Firstly, employers in the non-Labor states derived a comparative advantage from having their employment conditions prescribed by state authorities. Secondly, the CCEA, notwithstanding the increasing signs to the contrary, continued to hope for the implementation of some universal wages boards system. Thirdly, they saw Hughes and Higgins as unsuitable architects for instituting a national system of uniformity. Prime Minister Hughes had led Labor's parliamentary initiatives to overcome the High Court restrictions on the Arbitration Court. Employers' regard for Higgins was sufficiently low as to seek his removal through parliament where it was even suggested that hanging might be the appropriate penalty for his actions (*CPD* vol. 83:2859 26/9/17). A frequent CCEA complaint was Higgins' anti-employer bias, which, notwithstanding its 'patent obviousness', the Council continued to bring to the public attention:

> The bias exhibited by Mr Justice Higgins since the establishment of the Arbitration Court towards employers calls for our utmost condemnation . . . There is not an employer who feels that he can get justice when appearing before him. We ought to seek his removal because the Arbitration Court has been the means of causing more strife and ill-feeling, and is likely to continue doing so as long as the present judge holds his position. (CCEA Conference 19/9/17:108)

The formation of the National Party in 1917 gave the CCEA hope that favourable legislation could at last be expected. In August it engaged legal counsel to 'prepare the basis for a new arbitration Act defining the limits of state and federal industrial powers'. The basic scheme envisaged was the drawing up of a list of industries considered 'national' and so under federal industrial jurisdiction. All other industries were to be handled by state authorities. For its part the Council considered only two industries to be 'national' — shipping and shearing. Industry-based employer organisations saw things differently, with many finding it advantageous to come under the authority (and imposed uniformity) of the Arbitration Court and thus remove wage competition from the market. This gravitation towards the federal jurisdiction is reflected in the employer association registration figures. Up to 1911 only one association — the Commonwealth Steamship Owners' Association with six members — was registered. By 1920 six other associations 6170 members) had registered and over the next 5 years a further 20 registrations took place.

As the CCEA lost the battle to reduce the Arbitration Court's influence, or to remove compulsory arbitration from the statute books, or to rationalise the dual arbitration system, more and more associations came to an accommodation with federal arbitration and sought uniformity through federal awards. Higgins' departure in 1921 hastened this trend. Thus for the CCEA there was increasing pressure either to accommodate itself to the federal jurisdiction or else to find a viable alternative. Not surprisingly in view of its history of Arbitration Court opposition it chose the latter approach. Its suggestion that special industries be designated as 'federal' and the rest left to the states was seriously considered at subsequent Premiers' Conferences, which were also seeking some political solution to the problem of overlapping awards. The Premiers failed to put such a plan into action because, like employers, they could not agree on the criteria for determining which industries ought to come under federal jurisdiction.

A National Union Bill, which attempted to allot specified industries to the Arbitration Court and leave the rest to state tribunals, also met with failure. This Bill was the one major show of employer cohesion during the period and involved not only the CCEA and its affiliates, but also the ACMA and 22 other associations (CCEA Conference 11/10/20:80–98). In November 1917 the Bill was handed to Hughes (now leader of the Nationalist Party following Labor's split on conscription), who had promised to give it 'careful attention'. Hughes, however, had his own solution to the increasing industrial dislocation. The *Industrial Peace Act* and amendments to the *Conciliation and Arbitration Act* were enacted in 1920 but the CCEA complained that 'of the practical and useful amendments suggested in our draft Bill practically no notice has been taken' (ibid, President's Report:2). The CCEA was opposed to the *Industrial Peace Act*, which established special tribunals to deal with specific industries. Delegates considered that such tribunals had the potential of creating flow-on problems for other industries. They also saw these tribunals as a method of enlarging the federal jurisdiction by stealth (ibid:56–9). The Act did not survive Hughes' loss of office as Prime Minister in 1923.[9]

The industrial front

By the time the *Industrial Peace Act* was enacted the centripetal tendencies operating in the Arbitration Court were such as to force the CCEA into greater direct involvement with matters coming to that Court. By 1920 the piece-meal case-by-case approach that characterised Arbitration Court operations began to give way to 'test' cases, that is, cases designed for general application. In that year Higgins initiated a test case in relation to standard hours of work and in the following 2 years test cases were held in relation to the basic wage. Such cases necessarily involved greater employer co-ordination. The areas of basic wage determination, standard hours of work, and secondary wage determination illustrate the increasing centralism of the Court's activities.

Basic wage determination

As already noted, the Harvester judgement, which provided the standard for subsequent basic wages, was initiated as a test case — the 'fair and reasonable' standards determined were to be applied to all those employers seeking exemption under the *Excise Act*. The generalised application of the Harvester Standard, however, became difficult with the circumscribed role initially forced on the Arbitration Court. All that Higgins could do was insert the basic wage into those few awards, restricted to the maritime and pastoral industries, that came to the Court for adjudication.

These circumstances changed after 1914 as the Court's work-load increased and as inflation threatened the real purchasing power of the 'sacrosanct minimum' basic wage. During the war the number of Commonwealth awards in force quadrupled from 18 in 1914 to 85 in 1918. The rate of increase in work-load is indicated by the fact that in 1916 as many awards were made as had previously existed and in addition some 33 agreements were certified. In the following year 33 new awards were made and 135 agreements filed. This increased work-load necessarily reduced the President's capacity to 'work value' the different cases coming before him; and caused him to rely more heavily on the comparative wage justice, an approach that built on previous cases. While this increased work-load may be considered to have affected the secondary wage component more than the standardised basic wage component, the inability of the Court to make a common rule or to vary awards during their currency, and the different terminal dates of awards, necessarily meant that the basic wage component varied from award to award. It was the Court's practice to insert the 'Harvester Equivalent' in awards being renewed or being made for the first time. The publication by the Commonwealth Bureau of Census and Statistics of a Retail Price Index in 1912 brought about greater uniformity since it provided, for the first time, an objective yardstick for cost of living increases (Higgins 1922:53). The reduction of real wages due to the exigencies of war (Sells 1924:926–7), and criticism of the Harvester Standard following the 1914 New South Wales Living Wage Inquiry (14 *AR*(NSW) 29), however, were the causes of significant industrial strife from 1915 on. In many instances employers agreed to index the basic wage in line with the Retail Price Index (Anderson 1929:269). By 1919, awards that had previously been made for up to 5 years were being renewed annually (EFNSW *Annual Report* 1919-1920). Amendments to the Act in 1920, which provided that awards could be varied during their currency, enabled unions to mount aggregated or test cases. Thereafter, basic wage regulation was no longer on an award-by-award basis. The Arbitration Court held test cases in 1920, 1921, 1922 and 1923. The 1922 introduced, and 1923 case confirmed, the adoption of the system of automatic quarterly cost of living adjustments (ACOLA). The system of ACOLA adopted, which required that the base being indexed itself be the subject of periodic review, was a stimulus to the formation of the Australian Council of Trade Unions and for greater involvement by peak employer organisations with Arbitration Court proceedings.

Standard hours of work

The determination of standard hours of work also became the subject of test cases rather than of sectional claims. As late as 1919 Higgins J confirmed 48 hours as the general standard. In some cases, however, 'where the nature of the trade required it' hours had been set at 52 per week (Higgins 1922:56–7). In other cases standard hours of work were reduced where there were 'some strong and distinctive reasons for reductions' (10 *CAR* 185). Such distinctive reasons included the needs of building workers 'to follow their job' (7 *CAR* 226), the rigours of underground work and work associated with smelters (10 *CAR* 185, 11 *CAR* 636), and for women in the clothing industry, for reasons of 'health, efficiency and output' (13 *CAR* 705–6). In 1919, following the tendering of medical evidence claiming that the dusty and shift-work conditions of flour millers rendered these employees 'less healthy and more liable to infection', standard working hours were reduced in that industry (14 *CAR* 27–8).

The major departure from this piece-meal approach took place in November 1920, by which time a Royal Commission in New South Wales was reviewing the 48-hour working week. In the Timber Workers case (14 *CAR* 845) unions made similar claims to those that had proved successful in the Millers' case. Higgins, however, found 'no exceptional facts in the industry which would justify reduced standard hours'. Rather than dismiss the case outright, he chose to use it as a test case to determine whether a

44-hour standard week ought be the norm in similar industries, particularly those industries that involved the tending of machines. Higgins invited the views of employers and employees generally as well as those of the government in determining whether or not the standard 44-hour week ought to be implemented. The CCEA determined to prevent the case from becoming a test one. It decided it 'would not accept representation before the Court in the manner suggested by Mr Justice Higgins, which placed employers more or less in the position of defendant litigants' (CCEA Conference 11/10/20, President's Report:6). The Council briefed legal representation, which argued that the matter should not be decided by the President but 'by a judicial tribunal assisted by statistical experts'. The timber workers were successful in having hours of work reduced. The findings in this case were also used to justify a 44 standard hours working week in the Engineers case (15 *CAR* 320) initiated in the same year.

The Hughes Government also set about ensuring that the Timber Workers' case would not be used as a test case, and with greater success than the CCEA. It chose not to intervene in the case but had the Act altered to provide that, in any cases not already before the Court, any alteration of standard hours of work had to be considered by a Full Bench of three judges. This amendment prevented Higgins from applying his decision in the Timber Workers' cases more widely, and employers subsequently successfully appealed to a Full Bench to have the timber workers and engineers revert to 48 hours (16 *CAR* 649). The very act of instituting Full Benches to deal with major matters invited a co-ordinated union and employer response.

Secondary wage determination

The secondary wage, which was designed to facilitate different rates of remuneration according to the differing and changing characteristics of different occupations, also began a transformation from being sectionally and independently determined to one of centralised regulation. This process can be seen as taking place on an occupational, regional and inter-industry basis.

The Arbitration Court's initial approach under O'Connor J when confronted with the 'mysteries of the several arts and crafts' was to rely 'on the distinctions in grade between the employees as expressed in wages by the employers for many years' (2 *CAR* 65). Higgins J also approved of awarding existing differentials (Hancock 1979). This approach, however, came into conflict with his belief that 'awards must be consistent one with the other or else comparisons breed unnecessary restlessness, discontent and trouble'

(Higgins 1922:41). In many cases Higgins found that employers could not agree on the 'distinctions in grade' (7 *CAR* 6). As different industries came under the federal jurisdiction Higgins found many conflicting 'distinctions in grades as expressed by state awards and determinations' (10 *CAR* 484). The Builders Labourers' Award discussed earlier was one of many in which rates were standardised in the same city, between regions, and between states irrespective of previous regional differentials.

As the Court's jurisdiction expanded so too did its reliance on comparative wage justice to determine the secondary wages for different occupations. Comparative wage justice had inter-occupational, inter-industry and trans-industry potential for creating a unified wages system employing generally applicable, rather than case-by-case considerations. In the Harvester case, for example, having fixed the margin for fitters, Higgins fixed the same rate for a number of other occupations on the grounds that they required the same degree of skill (an extremely subjective criterion) and training. These occupations included those of millers, borers, slotters, gear cutters, turners, bar drillers, lappers, precision grinders, brass furnishers, boiler makers and metal moulders. Since the length of training was a reasonably objective measure, other unrelated occupations requiring apprenticeships — those of carpenters, joiners, tailors, printing compositors, butchers, coopers, etc. — were given the same secondary wage. The outcome of Higgins' concern to remove anomalies was that once relativities were fixed, movements in any of these occupations engendered wage movements for other occupations. 'Unions', wrote Hutson (1971:156), 'developed considerable ingenuity in drawing parallels between classifications, while the hunting down of anomalies became a popular sport'. Hancock (1930:151) noted that unions further 'developed the subtlety of medieval theologians in arguing about the fine points' of classifications and anomalies.

Not unnaturally in a system in which unions could exploit secondary wage movements in one area to seek flow-ons to others, a major union objective was to seek the award that would maximise such flow-ons. One of Higgins' last functions was to determine the Engineers' Award, which, for the next half century, would form the bench-mark federal award.[10] The log presented by the Amalgamated Society of Engineers sought minimum rates of pay for over 50 different occupations, all of which would have intra-award (vertical) relativities as well as inter-award (horizontal) relativities. Over 700 employer respondents were cited in the award and these represented a diverse range of industries, so diverse that Higgins felt it necessary 'in mere justice, to allow no less than eighteen advocates separately to cross-examine the union's witnesses from separate points of view' (15 *CAR* 300). It was to be expected that such a bench-mark award, with its global implications for employers generally, would be the subject of co-ordinated employer activity. As with the basic wage and standard hours of work, the secondary wage was to prove a siren song for Central Council tribunal involvement.

ORGANISATIONAL DEVELOPMENTS

CCEA developments

As the scope of industrial legislation and that of industrial tribunals extended, so too did the federations' and the CCEA's concern for the lack of a united front by employers towards union hostilities, over-award payments, uniform employment standards and the like. The federations, which had been conceived as the employers' equivalent of the Trades and Labour Councils, soon discovered they lacked the authority or sufficient general support for them to be much more than useful forums during periods of perceived legislative or industrial threat, or to provide industrial services to less well endowed affiliates unable to establish their own industrial departments. With one minor exception,[11] however, the federations showed remarkable internal stability and for most of the period employers acknowledged the division of labour between the federations and Chambers of Manufactures and Commerce. In Victoria this work demarcation was obscured in 1919 when the VCM established its own industrial department and became the major negotiator with the Victorian Trades Hall Council. Arguably, the VCM moved in this direction because the VEF had not followed its New South Wales counterpart in establishing an industrial department and because of its preoccupation with political rather than industrial considerations at that time.

Internal stability proved less easy for the CCEA and by 1920 three disaffiliations had already taken place. The first of these occurred in 1908 when the EFNSW resigned over the question of finances. By 1905, this federation had expended between $40 000 and $60 000 in fighting the New South Wales arbitration system (*Liberty and Progress* May 1905:43). Notwithstanding the fact that at that time the federation's membership included many of the largest metropolitan enterprises, the raising of sufficient fighting funds was never an easy matter. In fighting the Jumbunna case (1908) the CCEA had levied all affiliates on the population basis normally used for such purposes. The EFNSW objected to being financially committed without its prior consent and resigned in protest (CCEA Meeting 13/2/08). It rejoined when new rules were adopted in October 1908. These rules severely circumscribed the CCEA's financial independence. They provided for an annual operating budget of only $400 and a further sum 'not exceeding [$400] to meet expenses connected with conferences, legal and other special matters' (CCEA Meeting, 5/8/08).

The mendicant role forced on the CCEA as a result of this rule change affected its efficiency and reduced its activities. It was not able to engage a full-time Secretary or Industrial Officer, while the need for careful financial management caused it to prevaricate on a number of cases of importance to the CCEA's goals.

The second resignation was that of the VEF in December 1912. CCEA President E. Smith refused to deal with a particular matter sponsored by the VEF on the grounds that the CCEA's constitution did not allow it to do so. The VEF resigned in protest (CCEA Meeting 2/12/12). Six months later the EFNSW again resigned in protest against the CCEA exercising its authority independently of affiliates. The CCEA had authorised the publication of legal opinion critical of the referendum proposals calling for the handing over of industrial powers to the Commonwealth. As was the pattern with the EFNSW when under state Labor Governments, it was then favourably disposed towards the federal jurisdiction.[12] Its resignation reduced the CCEA to only two affiliates during a time of significant national industrial legislation and activity. The problem was overcome at a conference of delegates, which formulated a new set of rules further restricting the CCEA's independence and at which the VEF was pacified by the removal of E. Smith and R. S. Walpole, who had been President and Secretary respectively, since the CCEA's inauguration (CCEA Meeting 17/6/13).

As Melbourne was then the seat of Commonwealth government as well as the locus of Arbitration Court activities, it was also the logical place for the CCEA's location. Until the removal of Smith and Walpole the VEF effectively controlled the CCEA, much to the EFNSW's displeasure. All executive positions (President, Secretary and Treasurer) were held by members of the VEF. In addition the CCEA's offices were located with the VEF and until 1909 it was common for state federations to nominate VEF members to represent them at Council meetings to avoid travelling expenses. In 1913 The Federated Employers' Assurance of Western Australia Ltd, a mutual defence society, established the Western Australian Employers Federation (WAEF) (FEAWA Ltd, Report to Shareholders, August 1913). This action followed the advent of the first Labor government in that state, and amendments to the *Industrial Arbitration Act* in 1912. The CCEA had earlier tried to coax the Western Australian Pastoralists' Association, the Western Australian Chamber of Mines, and the Perth Manufacturers' and Producers' Association into forming a federation but with no success (*Liberty and Progress* April 1904:10). Until the WAEF was admitted to membership of the CCEA in February 1914 the Chamber of Mines provided a Western Australian input.

In response to a combined waterside workers' and carters' action against the Union SS Co. and the Huddard Co. over the employment of non-union labour, an employers' federation was formed in Tasmania in 1908 and immediately sought Central Council assistance in mounting a High Court challenge against the unions. The CCEA gave financial support to the Tasmanian appeal (which was unsuccessful and cost about $1000) but it was not until 1915 that this federation affiliated with the CCEA. Its membership was short-lived. In 1918 it advised that 'it had decided to withdraw from the Central Council as a prelude to the dissolution of the Federation'. The CCEA unsuccessfully attempted to resuscitate the Tasmanian Employers' Federation but in 1920 'regretted that the evident lack of co-operation on the part of employers in the Island State leaves it without an Employers Federation' (CCEA Conference 11/10/20, President's Report: 7). This state of affairs continued until 1952.

Indemnity funds

For the federations, and more especially the CCEA, the availability of finance was a major factor in determining the scope of industrial activities. The major source of income was membership fees although special levies were provided for in the various rules. Means of securing an adequate income to finance arbitration and other cases became an important consideration. The major method introduced to provide for such cases was the establishment of indemnity funds.

The first of these funds was established in South Australia in January 1912. Contributions in 1913 amounted to $9844 and by 1917 the fund had 'gone over the [$40 000] margin with absolute cash in hand'. The fund was then earning $2000 in interest and it was confidently predicted would soon be self-supporting. By 1920 the fund reported an accumulated cash balance 'in excess of [$50 000]'. The fund was open to all employers, and administered by trustees independently of the federation. Trustees referred cases in which employers sought funding to the federation, which, if it approved the expenditure, undertook the case. The federation's approach was to hold a meeting of employers affected and 'carry a resolution that all the respondents named in the plaint should bear the costs based on the number of employees'. Those belonging to the fund were reimbursed, thus providing an incentive for the other employers to join (CCEA Conference 25/9/17:151–3).

As already noted, the WAEF was actually formed, not by meetings of employers, but by the Federated Employers' Assurance of Western Australia. This Assurance company provided the federation with the funds needed for its industrial work (FEAWA Circular to Shareholders 14/8/13).

The SAEF and WAEF delegates to conferences made great claims for their funds and attributed to these the relative industrial stability in their states. They were critical of the other states that did not have such funds and that, as a result, they claimed, became wage pace-setters. They frequently called on other federations to establish similar funds. Thus, at the 1917 Conference (p.152) it was moved:

> That the frequency of the calls on the finances of the Employers Organisations to meet the legal costs testing the validity of Acts of Parliament and for the general protection of Employers during strikes and otherwise has made it imperative that a proportionate system of contribution by employers should be established both for State and Federal purposes and that this Conference pledges itself to support a method similar to the Employers' Mutual Assurance Fund Ltd now registered in South Australia and Western Australia. (ibid:152)

In 1917 the VEF attempted to establish such a fund in concert with the VCM, Melbourne Chamber of Commerce, Chamber of Mines and the associations of 'Warehousemen, Carriers, Grocers, Hardware Merchants and Mill owners'. Members were to be levied at 50 cents per $200 paid in wages and the fund was to be jointly administered by the Secretary of the VEF and that of the VCM. Rather than register as a company, thus having to file a balance sheet with the Registrar General 'for any Trades Hall men to see what monies we have', the Victorian scheme was established as a non-profit company. The VEF anticipated that funds of $500 000 would be available within 4 years 'and if we get a big fund like that, organised labour should be very chary about starting a strike' (ibid:154–5). Like other joint ventures at this time, this one proved futile.

At the 1917 Conference W. Brookes, President of the EFNSW, considered that 'taking into consideration big and small associations and companies over [$200 000] a year was spent on industrial matters'. Brookes claimed that no fund had been established but 'had been the subject of consideration on several occasions' (ibid:156). EFNSW *Annual Reports* do not support Brookes' latter contention. A fund was established in 1913 (EFNSW *Annual Report 1912–13*:18). In the reports for 1912–13 to 1914–15 the federation complained that the fund 'was overlooked by those whom we thought would come into it'. The fund went out of existence, probably in 1916. Financial problems persisted with the major federations and by implication the Central Council.

As the federations in the two major states struggled to establish indemnity funds the Chambers of Manufactures moved into the field of insurance. By 1914 Workers' Compensation Acts had been enacted in New South Wales and Victoria. The federations did not respond to these Acts other than by way of negative criticism. The chambers responded in a more practical way. In 1914 both the VCM and the CMNSW established insurance companies to cope with employers' needs under the compensation legislation. The Victorian company (Chamber of Manufactures Insurance) also branched into other areas of insurance. In both cases these companies provided their chambers with a lucrative source of income. The VCM received commission of $2194 in 1914 and this had grown to nearly $6000 by 1920 (Matthews 1971:66). By the latter date the Mutual Accident Indemnity Insurance Company was contributing over $2000 a year to the CMNSW's coffers (ibid:67). The finance generated by these insurance companies enabled the chambers to extend their operations. In 1919 the VCM appointed three new full-time officers, one of whom was an industrial officer (ibid:68). The VEF was not in a position to appoint an industrial officer until 1927, the year in which it established an imitative insurance company (ibid.).

Industrial services

Unlike the VEF, whose major preoccupation was political, the EFNSW quickly came to recognise the need to provide basic industrial services if it were to remain viable. In 1914 the President's Report noted the large number of 'sectional associations' created to deal with the 'increased application of arbitration laws to every section of Employers'. If sectional action continued, and if the 'tendency in some organisations to keep aloof from the Federation' became widespread, the President predicted that the federation 'would soon develop into a mere academic institution'. He urged the federation to 'take such action as may make it of practical use to members and retain its position as the authoritative mouthpiece of all employers as far as industrial legislation and action is concerned' (EFNSW *Annual Report 1914–15*:15). The federation responded with two positive moves: the restructuring of Council's Executive to give affiliated associations greater involvement, and the creation of an industrial department through which affiliates could channel their industrial activities.

The Executive restructuring increased the already large Executive of 19 (all of whom were elected at the annual general meeting) by adding to it nominated representatives of affiliated associations. There were 15 nominated representatives in 1915–16 resulting in an Executive of 34 members (EFNSW *Annual Report 1915–16*:1).

In 1915 the federation established its Industrial Department with J. F. Kirby, a former inspector with the Department of Labour and Industry, as the Industrial Officer. The scope of this Department's activities was a wide one:

> To advise members as to the correct interpretation of Acts, Awards, Agreements and Regulations.
> To advise shop-keepers in the carrying out of the Early Closing Act.
> To advise Factory Proprietors re the proper method of guarding machinery, also in respect of ventilation, space accommodation, etc., as required by the Act or Regulations.
> To supply employers, at their request, with Awards, and variations, when gazetted, with an interpretation of any new matter that may seem to be ambiguous.
> To instruct Members how to keep the time and pay sheets as required by the Act or Regulations.
> To assist the respective industries connected with the Federation in the Preparation of cases for Courts or Boards.
> To keep in touch with all proposed new Labour legislation, and advise re same.
> To record all important judgements of Industrial Courts which may be of service to respondents in further cases.
> To assist in bringing threatened industrial upheavals and strikes to an amicable conclusion. (ibid: 12)

Subsequent *Annual Reports* indicate that employers made extensive use of these industrial services, particularly in relation to award making. Kirby was an employer representative at the New South Wales Living Wage Inquiries as well as that into hours of work. In 1920 the Industrial Department began publishing *Industrial Bulletin* (subsequently called *Employers' Review*) as a monthly journal that informed readers of award variations, industrial legislation and the like, and in which it attempted to counteract left-wing union propaganda with its own free enterprise rhetoric.

The common front

The rapid growth of the union movement, its apparent cohesive organisation, its syndicalist and One Big Union elements, the extension of federal awards and the increased number of major inquiries, all brought calls for better forms of organisation between the many disparate employer associations, their federal bodies, and the peak national councils. As early as 1910 CCEA deliberations were directed at getting employers to hold 'the common front' and not pay over-award payments (CCEA Meeting 11/12/10). In 1912, a year of syndicalist strike activity, the CCEA adopted a plan to counter 'the general strike tactic' (CCEA Conference 25/9/12:12). By 1915 consideration was being given 'towards securing more cohesion between large and small employers' (CCEA Conference 24/4/15:8). The federations, which in their formative years represented mainly the larger employers, increasingly came to represent the smaller and medium sized firms, which needed as much protection from the industrial activities of larger establishments as from unions or industrial legislation. The larger firms were able to register as industrial organisations in their own right and, in many cases, opted to join sectional associations rather than the federations. Though some of these associations were affiliated with the federations, they acted independently. Thus, though the shipping and pastoralist associations had earlier been the mainstay of the federations, by 1917 the latter were complaining that these associations were 'doing their own thing, and likewise the colliery owners and Mine Managers Association' (CCEA Conference 18/9/17:15). By then wage inquiries had already been instituted in New South Wales and Queensland and both employers and unions were calling for a federal basic wage review.

These inquiries intensified the need for cohesion between employers. Speaking of the New South Wales experience W. Brookes noted:

> The chief point when you have a Commission inquiring into an important matter . . . which has an absolute bearing upon the whole of the wages to be paid in the States and the Commonwealth, is that the employers as a body cannot afford to let it go without the most strenuous attention . . . If it is a big inquiry, it means a lot of labour and very great cost.

'The 1914 Inquiry', Brookes added, 'cost over [$10 000]' (CCEA Conference 20/9/17:133–4).

One proposal for overcoming the problems of co-ordinating the presentation and financing of cases, as well as to provide a united front against strike action, was the creation of an Employers' Industrial Disputes Council. The object of such a council was to be 'the securing of a powerful Central Council of Employers representing important industries to deal with any serious industrial disturbances arising at any time'. It was suggested that the Council comprise representatives of the Central Council, the Associated Chambers of Commerce, the ACMA, and 'of such large employing interests as Shipping, Colliery Proprietors, Pastoralists, and other large groups of industries'. The Council noted that in order to be 'entirely successful it would be necessary for similar councils to be established in each state'. The 1917 Conference called for the establishment of state councils (ibid: 141–8). Only in New South Wales was there an (unsuccessful) attempt to establish a council (EFNSW *Annual Report 1917–18*:16–7).

The 1920 Conference again deliberated on the question of greater employer solidarity and two papers were presented on this subject. In his paper entitled 'Proposals for Improving Organisation of Employers', VEF President T. R. Ashworth described the Victorian situation in which the VEF was the 'connecting link between 53 affiliated separately organised trade sections with a membership of about 8000'. The VCM had about 1700 members organised into trade sections and the Chamber of Commerce had about 600 members and eight affiliated bodies. The Chamber of Mines had 150 individual and corporate members. The Chamber of Agriculture had 139 branches with an undisclosed membership. In addition, there were 'at least 31 other independent sections of employers' with a combined membership of about 4000. 'There is not', complained Ashworth, 'a connecting link between the 36 independent employers' bodies, no organisation which can speak and act for employers as a whole in the same way that the Trades Hall Council can for employees'. This, according to Ashworth, resulted in 'friction, waste of energy, loss to employers and ultimate social loss' (CCEA Conference 11/10/20:103–78 and Appendix A).

Samuel Perry's paper ('Organic Co-operation of Manufacturers and Employer Federations: Proposed Federal Council') explored unitary and federal systems for a Commonwealth Council of Employers in which industrial, commercial and manufacturing interests would be compartmentalised into separate departments (ibid: 100–2 and Appendix A). His federal model foreshadowed, in many respects, the approach adopted by the Confederation of Australian Industry over 50 years later. It is reviewed more fully in the next chapter.

Both papers made it clear that neither the federations nor the CCEA were performing the industrial co-ordinating role for which they had been instituted. In the case of the VEF a further consideration made employer solidarity more pressing — the independent industrial role then being exercised by the VCM. In the absence of VEF industrial leadership the Melbourne Trades Hall Council had begun the practice of attempting to resolve disputes by negotiations with the VCM. Apparently, claimed T. R. Ashworth, 'it is the intention of the Chamber, a body which represents about one-tenth of the organised employers, to confer with the Trades Hall Council which represents practically the whole of organised Labour'. The

VCM had, in fact, filled a vacuum created by the VEF's own incompetence. The VCM was also called in by Higgins J to represent employers at the Timber Workers' (standard hours) case after the CCEA declined to give evidence (14 *CAR* 846). Ashworth prophetically noted that the key to greater unity was the Chamber of Manufactures.

The Conference considered that one method of bringing about greater cohesion would be to accommodate 'all employer associations in one building'. A resolution was passed recommending that each federation 'take steps to acquire a building to accommodate the various Employers' Associations' (CCEA Conference 11/10/20:135–6). The major resolution passed called on the CCEA to convene conferences of employer groups aimed at closer cohesion:

> That the Central Council be requested to convene from all States a Conference of organised bodies of employers including the Chambers of Manufactures, Commerce, Mines and Agriculture, Master Builders, Pastoralists, Ship Owners and the Employers' Federations for the purpose of formulating proposals for the closer organisation of employers. (ibid : 107)

Not withstanding the various wages and standard hours inquiries (1920–23), the Basic Wage Royal Commission (1920) and the industrial Peace Conference (1922), which necessitated a combined employer input, nothing came of this proposal. The CCEA referred the matter back to the federations, requesting them to convene state conferences. Only the VEF appears to have held a conference. The EFNSW's criticism of this Conference served to widen the breach between employers (CCEA Meeting, 2/3/21). Further, by 1920 the Chambers of Manufactures embarked on a second generation of protection for those industries created under the stimulus of war (Hagan 1981:25–30). They were wary of any united front overtures that might obstruct their drive. Thus employers moved into the 1920s with little cohesion — cohesion that had been the rationale for bringing into existence the employers' federations and the Central Council of Employers of Australia.

Summary and conclusion

By 1920, though the New Protection had been eradicated, compulsory arbitration had been confirmed as the institutionalised method of dispute resolution in the Commonwealth and in most states. Wage determination had also largely passed over to these industrial tribunals, in the case of the Commonwealth Court of Conciliation and Arbitration as an incidental part of its dispute prevention and settlement function. The extension of the federal jurisdiction as the result of liberal High Court decisions after 1913, the attractive minimum standard established by the Harvester case, and the ability of unions to take advantage of federal awards without necessitating a severance from the state tribunal systems as the result of the Bootmakers' case, inevitably led to centripetal forces that centralised wage determination and sought to institute a system of uniformity and consistency.

The CCEA adjusted slowly and negatively to these developments. Its organisational structure was poorly equipped to handle an extension of the federal jurisdiction. Its expensive and successful early High Court litigation against the Arbitration Court lulled it into a false sense of security, which, in turn, made it easier for affiliates to emasculate its authority and resources. The financial and autonomy losses suffered by the CCEA in 1908 and 1913 left it unable to do much other than react negatively to industrial developments.

Just as the federations' support of the CCEA was largely token until some matter requiring national co-ordination arose, so too federations found their own support reliable. As major companies took out state industrial registration in their own right, and as sectional associations handled their own industrial matters, the federations' influence waned. The EFNSW responded constructively to this situation by creating an industrial department and by providing a practical service rather than merely the support of ideologically charged rhetoric. In Victoria it was the VCM that established such a department, a move that rejected the traditional demarcation between the role of the chambers and that of the federations. The two Victorian organisations were to vie for recognition as the employer mouthpieces on industrial affairs — a situation that was to be replicated later in New South Wales, South Australia and nationally. By 1920 the situation had been reached where the CCEA simply referred matters sent to it back to affiliates, thus leading to either no action or to different approaches in different states. In other cases the CCEA chose to ignore appeals to handle matters of national import to employers.

The High Court failures and the inability of the CCEA to extract favourable legislation under Labor Governments, and the Nationalist Government headed by the parliamentary champion of federal arbitration, meant failure for the limited objects of the CCEA, which were conceived in terms of legislation and litigation. By 1920 the CCEA could boast little success on the legislative, legal or organisational fronts. Most importantly it had failed to prevent an expansion of the federal system or to come to terms with that expanded system. It had failed to remedy the overlapping of industrial awards, overlapping that, ironically, had been made easier by its own successful High Court action in 1910. The removal of the menace of overlapping awards was to be the Central Council's obsessive pre-occupation of the 1920s.

Notes

[1] Legislation forming part of this 'consistent policy' included the *Immigration Restriction Act* 1901, the *Defence Act* 1903, the *C&AA* 1904, the *Customs Tariff Act* 1902, the *Pacific Islanders Act* 1901, the *Sugar Bounty Act* 1905, the *Bounties Act* 1907, the *Excise Tariff (Spirits) Act* 1906, the *Australian Industries Preservation Act* 1906, the *Excise Tariff (Agricultural Machinery) Act* 1906, the *Trades Mark Act* 1905, the *Excise Procedure Act* 1907, the *Customs Act* 1907, the *Excise Tariff Act* 1908 and the *Manufacturers Encouragement Act* 1908.

[2] Meetings referred to are those of the Executive Committee.

[3] In 1906 the High Court declared that a union of state government railway employees could not come under federal jurisdiction (3 *CLR* 809).

[4] The appointments were Charles Powers, G. E. Rich and F. Gavan Duffy. A. B. Piddington, Labor's first choice, resigned without ever sitting, as the result of agitation by the legal fraternity.

[5] The case concerned the ability of unions to make employers not engaging unionists respondents to awards. The success by unions had the potential to negate the lack of common-rule provisions in the federal jurisdiction.

[6] This seemingly high figure is no doubt inflated by the common-rule application of state award employees, and by the fact that most federal award employees at this time also came under state awards.

[7] Higgins announced his resignation in September 1920. His resignation was to take effect after completion of 'certain matters partly heard' (Higgins 1922:172).

[8] The only paid appointment, other than that of part-time Secretary, was that of Walpole appointed as 'adviser to the President' when relieved of the Secretary's position in 1913. The position seems to have approximated that of a research officer. Walpole had been part-time Secretary from 1904.

[9] The Act became a dead letter under the Bruce Government and was finally repealed together with a long schedule of other outdated Acts, by the *Statute Law Revision Act* 1950.

[10] The Engineering Award was subsequently named the Metal Trades Award and then the Metal Industry Award.

[11] As already noted, the VCM disaffiliated from the VEF in 1905.

[12] The ambivalence of the EFNSW concerning federal/state regulation under Labor Governments is developed more fully in Plowman (1983).

3

RIVAL SHOPS 1921–1929

The previous chapter outlined developments from 1907 to 1920. During this period the major activity of the Central Council of Employers of Australia was to restrict the federal arbitration system. Until 1913 the CCEA was successful on this front. Thereafter its High Court challenges merely opened the way for an expanded federal jurisdiction. The High Court's test of legal inconsistency adopted in 1910 allowed for a situation of overlapping federal and state awards. This enabled unions to treat tribunals as 'rival shops', to seek award variations from one tribunal in the knowledge that it could not reduce standards already determined by the other tribunal; to pick the most favourable combination of employment standards from their federal and state awards; and to jettison federal awards when it suited. The rationalisation of dual regulation became a major preoccupation of both employers and legislatures during the 1920s. Attempts to rationalise dual regulation included increasing the Commonwealth's industrial powers by the conferring of such powers by the states or by referendum, and, conversely, the Commonwealth vacating the industrial field in favour of the states. These developments are reviewed in the first part of this chapter. It also examines the emergence of basic wage and standard hours test cases during the period. Such test cases necessitated union and employer co-ordination. The organisational developments of the Central Council and its activities to bring about a 'closer organisation of employers' are reviewed in the second part of the chapter.

Dual regulation

By 1921 High Court decisions had facilitated an expansion of the federal jurisdiction beyond the level that employers considered constitutionally permissible. This expansion continued until halted by the State School Teachers' case of 1929 (41 *CLR* 569). It created a situation of overlapping federal and state regulations. As a result of the Whybrow case (1910) the Arbitration Court was precluded from making a common rule binding all employers in a particular industry. Further, as the result of the Holyman's case (1914) the Arbitration Court could not make an award for non-unionists employed by respondent employers. Thus, where federal awards regulated industries they could not do so to the exclusion of state awards. The latter catered for those employed by non-respondents and regulated employment conditions for non-unionists.

The nuisance value of this dual system of regulation was compounded for employers by the test of legal inconsistency adopted by the High Court in 1910, namely the ability to satisfy the requirements of both federal and state laws simultaneously. In the Whybrow case the High Court held that a federal wage of 50 cents per day was not in conflict or inconsistent with a state wage of 48 cents per day. The Court observed that, by paying the higher rate, an employer automatically observed the lower rate and consequently no inconsistency could arise. This test of inconsistency enabled unions to pick the most favourable combination of employment conditions from the state and federal provisions. Thus they were not exclusively bound by either the federal or state standards, could opt for the best combination of standards derived from both sets of prescriptions, and could repudiate federal award provisions when it suited. The proportion of employees regulated by federal awards thus varied depending on the attractiveness of federal regulation vis-a-vis state regulation.[1]

As well as problems of award instability, the dual tribunal system also led to the major problem of flow-ons between jurisdictions. This is illustrated by the 1914 federal Builders' Labourers' Award discussed in the previous chapter. The *Annual Report* of the EFNSW for 1914-15 (p.4) complained of this new federal award:

> In this case Higgins J raised the wages from 9/- to 11/- per day and also reduced the hours from 48 to 44 per week with the provision for a one hour meal break. Seeing that at the time all the skilled tradesmen in the industry are working a 48 hour week (with a 3/4 hour lunch break) it can be easily seen how difficult it is for employers to carry on their work satisfactorily, as these unskilled labourers have to attend upon the skilled men, and are not available for nearly one hour before the skilled men leave off work.

The report noted that of 3000 builders in New South Wales only 170 were bound by the federal award, thereby causing 'friction and dissatisfaction all round'. The relevant state award had been made for 3 years, the federal award for 5 years. Their concurrence involved 'starting and knocking off men at different times, payment of overtime to some and not to others, while others again are out of employment' (ibid.).

As well as the inconvenience and friction caused by the two awards the federation was also concerned about the pace-setting implications of the federal award. Tradesmen in the New South Wales building industry had begun to demand the 44-hour week as well as a restoration of the previous wage relativities between tradesmen and labourers. The federation lamented:

> Should 44 hours become the standard week's work in the building trade, other industries may be expected to follow suit. The importance of the reduction of four hours per week per unit of industrial population, therefore, becomes a question of the greatest public importance . . . Justice Higgins in granting 44 hours to labourers, did so knowing it would be used as a lever to enforce the same limitations of working hours in other industries. (ibid.)

The pace-setting potential was not confined to the Arbitration Court. After the recession of 1921–22 it was industrial legislation in the Labor states of Queensland and New South Wales that set the pace. In many instances unions merely allowed their federal awards to expire, refused to submit an interstate log of claims (that is, create an interstate dispute with employers in these two states) and thus reverted back to state awards. This is instanced by the AWU case. This union had been the applicant to the Pastoralists' Award, which had regulated employment in the industry for the mainland states except Western Australia since 1907. The federal award had been renewed in 1911 and 1917. The latter award was due to expire in 1921. In 1920 the AWU authorised its Queensland branch to seek a state award at the expiration of the 1917 award so that members in that state could avail themselves of the 44-hour week then prevalent in Queensland. When the union served its federal log of claims it did so only in relation to New South Wales, South Australia and Victoria, thus excluding Queensland from the federal dispute. Employers asked the Arbitration Court to exercise its authority under section 20 of the Act and order the Queensland Industrial Court to cease handling the matter. Higgins held that he could not make the order asked by the pastoralists. The Queensland tribunal was dealing with an intra-state dispute and the Arbitration Court could not displace the tribunal's award. Despite this, Higgins left little doubt concerning the problems caused by such union tactics:

> although I have to dismiss the application, this case puts into glaring light the inconvenience and danger of the constitutional position. Here are two tribunals — one constituted by the Commonwealth and one constituted by a

> State — handling the same subject matters independently, as if the other tribunal did not exist. There is no co-ordination, no interdependence between the Courts, and the disputants are only apt to treat the Courts as rival shops. This position involves grave danger to industrial peace, and to the continuity of operations in industries. But I cannot see how the position can be avoided without a change of the Constitution. (14 *CAR* 369)

Though union state branches could opt out of federal awards by ceasing to be parties to interstate disputes at their expiration, employers in any particular state had more difficulty in convincing the Arbitration Court that the settlement of intrastate disputes with state branches of unions was a ground for the Court exercising its discretionary powers under Section 38 of the Conciliation and Arbitration Act to leave the matter to the state Authority. This is instanced by Arthur's case of 1917. The Federated Carters' and Drivers' Industrial Union had created an interstate dispute that included South Australian employers. These employers were also parties to a state log of claims with the same union. When the matter came before the Arbitration Court, South Australian employers claimed not to be part of an interstate dispute on the grounds that the state Industrial Authority had already heard and settled the dispute. Powers J determined that he would not recognise the decision of the state Authority, even if the subject matter in the federal and state claims were identical, unless the parties had previously agreed to accept the findings of that Authority as a settlement of part of an interstate dispute. Unions were not likely to agree to a situation in which they forsook the option of improving on state conditions by subsequent recourse to the federal jurisdiction. Powers added that he had 'never had a case in which employers have had greater cause for complaint of the effect of federal and state arbitration awards operating in the same industry'. As with Higgins, however, he claimed the solution was one for the legislatures rather than the tribunals: 'It is for the State Parliaments (or the people if Federal Parliament again submits the question) to say whether Federal Courts are to regulate all industrial matters, or whether both Courts are to continue to do so' (11 *CAR* 831).

At the federal level non-Labor Parties held office until October 1929 and could have been expected to implement legislative changes urged by employers. The Bruce–Page administrations did attempt rationalisation by way of Premiers' Conferences, referendum, and legislation. The Premiers were obdurate, the referendum unsuccessful, and legislation of limited value until the High Court's adoption of a new test of inconsistency in 1926. Following this the legislation of 1928 went a long way towards rationalisation but in a situation of deepening depression employers called for greater action. In attempting to remove the Commonwealth from the industrial field Bruce brought about his own downfall — the fourth Prime Minister to founder on the rocks of industrial arbitration.[2]

As early as 1917, Premiers' Conferences attempted a political solution to the problem of dual awards. In a situation where neither the states nor the Commonwealth would cede any existing industrial powers, the compromise proposed was the assignment of specified industries to the Commonwealth with all other industries being handled by the states. In 1918 New South Wales Attorney General Beeby proposed assigning jurisdiction to the Commonwealth over the following industries:

(a) Seamen, and all labour employed on ships except those engaged in intra-state trade.
(b) Wharf labourers and coal lumpers.
(c) All employees engaged in shearing of sheep, and all labour connected therewith.
(d) All employees engaged in the production of sugar.
(e) All employees engaged in the coalmining industry. (Lee 1980:110)

Unable to agree on this allocation, the Ministers referred the matter to the Treasurers' Conference of July 1918. At this Conference the Commonwealth proposed an extension of Beeby's list to include 'boot and shoe, jam, biscuit, meat processing, meat packing, and other such manufacturing industries as the Interstate Commission may from time to time declare to be materially affected by Interstate competition' (ibid). Though 'agreement in principle' was reached, little eventuated from the Conference.

Convinced that there was little hope that the Arbitration Court would be abolished while Hughes remained Prime Minister, the Central Council saw virtue in confining the federal jurisdiction to specified industries. In its view, however, the list of federal industries ought to be confined to shearing and shipping.

The CCEA submitted at the Premiers' Conference of 1923 the need to 'take prompt legislative action to amend the existing system of industrial arbitration with the object of relieving the industries of the Commonwealth from the intolerable conditions brought about by the overlapping and conflicting of awards'. It added that it was essential that 'the jurisdiction of the federal Arbitration Court be strictly confined to industries which are purely federal in character like shearing and shipping' (CCEA Meeting 1/3/23).[3] The Premiers' proposed solution was not to the CCEA's liking. This involved amendments to the Constitution:

To provide that the States by agreement may decide upon a list of industries to be deemed Federal, which list may be revised at intervals of not less that five years and that a new tribunal representing the Commonwealth and States should be established with power:

(a) To revise this list at the intervals aforesaid.

(b) With regard to such Industries to extend the Commonwealth Industrial power to industrial conditions generally.

(c) To revise the determination of State Industrial authorities or to make an order where there is no State Industrial authority. (CCEA Conference 1923:42)

The proposed constitutional changes made it possible, in fact probable, that more industries that those contemplated by the CCEA might come under federal control. The CCEA Conference of 1923 condemned the proposals, claiming they would 'not afford relief which is desired to stop the complications which exist owing to dual control of industrial matters . . . but rather will the proposals — embodying as they do provisions for the establishment of any additional tribunal — tend to create further delay and confusion' (ibid.). The Conference also created an Industrial Arbitration Propaganda Committee in order to conduct 'a rigorous publicity campaign through the daily papers in each state respecting overlapping of state and federal industrial arbitration and the necessity of a clear line of demarcation being drawn between such legislation as intended by the Constitution'. By March 1924 this Committee had spent $2000 in commissioning articles, which were published in the principal morning papers in each capital city on 26 March. Copies of the articles were also sent to each member of parliament and to 'others interested in the question' (CCEA Meeting 15/2/24). In June of the same year CCEA President Senator Drake-Brockman, then Government Whip in the Senate, arranged a private CCEA deputation to the Prime Minister (CCEA Meeting 16/6/21). Bruce intimated that without the support of the Premiers he could do little to bring about that demarcation requested by employers.

At the 1925 Premiers' Conference Bruce was confronted with four new Ministries and five Labor Governments. Unable to make any headway with this new configuration of power brokers he decided to seek increased Commonwealth industrial powers by way of referendum. This was held in 1926. The enlarged and exclusive industrial powers sought would have resulted in the unification of industrial regulation and would have brought an end to the problems of overlapping jurisdictions. However, only employers in the 'traditional' Labor states of New South Wales and Queensland supported the constitutional changes. Despite a majority in these states voting in support of constitutional changes, the referendum was lost.

Though the referendum had been unsuccessful, 1926 was the year in which some relief was provided against the concurrency of federal and state awards for the same employees. In the Cowburn case of that year the High Court adopted a different test of inconsistency, that of 'covering the field'. This new test forced unions to choose between federal or state awards. It held that federal awards were paramount and, to the extent that they intended to regulate industrial matters, it was inconsistent for state regulation to be also invoked (37 *CLR* 466). For employers who chose federal regulation, this decision meant that unions under federal awards could be denied access to state awards.In 1928 the Act was amended to give federal awards exclusive coverage over matters in those awards. Unions now had to choose between jurisdictions. Thus, this case removed an important problem associated with dual regulation.

Surprisingly, little joy was expressed by employer groups at this landmark decision. With the exception of those in New South Wales and Queensland, employer bodies saw Cowburn as offering relief in the wrong direction, namely at the expense of state regulation. Further, though this decision did remove one serious problem, others remained. The pressures for flow-ons between jurisdictions had not been removed by the Cowburn case and, until such time as the CCCA could make a common rule, dual awards could not be eliminated. Even in this area, however, by way of the Burwood Cinema case (1925), the High Court went a long way in providing relief for employers prepared to plump for federal regulation. In this case the majority held that employers could be involved in an industrial dispute even though they employed no unionists (35 *CLR* 528). This decision over-ruled Holyman's case and enabled unions to secure the same practical effect as a common-rule provision by merely roping-in all employers in respect of unionists and non-unionists. The combined effects of the Cinema and Cowburn cases, if desired by either unions or employers, would have put an end to dual regulation in their respective industries, or at least in those establishments covered by federal awards. Unions were ambivalent about federal control in a period when the shorter working week prevailed under state regulation. Employers were less ambivalent and refused to turn to the Arbitration Court as their industrial Mecca.

By the beginning of 1929 recession and strikes added to the government's industrial relations problems. In January 1929 timber workers began a 10-month strike in response to an adverse award determination. For Bruce, this long-lasting and costly strike by an otherwise non-militant union that had been a docile client of the Court for over a decade, was but another in a long list of industrial setbacks experienced by his government. Parliament increasingly came to consider economic deterioration as the product, rather than the possible cause, of worsening industrial relations. This view was supported by the report of the British Economic Mission whose views, according to ex-Prime Minister Hughes, were suspiciously close to the submissions of the employers' federations (Groom 1941:255). The report claimed: 'a change in the method prevalent in Australia in dealing with industrial disputes appears to us to be essential' (*Commonwealth Parliamentary Debates* 1929, vol.2:1248).

Bruce's decision to abandon federal arbitration came at the Premier's Conference of 1929, where he threw down the gauntlet to the states: either they referred industrial powers to the Commonwealth or the latter would repeal its arbitration legislation. None of the states proposed surrendering their industrial authority. Bruce acted to divest the Commonwealth of arbitration by introducing the Maritime Industries Bill in August 1929. This Bill provided for the repeal of both the *Conciliation and Arbitration Act* and the *Industrial Peace Act* and for the regulation of the stevedoring and maritime industries under the Trade and Commerce powers of the Constitution by way of round table conferences of employer and employee representatives. In September the Second Reading Bill was carried by only four votes in a House in which the Government nominally had a majority of 12. The next day the Government was defeated in the House by one vote. The ensuing election centred around compulsory arbitration and two other minor matters.[4] The outcome proved disastrous for Bruce. He not only lost government but also his seat of Flinders.

Test cases

Until 1921 the Commonwealth Court of Conciliation and Arbitration had held few test cases. Higgins J had sought to make the Harvester case into a general one but, in addition to the High Court challenges initiated by employers, the inability of the Arbitration Court to vary awards during their currency necessarily restricted the Court's use of test cases in the area of wages. The most Higgins could do was to bring together awards expiring about the same time and determine a common basic wage for these awards (Higgins 1921:83).

Changes to the Act in 1921 provided for the Full Bench to determine certain disputes.[5] This gave such disputes greater 'precedence' and thus test-case value. More importantly, other changes to the Act provided that awards could be varied during their life-times. This made it possible for unions to mount joint applications for wage adjustments. It also made it possible for federal standards to be readily transmitted by way of test cases. In the same year, the new President of the Arbitration Court (Powers J) directed that the many unions seeking adjustments to the basic wage(s) on the basis of the Piddington Commission's Report should be jointly represented by one advocate and that employers should do the same (15 *CAR* 838). The prototype national wage case was thus inaugurated. Other cases followed and were important, not only for establishing wage levels, but also for the criteria and adjustment mechanisms adopted. Of special interest was the Full Court's adoption of automatic quarterly cost of living adjustments for the basic wage in October 1922.

Test-case developments also took place on the hours front. Until 1920 the Court had adopted the 48-hour week as its standard. As noted in the previous chapter, in 1920 Higgins had reduced working hours for timber and engineering workers, but a Full Bench reversed these decisions in the same year. The 48-hour standard remained until the Main Hours case of 1926, a case that 'was looked upon as a test case, and it was generally understood that the decision of the Full Court in this case would have a strong bearing on other applications for a reduction in weekly hours of work' (Anderson 1919:59). It restored the 44-hour week for the benchmark engineers' award. Further, the Court intimated that 'in industries which were similar, in their conditions as to leisure or want of leisure, to the engineering industry, the Court would probably apply a similar reduction in hours' (24 *CAR* 906). Following the Main Hours case, a 44-hour week was granted to workers in the metal, glass and printing industries. Because of the worsening economic climate, however, unions were unsuccessful in any applications for reduced working hours after 1927. They had to wait until 1933 before seeking any further extension of the 44-hour working week (CAI 1980: 11).

Unions quickly adjusted to the new 'test case' environment and organised to maximise its returns. In 1923 federal unions formed the Commonwealth Council of Federated Unions, whose charter was to prepare and present claims relating to hours and the basic wage. In 1925 the Trades and Labour Councils formed the Commonwealth Industrial Disputes Committee with 'power to take hold of and handle every dispute likely to extend beyond the province of any one State'. The formation of the Australian Council of Trade Unions (ACTU) in 1927 represented a compromise arrangement between these two federal organisations. The employers' organisational response is reviewed below.

ASSOCIATION COMPETITION AND CO-OPERATION

Industry associations

When the Central Council of Employers of Australia (CCEA) was formed in

1904 it was envisaged that it would represent the national interests of employers as a confederation of state federations to which would be affiliated the many trade associations. This scheme did not materialise because of the separate organisation of manufacturers. The CCEA's national role was further reduced by the dissolution of the Tasmanian Employers' Federation in 1920. By this date another challenge to the federation's industrial role was emerging. A number of trade associations were diversifying into industrial relations and bypassing federations in their tribunal dealings and negotiations with unions. This development also impacted on the CCEA, since many of these associations formed national industry/trade associations and, in many instances, sought federal registration. At the least, national co-ordination now involved not merely a commonality of purpose on the part of federations and between the Central Council and the Associated Chambers of Manufactures of Australia, but also a common approach with national associations.

The 1923 Conference considered these developments and the 'Necessity for more active support by Employers to their respective Federations'. This, in the VEF view, was the 'most important matter before the Conference'. President Fairbairn claimed that membership problems would continue 'until the Federations in the different States get a proper fighting fund' along the South Australian and Western Australian lines. The WAEF considered that its fund was 'a very big factor in enabling us to obtain members of the Federation'. 'One benefit of the Fund', the SAEF Secretary claimed,

> is that we have only one industrial body, that is the Employers' Federation. The Chamber of Manufactures and the Chamber of Commerce have their own work to do but they never touch or interfere with industrial matters which are left entirely to the Federation. In the other States you have five or six bodies acting in industrial matters and I contend we should direct our efforts at getting one body to look after employers' interests in industrial matters. (CCEA Conference 14/8/23)

Both the VEF and EFNSW had found through experience that such funds were difficult to implement in their states. The drift of members to specialist organisations continued, as did the inroads of these organisations into that area considered the domain of the CCEA. Federal registration figures provide one index of these trends. To 1920 only five employer organisations had been registered, one by proclamation.[6] In addition to the Commonwealth Steamship Owners' Association, which had been registered in 1905, the Federated Picture Showmen's Association (1912), the United Licensed Victuallers' Association (1914) and the Theatrical Proprietors' and Managers' Association (1917) had also successfully sought registration. Between 1922 and 1929 a further 23 associations were registered. These catered for a range of industries and occupations such as timber merchants, bonded stores, brick carriers, printers, metal fabricators, pastoralists, showmen, shearing contractors, abattoir operators; furniture makers, and jam and glue manufacturers (Appendix 1).

By 1927 federations were voicing concern that the activities of industry associations were affecting their own work. In July of that year, the CCEA considered a letter from the SAEF to the EFNSW 'deprecating the action of the New South Wales Metal Trades Employers' Association in formulating a log and serving same on the Stove Makers' Union, and purporting to be acting on behalf of New South Wales, Victorian and SA employers'. The SAEF pointed out that the CCEA 'had emphasised from time to time the absolute necessity for unity of action and that it is considered that they [SAEF] should have been consulted before the log was served on the Union'. The Chairman 'regretted that a body in New South Wales had taken such action' but pointed out that the MTEA was not an affiliate of the federation and therefore not amenable to federation influence (CCEA Meeting 11/7/27). The EFNSW was asked to try to arrange 'some cohesion with the MTEA', a matter in which the Chamber of Manufactures had more success. Increasing competition was a fact of life, which federations and the CCEA were forced to accept.

CCEA discord

In 1913 the former VEF President, Senator Fairbairn, was elected President of the CCEA. He continued as President until 1924, when he was appointed Victorian Agent General to London. Before retiring he was asked to suggest somebody 'similar to himself who was independent of any Federation' as his successor. He suggested Brigadier General Drake-Brockman C.B., C.M.G., D.S.O., a Senator from Western Australia. On Fairbairn's invitation Drake-Brockman began to attend meetings to 'be given every opportunity of being brought in touch with the work of the Council'. This practice was regularised when the SAEF appointed him as one of its delegates.

Fairbairn's resignation was discussed at the June 1924 meeting, by which time he had been in England for some time and Vice-President Brooks (EFNSW) had become Acting President. At the meeting Drake-Brockman was appointed President, the EFNSW intimating 'that it regretted that the Constitution of the Council debarred the Hon. Wm Brooks

(Vice-President) from being appointed and expressed the opinion that the Rule in question (No. 3) should be altered' 9CCEA Meeting 16/6/24).

The EFNSW quest for rule changes was reawakened in 1926 when Drake-Brockman resigned as President to become a judge of the Arbitration Court. W. Brooks again became Acting President and the EFNSW lobbied to have him made President. The matter was considered by the Executive in July, when the EFNSW and WAEF supported Brooks' nomination. However, the SAEF and VEF successfully had the matter deferred to the next Annual Conference 'when suggested amendments to Rules having a bearing on the appointment of President would be under consideration' (CCEA Meeting 11/7/27). Within a month the CCEA was in the anomalous situation of having an Acting President whose own organisation had given 3 months notice of its intention to resign.

The resignation notice was intended to exert pressure on the other federations to accept the EFNSW restructuring proposals. It was also an expression of EFNSW frustration at its inability to get industrial policies accepted by the CCEA. The nature of the EFNSW's difficulties was highlighted by the *Sydney Morning Herald*, which noted:

> There was a feeling among members in New South Wales that the bodies in the other States did not fully realise the handicaps under which New South Wales employers were carrying on their businesses. The conditions in the mother state were entirely different from those prevailing in the other States, and, although New South Wales represented 45% of the interests involved, the voice of the New South Wales Federation was not heeded in the Federal Council. It had, therefore, been decided that employers in New South Wales, having to shoulder burdens which did not exist in other parts of the Commonwealth, should fight their battles on their own account, unfettered by influences from other quarters. It was also decided that the Constitution under which the Federal Council operated was not of a character that gave New South Wales interests the opportunity to receive assistance in dealing with the special difficulties that had to be faced. (*SMH*, 23/8/27)

The 'handicaps' referred to were those resulting from Labor Government legislation, which New South Wales employers considered placed them at a comparative disadvantage with competitors in other states. This was particularly so in relation to standard hours of work, which had been reduced to 44; the state living wage, which was generally higher than the federal basic wage; and child endowment, which was financed by a 6 per cent levy on employers. The EFNSW had sought respite from these imposts by seeking federal standards. Though the QEF tended to support the EFNSW in this line, the majority of federations could not accept the New

South Wales policy, which meant turning their backs on two decades of espousing the curtailment of federal regulation. Their position was summed up by VEF President Ashworth, who noted that 'extremists like Lang and cranks like Piddington [should] not be allowed to fasten uneconomic legislation on the whole of Australia because they have succeeded in doing so in New South Wales'. Further 'it was unreasonable to expect other federations whose state industrial tribunals were working well to give them up because those in New South Wales were working badly'. Whether the EFNSW considered that rule changes, which implied loosening of VEF control over the CCEA Executive, would change this situation is not clear. It decided to remain with the CCEA until such time as it had the opportunity to seek such changes. If unsuccessful, it would put into effect the intention to resign.

The Perth Conference was held in November 1927 and the EFNSW sought amendments to Rule 3 to provide:

> The affairs of the Central Council shall be managed by an Executive Committee consisting of the President of such Central Council, and two Representatives elected by each Member of the Central Council from amongst its members. The President shall be elected by and at the Annual Conference and shall be a nominee of members in rotation . . . The order of rotation of States in nominating for the Presidency shall be as follows: New South Wales, Victoria, South Australia, Queensland and Western Australia.

This proposal implied four significant changes to the existing situation. In the first place it reversed the 1913 decision to appoint 'outsiders' to the position of President. The second change was that Presidents would be rotated among federations. The third change was the potential to erode the Victorian presence on the Executive. The fourth change, one that met with disapproval from some delegates, was that it allowed a single federation, rather than the CCEA Conference, to determine the incoming President.

Despite vigorous VEF opposition the rule changes were accepted. Brooks, who had spent 2 years in the position of Acting President, was elected President. The EFNSW withdrew its intention to resign notwithstanding the fact that only the QEF supported its motion for a 'uniform basic wage for Australia' (CCEA Conference 14-15/11/27).

Within a short time of determining the manner of appointment of the President, friction between the EFNSW and VEF ensued over the appointment of the CCEA Secretary following the deaths of Secretary L. Smith and part-time Advisor R. Walpole. At the 1928 September Executive it was decided to appoint Mr F. Lee, a former employee of the VEF, as full-time Secretary (CCEA Meeting 10/9/28). The VEF, which had opposed the appointment, subsequently wrote protesting against the 'appointment of Secretary being made without the matter having been notified to the member Federations'. It sought a review of the situation. The EFNSW took exception to the matter being raised, claiming that 'if the Central Council has to get the approval of the Victorian body before anything can be done it is time the Central Council was terminated' (letter, EFNSW Secretary Schwilk to VEF Secretary Serle, 30/11/28). The VEF considered the EFNSW approach 'as an improper slur' and that 'the motion for deletion will only be regarded by the Executive of the VEF as uncalled for and hurtful' (letter VEF President Ashworth to EFNSW Secretary Schwilk 19/12/28).

By this time recession had forced federations to economise. The QEF gave notice of financial difficulties and sought a reduction in its annual quota to the CCEA (letter, QEF Secretary Benjamin to CCEA Secretary Lee 25/4/29). The VEF suggested that 'with a view to the curtailment of expenses . . . the Secretary of the Central Council shall be the Secretary of the Federation in the State in which the President for the time being resides, but that for the purposes of expediency the meetings of the Central Council be held in Melbourne' (letter, VEF Secretary Mann to CCEA Secretary Lee 18/5/29). By the time the Executive met to consider this suggestion, Lee had tendered his resignation. The fact that he left to take up the position of Secretary of the prestigious ACMA would indicate that his choice as CCEA Secretary had been a sound one.

In May 1929 the CCEA Executive again considered the appointment of a Secretary. It was decided that Thomas Maughan, Secretary to the Australian Mines and Metals Association (AMMA) and a long-time WAEF delegate to Council meetings, be appointed Honorary Secretary until such time as the Council further considered the matter. Only the VEF objected to this proposal (CCEA Meeting 27/5/29). By that time VEF President Ashworth had played out his brief innings as CCEA President, during which he showed an immense dislike for Maughan.[7] The latter was to remain Secretary until his resignation in 1940.

T. R. Ashworth had been the major driving force behind the VEF since becoming its President in 1921. He relinquished this position in 1924 but was re-elected in 1925. He was instrumental in having the then VEF wound up voluntarily in 1924 and a new organisation of the same name established. This organisational change transformed the VEF from a non-Labor political organisation into an industrial one. Its journal, *Liberty and Progress*, which was subtitled 'The Anti-Socialist Organ of Australia', was retitled the *Employers' Monthly Review* in 1927. By that time the VEF had acquired its own property and established its own insurance company,

Federation Insurance. In 1927 a General Secretary was appointed as well as two industrial officers. The latter included L. Mann, a barrister with Arbitration Court experience, who took over the position of General Secretary in 1929. Together with C. H. Grant of the VCM, Mann had control of the conduct of the basic wage cases on behalf of employers in the 1930s.

Despite these achievements, T. R. Ashworth succeeded in alienating many employers because of his independent and unpredictable outlook. Thus, in 1926, and notwithstanding his opposition to EFNSW policy on uniform industrial standards, as a member of the Royal Commission into the Constitution he joined with union and ALP members in the minority report in arguing against the return of industrial powers to the states. Ashworth succeeded in offending many VEF members, and between 1920 and 1929 11 of its 53 affiliated associations left the federation (Matthews 1971:62). The VEF also lost the support of many large companies as the result of Ashworth's attacks on the Nationalist Party, a paradox considering his efforts to depoliticise the VEF. In 1929 he further alienated employers by again siding with the two Labor representatives in the Minority Report of the Royal Commission on the Constitution. By that year he had been ousted as President of the Central Council and attempts were in hand to remove him from the Presidency of the VEF.

The 1927 CCEA rule changes, which provided for a rotation of Presidents from among the federations, gave the VEF nomination rights at the Annual Conference of October 1928. Ashworth was nominated to the position in his absence. At a time of financial and economic uncertainty, and a time when the CCEA needed a respite from its internal conflicts, Ashworth used his position in a way that incited federations to seek his removal. His first action as Chairman was to call for credentials of representatives in a move to embarrass T. Maughan whom he considered 'a disruptive influence in the industrial life of Victoria and an obstacle to the organisation and leadership of the VEF'. Maughan had been an alternate delegate for the WAEF for many years, a situation accepted by other federations. The calling for official credentials threatened not only Maughan, but also C. L. Hewitt, a Melbourne-based QEF delegate since 1908. Ashworth's move was blocked by Council, which 'decided to recognise both representatives as having full status at the meeting' (CCEA Meeting 29/12/28).

Ashworth's next move was to circularise a number of 'Statements by the President' between December 1928 and January 1929.[8] The federations found these both biased and offensive. The WAEF complained about

Ashworth's abuse of his position and suggested he take a leaf out of his own book and resign as President of the VEF while President of the CCEA, and that any future Statements not be despatched under VEF letterhead (letter, WAEF President Temperley to CCEA President Ashworth 30/1/29). The EFNSW again tendered its resignation and set about seeking support for dissolving the federal body (telegram, Andrews to Maughan 13/2/29). The federations, including the VEF, exerted sufficient pressure to force Ashworth's resignation (CCEA Meeting 27/5/29).

By the end of 1929 Ashworth was also facing pressures to resign as President of his own federation. Despite considerable opposition, the disaffiliation of a number of associations, and the resignation of eight of the 11 elected members of the Executive, he continued as President until February 1934. He died some months later after a long illness.

Closer organisation of employers

Amendments to the Act in 1921, which allowed awards to be varied during their currency, led to Basic Wage and Standard Hours cases becoming 'test cases', cases designed to provide new bench-marks for all federal awards. Federal unions responded to the changed conditions by forming the Commonwealth Council of Federated Unions in 1923 with the task, *inter alia*, of handling Basic Wage submissions. This Council was absorbed by the ACTU 4 years later. These developments spurred greater efforts by the Central Council to develop 'the closer organisation of employers'. As noted in the previous chapter, such activities had occupied much of the deliberations of the 1920 Conference. Two papers had been read at that Conference proposing a basis for reorganising the structure of existing associations for the purpose of 'closer organisation'. In both models the Central Council and federations were important linchpins. The first paper was by S. Perry, a member of the SAEF, who outlined various 'schemes which will illustrate the possibilities in the direction' of reorganisation. The first scheme was a unitary one in which all 'employers shall become members of a general State Association which shall be governed by an elected Central Council'. Members would be organised into trade sections, which would be grouped into 'Chambers of Manufactures, Commerce, Agriculture, Mines, Building and such other bodies as may be determined'. Provision would be made 'for linking up the sections, Chambers and State Associations with similar bodies in other States in each case in which it is deemed expedient'. This method of organisation is depicted in Perry's Figure 1 (Fig. 3.1). He considered this unitary system would not give different groups the degree of autonomy they desired, and he recommended against it.

Figure 3.1 Unitary model of employer co-ordination (1920)

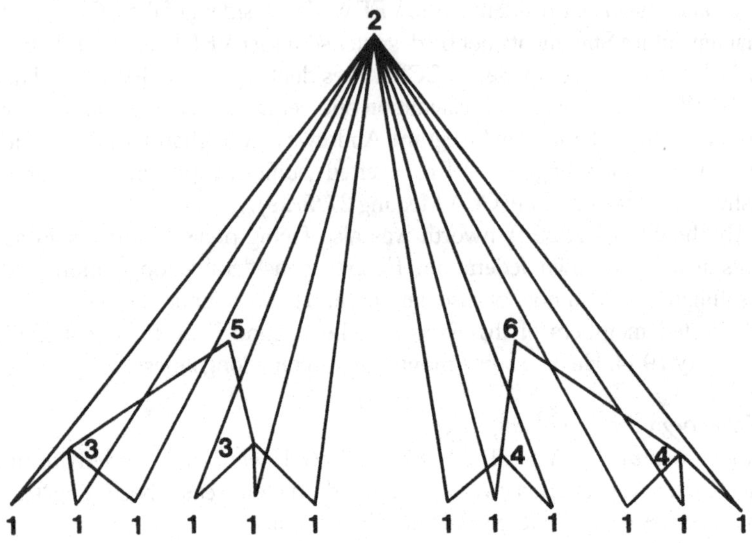

1 Individual employers 2 State Employers' Association 3 Trade Association (Manufacturing) 4 Trade Association (Commercial) 5 Chamber of Manufactures 6 Chamber of Commerce. Lines indicate connections between the various individuals and groups. The 12 employers are first directly connected with The Central State Employers' Association as members. The Association then organises them into Trade Associations and Chambers as shown.

Perry suggested three other systems of 'organic' reorganisation. The first of these he classified under the heading of 'ideal federal scheme', which is illustrated in his Figures 2 and 3 (Figs. 3.2 and 3.3). These variants proposed that employers combine into state Trade Associations, which, in turn, would be grouped into Chambers of Mines, Commerce, Manufactures, Building, Agriculture and so on. The purpose of these Chambers would be 'the promotion of the common interests of its members within the State'. Within each state there would also be a State Central Council of Employers composed of either representatives of the Trades Associations (Fig. 3.2) or representatives of the chambers (Fig. 3.3). Its role was 'the protection of the interests of Employers within the State'. An Indemnity Company would be formed in each state with the object of compensating employers for any losses sustained through industrial disputes. A Federal Council would be established for each of the chambers to 'deal with Interstate questions affecting its members'.

Figure 3.2 Federal scheme I for employer co-ordination (1920)

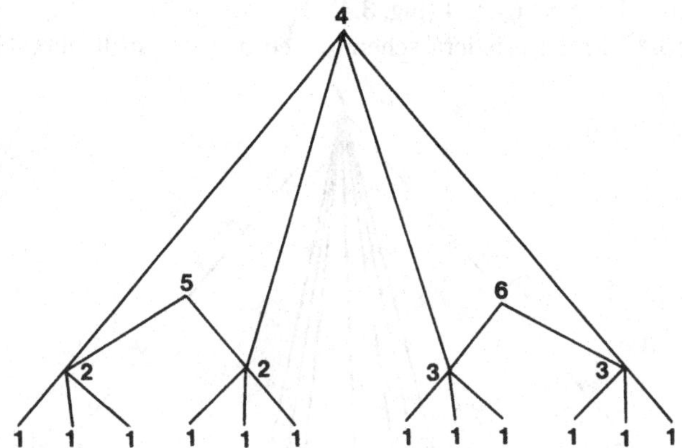

1 Individual employers 2 Trade Association (Manufacturing) 3 Trade Association (Commercial) 4 State Central Council of Employers 5 Chamber of Manufactures 6 Chamber of Commerce. Employers are first formed into Trade Associations. Each Trade Association is connected as a member with a State Central Council and a Chamber.

Figure 3.3 Federal scheme II for employer co-ordination (1920)

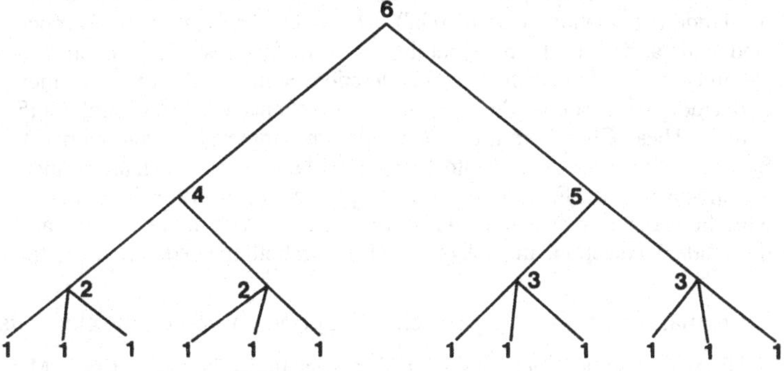

1 Individual employers 2 Trade Association (Manufacturing) 3 Trade Association (Commercial) 4 Chamber of Manufactures 5 Chamber of Commerce 6 State Council of Employers. Employers are first formed into Trade Associations. Trade Associations are joined into Chambers. Each Chamber is connected to State Central Council.

In addition there would be a Federal Central Council of Employers composed of representatives of the State Central Councils. This body was to 'deal with questions of common interest to employers throughout Australia'.

The fourth schema was entitled 'Practical Scheme on Federal Lines'. It is illustrated in Perry's Figure 4 (Fig. 3.4).

Figure 3.4 Practical federal scheme for employer co-ordination (1920)

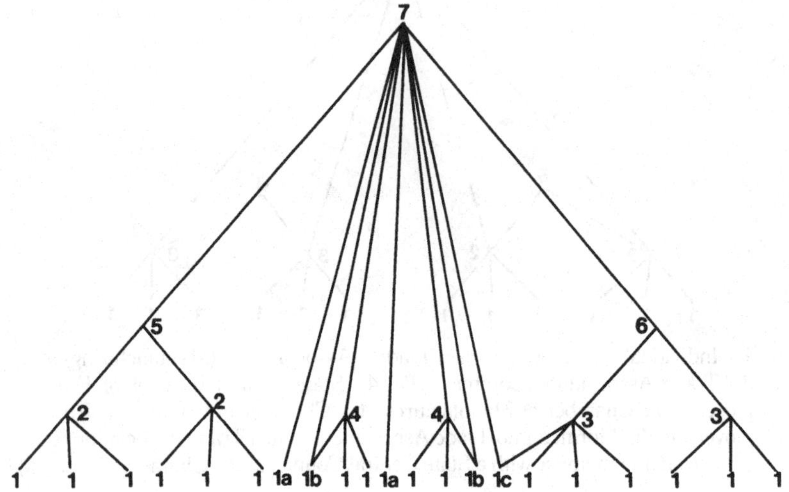

1 Individual employers 2 Trade Association (Manufacturing) 3 Trade Association (Commercial) 4 Trade Association (not associated with a chamber) 5 Chamber of Manufactures 6 Chamber of Commerce 7 State Employers' Federation. Some employers are formed into Trade Associations (2 and 3), which are connected with Chambers (5 and 6). These Chambers are connected with Employers' Federation (7). Some employers are formed into Trade Associations (4), which are connected directly with the Federation. Some employers (1a) are directly connected with the Federation and others (1b) are connected with the Federation and the Trade Association, and still others (1c) with both the Federation and the Chamber.

This schema, which was Perry's preferred option, involved nine elements:

1 All existing bodies, including all trade associations, the Chambers of Manufactures, Agriculture, and Mines, shall be invited to join a State Federation of Employers.
2 The members of the Federation shall be individual employers, firms, or companies hereafter referred to as individual members and organised trade associations and Chambers hereafter referred to as affiliated bodies.
3 The Federation shall be governed by a Council; each affiliated body shall be entitled to one representative on the Council for each 500 members or fraction thereof.
4 Each affiliated body shall subscribe a sum of five shillings per member to the funds of the Federation.

5 The subscription for individual members shall be one guinea, firms 2 guineas, and Companies, 3 guineas, and they shall be jointly entitled to one representative on the Council for each 100 members.
6 A general Executive consisting of President, Vice-President, and ten members shall be elected by the Council.
7 A Central Disputes Committee of ten members shall be appointed by the Executive. Each trade section and Chamber may have its own Industrial Disputes Committee, which shall attend to minor domestic troubles. Important disputes and those affecting the general interests, shall be delegated to the Central Disputes Committee.
8 The Employers' Federation shall either be dissolved so as to make way for the proposed Federation, or it shall have its constitution amended, so as to give effect to the above proposal and such modification thereof as may be hereafter determined.
9 There shall be a Commonwealth Council of Employers composed of representatives of the State Federations. (CCEA General Conference 11/10/20, Appendix B)

The second paper was by VEF President Ashworth and entitled 'Proposals for Improving the Organisation of Employers'. Ashworth articulated many of the problems associated with the lack of co-ordination by the various employer bodies in his state. He also considered the central role federations should have in bringing about greater co-operation. He successfully moved the resolution 'THAT the Central Council be requested to convene from all States a Conference of organised bodies of employers including Chambers of Manufactures and Commerce, Mines and Agriculture, Master Builders, Pastoralists, Ship Owners, and the Employers' Federations, for the purpose of formulating proposals for the closer organisation of employers' (CCEA Conference 11/10/20:102).

A committee was constituted in 1921 to give effect to this Conference recommendation. It decided that the VEF should pilot a scheme that would then serve as a model for other federations and states. The VEF held a conference of Victorian associations in December 1920 and February 1921. Little came of these meetings other than complaints by the EFNSW that 'the outline scheme drawn up in Victoria did not quite conform to the underlying idea of the Perth Conference' (CCEA Meeting 2/3/21). Despite this lack of success the CCEA persisted with its calls for 'closer organisation'.

Further 'closer organisation' resolutions were passed at the 1922 and 1924 Conferences. With the economic downturn of 1927 the CCEA Conference again called for greater unity:

That this Conference is of the opinion that it is essential to the adequate

> protection of the business and industrial sections of the community that the employers Federations in each State should intensify their efforts to bring about closer unity between employers and their organisations in both Federal and State activities. (CCEA Conference 1927:14)

A note of despair entered a similar resolution passed in 1928:

> That this Conference regrets that despite repeated resolutions of previous Conferences, no practical advance has been made in bringing about closer unity of employers – State and Federal . . . and that this Central Council convene a conference of employers Federal bodies to consider the question. (CCEA Conference 1928:6)

Despite such resolutions the Central Council was not able to formalise any machinery for closer organisation. It was essentially a federation of state organisations, as was ACMA. Though there were pressures for some form of national co-operation and organisation, they were not compelling enough to overcome the strong antagonisms between the dominant state affiliates of both organisations. At the national level, the question of tariffs also provided a barrier to closer relations between the Council and the ACMA.

In Western Australia and South Australia economies of scale had resulted in the chambers and federations coming to an acceptable working relationship whereby the former left industrial work to the federations. This was also the case, in the main, in Queensland, though the emergence of the Metal Trades Employers' Association (MTEA) reduced the federation's representative role. In Tasmania the Chamber of Manufactures had no federation to contend with. In New South Wales and Victoria, however, relations between the chambers and federations were strained by the chamber's establishment of an industrial relations department in the former state, and by the federation becoming an industrial organisation in the latter.

The New South Wales move was forced on the chamber because of the activities of the MTEA in that state. This Association was the successor of the Iron Trades Association, whose President had been instrumental in bringing the EFNSW into being. It seems to have disaffiliated at some time between 1915 and 1920, when it became reconstituted as the MTEA. The new organisation was active in Queensland as well as New South Wales. Between 1921 and 1924 the chamber negotiated with the MTEA for the latter to become a Division of the chamber. This was unsuccessful and in order to better compete with the MTEA, which was enticing chamber members, the latter established an industrial department in 1925. This reduced the federation's representative role at State Living Wage cases and in industrial representation generally. Having expended considerable resources to establish this department, the chamber was not amenable to federation moves directed at having it act in a subservient role.

In Victoria the VEF had been established, with VCM assistance, as an extra-parliamentary organisation. The chamber had filled the vacuum left by the lack of an industrially-oriented federation and had established an industrial relations service for its members in 1919. By 1925, the VEF had been transformed under Ashworth's direction into an industrial organisation and sought to have the VCM vacate the field. Despite the establishment of Federation Insurance, the VEF's resources were no match for those of the VCM. The older established organisation was certainly not prepared to play second fiddle to the VEF and reacted strongly to VEF attempts to poach on what it considered its industrial domain.

At the national level, the ACMA found itself closer to the ACTU and Labor Party view on tariffs and was not amenable to solidarity overtures that might jeopardise its affinity of views with those bodies. Other major obstacles to closer co-operation were the greater financial resources of the ACMA and the disdain in which it held the CCEA. To the ACMA, the CCEA was merely a loose-knit 'organisation comprised of a wide variety of employer organisations. It functioned under the aegis of the Australian Mines and Metals Association . . . Its secretary was Thomas Mangham [sic] of the Mines and Metals Association and its domicile was Melbourne. The council's interest in industrial matters was, in general, confined to such questions as the basic wage and standard hours' (Hall 1971:536). The CCEA had a greater vision of its role than that ascribed to it by C. R. Hall, the Secretary of the CMNSW. It saw itself as a special-purpose industrial relations council of employers. Other organisational factors also inhibited unity. In 1927 the ACMA voted to establish its secretariat at Canberra, the new seat of government. As part of this relocation the ACMA rules had been rewritten and the new power arrangements were to occupy a great deal of ACMA deliberations over the next decade or so, with the New South Wales chamber threatening to disaffiliate because of its inability to pursue a policy of uniform federal wages and standard hours against the opposition of affiliates in other states. As already noted, the CCEA experienced similar internal problems, over similar issues, at this time.

The inability of employers to bring into being any formal collaborative organisation during the period was demonstrated by the Industrial Peace Conference 1928–29 sponsored by the Commonwealth. VEF and CCEA President Ashworth commented of this Conference:

> Had the employers been as well organised as the trade unionists, a practical outcome would have been possible . . . On the side of the employers, the

> requisite leadership and organisation were lacking . . . In essence the aim of the Conference was an integration of the various sections of both employers and employees. The Conference was foredoomed to failure . . . an all-inclusive employers' federation does not exist. (CCEA 'Report of Interstate Conference', October 1929)

The Committee of Control re Basic Wage and Working Hours

Though the Central Council was not successful in bringing about 'closer organisation' by way of a greater integration of organisations around itself and the federations, it did have a high degree of success in rationalising employers' approaches to test cases that were initiated following the 1921 amendments to the Act. In 1921 the basic wage review for employees in the Gas Employees' Award was converted into a general review. A sub-committee consisting of P. C. Holmes Hunt representing the Gas Companies, T. Maughan (Mines and Metals) and Senator G. Fairbairn and L. Smith (President and Secretary of the CCEA respectively) handled the matter on behalf of employers (CCEA Meeting 3/6/21). At the next major case of 1922, F. Derham represented the VCM, and the CCEA, as well as the Australian Mines and Metals Association, the Metal Trades Employers' Association, the Master Carriers and the Municipal Association of Victoria. A second advocate, H. M. Adams, represented the company involved, three shipping organisations, the Timber Merchants' Association and the Master Builders' Federation. The fact that these two advocates appeared for so many associations indicates that some liaison did take place.

Between 1924 and 1928 unions threatened to apply for a general review of the basic wage formula. This consideration, and the Main Hours case of 1926, led to employers establishing a more formalised system of co-ordination and revenue raising by way of a Committee of Control. This had its origins in a meeting of five organisations initiated by the Central Council in August 1924. Senator Drake-Brockman chaired the meeting, other organisations involved being the Graziers' Federal Council of Australia, the Commonwealth Steamship Owners' Federation, the Mines and Metals Association and the Timber Merchants' Association. The 'Gas Companies' indicated an interest but an inability to attend. The ACMA was a noticeable absentee at this and subsequent meetings.

These associations met again a month later, by which time they had adopted the title 'Committee of Control re Basic Wage Case'. The number of organisations represented had increased to include the Gas Companies and CSR. Expressions of interest had also been received from the ACMA, the Associated Chambers of Commerce, the Northern Collieries, the

Federated Flour Millers' Association, the Associated Banks, and BHP. Three matters were discussed: finance, tactics and organisation. It was also decided that the 'original guarantors form a Committee of Control with power to add representatives from other bodies that agree to contribute and that any three form a quorum'. Senator Drake-Brockman was appointed permanent Chairman 'with power to act in cases of emergency'. The ACMA was levied $500 and the other organisations $300 each (Meeting of Employers' Committee of Control re Basic Wage Case, 8/9/24).

Within a fortnight of this meeting pledges of contributions had grown to $3771 (CCEA Meeting 29/9/24). By December 1925, though the case still had not come on for hearing, $4971 had been pledged (CCEA Meeting 14/12/25).

In May 1926, a special meeting of the Central Council was convened to discuss 'the 44-hour week position and the proposal of the Federal Government to remit the question of standard hours to the new Arbitration Court for review'. On the Chairman's suggestion it was resolved:

> THAT the Employers' Committee of Control appointed to represent the Employers' case in any application to the Federal Arbitration Court for the revision of the basic wage be requested to protect the employers' interests in any application that may be made to the newly constituted Arbitration Court for a reduction of standard hours below 48 per week and that the Committee obtain the necessary authority from the subscribers to undertake this additional responsibility. (CCEA Special Meeting 10/5/26)

When the matter finally came on for hearing the Committee briefed Counsel on behalf of 'employers in general'.

In September 1926 the Committee's title was enlarged to that of 'Committee of Control re Basic Wage and Working Hours' and it was authorised to handle the Main Hours case. Its membership had also expanded to include the Fire Underwriters' Association, Overseas Shipping Representatives Association, BHP, the Flour Millers Association, the Melbourne Woolbrokers' Association and the Melbourne and Metropolitan Tramways Board. At that time an amount of $6400 was promised. In view of the solicitor's report that the 'case was stretching out to an inordinate length', it was decided to seek more subscribers and to ask existing subscribers to augment their contributions. Several organisations agreed to the latter. The VCM increased its contribution from $300 to $1000 and the SAEF promised to recommend the payment of $500 from that state's Employers' Mutual Fund (Meeting of Contributors of Employers' Committee of Control re Basic Wage and Working Hours, 29/9/26). The Main Hours case eventually cost employers $16 172, which the Committee of Control had little difficulty in meeting (CCEA Meeting 21/3/27).

The Committee had success in increasing the number of contributors, and some 24 organisations were represented at the next meeting, which was convened under the CCEA's letterhead in February 1927. New members included the Victorian Master Printers' Association, the Master Butchers' Association, McKay Pty Ltd, the Master Tanners' Association, Vacuum Oil Co., Yellow Cabs Pty Ltd, British Imperial Oil, the Grocers' Association of Victoria, and the Theatrical Proprietors' and Managers' Association. The Implement Makers' Section of the VCM was also separately represented. The purpose of the meeting was 'to discuss what steps, if any, should be taken by Employers in the matter of the suggested revision of the Basic Wage and to consider whether the Employers should open the question or wait until the Labour Unions took action'. The meeting resolved that an Executive Committee of seven members be appointed 'to watch proceedings in the matter of the Basic Wage and should occasion arise to make a recommendation to the General Full Committee' (Meeting of Full Committee, Employers' Committee of Control re Basic Wage and Working Hours, 16/2/27).

The final meeting of the Committee of Control for the period was in August 1927. The main business was to finalise accounts for the Main Hours case. The VCM claimed that unions had made greater and better use of the press during the recent cases and recommended that employers 'should have machinery in readiness in the event of unions adopting similar tactics in connection with the Basic Wage'. It recommended that 'a small committee be appointed and empowered to arrange with some person to inspire or write any articles relative to the basic wage that may be necessary in the employers' interests'. This suggestion, with its hint of some on-going sub-committee, was left in abeyance until the next meeting of the Committee of Control. This *ad hoc* Committee did not meet again in the next 2 years. As recession set in and the likelihood of any union application for adjustments to the Basic Wage principles receded, so too did any impetus for changing the *ad hoc* nature of the Committee. It met again at the height of the Depression when it initiated moves for a reduction in the real basic wage.

Summary and conclusion

During the period under review significant developments took place that affected federal arbitration and national employer co-ordination. The High Court continued to be permissive of an expansion of 'the New Province', a factor that led to the CCEA and other organisations being less eager to initiate legal appeals. It was by way of the High Court, however, that employers did obtain some redress from the worst features of dual arbitration after political lobbying had been ineffective. Political action merely served to confirm the *status quo*: state legislatures refused to surrender any industrial powers, while the Commonwealth's attempts to do so cost Bruce the Prime Ministership. The period was also important because of the emergence of national test cases relating to the basic wage and standard hours of work. This development led to the union movement forming the Commonwealth Council of Federated Unions (1923) and then the Australian Council of Trade Unions (1927). The CCEA was active during the period in trying to reorganise employer associations, with a view to 'closer organisation'. On that front it was unsuccessful. Its schema envisaged a reduced industrial role for the ACMA and its state affiliates, a situation that the dominant chambers found difficult to accept. In addition, the CCEA's alliance with the anti-protectionist rural and commercial associations made the ACMA reluctant to give any primacy to the CCEA's industrial role. The CCEA's schema also involved other organisations dismembering their newly formed industrial departments, a move they resisted. For these and other reasons (including its internal instability) the CCEA's quest for 'closer organisation' was not successful. Its other venture, that of co-ordinating the employers' approach to national test cases, met with greater success. The Committee of Control re Basic Wage and Working Hours was the forerunner of a number of variously titled organisations seeking to ensure employer unanimity at such important cases.

Notes

[1] Accurate data to indicate the ebb and flow of the federal expansion do not exist for the period. Hancock (1979:6) indicates the initial growth by reference to wage data. In the period 1918–21 only 13.6 per cent of wage changes were effected by way of federal awards and agreements as against 62.4 per cent by those of state tribunals. In the period of 1922–25 the proportions were 29 per cent and 55.7 per cent respectively. By way of contrast, in the period 1926-29 nearly 59 per cent of wage changes had been effected by Commonwealth awards and agreements and only 30.4 per cent by state tribunals. As state regulation conceded the 44-hour week more quickly than the Arbitration Court, and as that Court initiated wage cuts during the Depression much earlier than state tribunals, its attractiveness dwindled. By then, too, the High Court had adopted a different test of inconsistency, which forced unions to choose between federal or state regulation. The proportion of the New South Wales work force under federal awards was reported to be 50 per cent in 1930 (*Employers' Review*, July 1930:13) and then fell away to about 40 per cent (ABCS 1965:56). The union retreat from the federal sphere coincided with employers' changed preference for federal, rather than state, regulation.

[2] The others were Deakin (1904), Watson (1904) and Reid (1905).

[3] Unless otherwise indicated the Minutes of Meetings are those of the Executive Committee.

[4] The other issues concerned the 'John Brown cases', where a large coal-mine owner locked out employees without being prosecuted, and the Amusement Tax on the film industry.

[5] The 1921 amendments to the Act required Full Benches to deal with disputes over standard hours of work. Full Benches were not required to deal with basic wage matters until 1926. However, several important wage cases, such as the decision to introduce AQCOLA, were determined by Full Benches.

[6] The *Conciliation and Arbitration Act* in its original form provided that organisations could be registered by proclamation. The Renmark Growers' Association was registered under section 158 A(3) of the Act in 1912.

[7] Reasons for Ashworth's antagonism were complex and hinted of jealousy. Ashworth claims that one of the major factors was that Maughan, an employee of an association, had been given the 'status of a principal' by the WAEF. Maughan, in fact, had a wealth of industrial and association experience. He had been Secretary of the Western Australian Chamber of Mines in 1904 and, in that capacity, had attended the interstate conference that had established the CCEA. When the WAEF was formed in 1913, Maughan became its first Secretary. He moved to Melbourne to take up the position of Secretary of the Mines and Metals Association. It was in that capacity that he was appointed an alternate WAEF representative at CCEA Executive meetings. As noted in the text he also became Secretary of the CCEA in 1929 and held this position until 1940. During much of the 1930s he acted as Chairman of the Committee of Control re Basic Wage and Standard Hours in place of the Sydney-domiciled President of the CCEA. His frequent written reports to the WAEF provide a useful insight into the operations of the CCEA for much of this period.

[8] Details of these circulars may be found in Plowman 1986.

4

DEPRESSION AND RECOVERY 1930–1939

The previous chapter reviewed CCEA developments during the 1920s. It also reviewed the emergence of national employer co-ordination machinery during the decade. The Committee of Control re Basic Wage and Working Hours was brought into being in response to the test-case environment that had been made possible by amendments to the *Conciliation and Arbitration Act* in 1921.

This chapter reviews the developments of the 1930s, years in which economic conditions dominated the political and industrial relations climate. The Great Depression was accompanied by a Labor administration, industrial legislation perceived as hostile to employers' interests, calls for piece-work and the abandonment of compulsory arbitration, and test cases to reduce the 'sacrosanct' and 'irreducible' basic wage.

The rapid economic recovery following 1934 led to a period in which employers were chagrined by the industrial legislative inactivity by non-Labor Governments, in which unions mounted test cases to restore the basic wage and reduce standard hours of work, in which the economy was progressively placed on a wartime footing, and in which employer associations abandoned their traditional hostility towards compulsory arbitration and became actively supportive of the tribunal system.

The economic developments are reviewed in the first part of this chapter. The second part examines CCEA developments that were dominated by a major schism over the question of industrial uniformity. This schism had the potential to destroy the CCEA. The second part of the chapter also examines employer industrial co-ordination by way of the Interstate Conference of Employers. This successor to the Committee of Control re Basic Wage and Working Hours unsuccessfully attempted to broaden the

Committee's charter to incorporate general industrial policy. The Committee had more success in co-ordinating activities designed to reduce the basic wage and prevent the subsequent rescission of the 10 per cent reduction. As was the case with the Committee of Control, however, the Interstate Conference operated on an *ad hoc* basis, and attempts to bring into existence a more permanent co-ordinating organisation met with little support.

Depression

The Scullin Government was sworn into office on 22 October 1929 — the day after the Wall Street stock-market crash, which signalled the beginning of the Depression. Within 2 years the prices of wool and wheat, commodities that accounted for a half and a quarter respectively of total export value, had fallen by 75 per cent. Deflation was accompanied by crippling unemployment, and 30 per cent of unionists were out of work by mid-1932.

As the economy deteriorated, employer calls for the abandonment of compulsory arbitration intensified. The CCEA Conference of 1928 had passed a unanimous resolution calling for the abolition of compulsory arbitration, a call repeated the following year, when it was resolved 'That this conference is of the opinion that compulsory arbitration has largely failed, and that it has not achieved the purpose for which it was introduced. Having this in view, we consider that it should be abolished' (*Employers' Review* 28/10/29).

The CCEA's sentiments were shared by other employer bodies. The EFNSW claimed that 'after many years of intimate association with compulsory arbitration it had definitely arrived at the conclusion that this form of legislation must be entirely removed if the country and our industries are to be rehabilitated' (ibid. 30/6/30). Arbitration, in this body's view, 'was a greater curse than droughts, prickly-pear or any other curse in Australia' and had 'done nothing else but cripple industry' (ibid. 30/8/30). It further contended that 'years of experience with our pernicious system of compulsory arbitration has clearly indicated to all carrying on industry that the system must operate to the detriment of all concerned. Under its aegis laws are passed which do not put one extra penny in the pockets of employees . . . Its actions and results are diametrically opposed to all our Economic Laws, and consequently the time must arrive when a change must take place' (ibid. 31/12/30). The ACMA expressed the view that arbitration was a burden that could only be supported during periods of prosperity and its abandonment was inevitable during a major recession (Hall 1971: 401–2). Its New South Wales affiliate was more emphatic: 'The evil which now obstructs our path to better conditions is without doubt compulsory arbitration. This must be suspended for it has now completely failed us' (ibid:445). The other major New South Wales manufacturing employer association, the Metal Trades Employers' Association, agreed: 'Away with it, and let us get back to the clear, open, economic rings' (Carboch 1958:192).

The evils attributed to compulsory arbitration were many. It was the major 'cause of depression in general; it reduces output since wages are paid to employees irrespective of their worth; it causes high unemployment, high tariffs, high production costs, industrial chaos and industrial conflict in particular' *(Employers' Review* 30/9/29). High on the employers' list of grievances was the system of wage fixation adopted by arbitration courts: this, by and large, did not incorporate the employers' preferred option of a system of payment by results. Thus the CCEA Conference of 1923 considered that 'the only system by which the great majority of the industrial workers in Australia can secure any substantial and any permanent increase in their earnings is by the unrestricted application of the principle of payment by results, with adequate provisions for the protection of a minimum standard in all industries'. This theme was re-echoed by the 1926 Conference: 'The material welfare of our people engaged in all spheres of industry can be improved only by increased productivity, and this can best be achieved by payment by results with a recognition of mutual obligation by all parties to promote and attain efficiency'.

In 1927 the Arbitration Court did attempt to insert piece-rates into the engineering and blacksmith's awards. The industrial disputation that resulted, however, led Beeby to vary the award in such a way as to allow unions to veto piece-work. Writing in 1929, Anderson noted:

> The conclusion of the struggle was that the unions refused to work under the piece-work provisions of the award, and there was apparently no power strong enough to compel them to do so, and there the matter stands. There is this to be said, however, that the position in regard to the adoption of an extended system of payment by results in Australia is worse today than it was before Judge Beeby's award, for there has been a trial of strength between the unions and the Courts and the unions have won. (Anderson 1929:454)

By 1930 employers were forced to change tack and seek a reduction in labour costs by way of the 'sacrosanct and irreducible' basic wage, which had been declared to be 'beyond bargaining'. These activities resulted in the 10 per cent wage reduction of January 1931. They were instrumental in the formation of the Interstate Conference of Employers, whose activities are reviewed below. They also stimulated legislative attempts by the Scullin

Government to block or retard any basic wage reduction by way of Conciliation Committees.

Within 6 months of gaining office the Scullin Government amended the Act in three ways. Strikes and lockouts were no longer prohibited — the first time since the original Act was passed that such actions were not illegal *per se*. The amended Act also enlarged the functions of Conciliation Commissioners. These had been introduced as auxiliaries to the judges in 1928. They performed conciliation functions under the charge of the judges and had limited autonomy. The Scullin amendments gave Commissioners the same powers as judges except in relation to Full Bench matters. The amendments also provided for Conciliation Committees consisting of representatives of the parties in dispute. These Committees were empowered to make majority decisions having the effect of awards. Where the parties could not reach a decision a Conciliation Commissioner was to make an award after a further hearing. Once appointed, Conciliation Committees ousted the jurisdiction of the Arbitration Court.

The latter provision was used by unions to counter the employers' moves to have the basic wage reduced. 'This', the *Employers' Review* noted, 'was a very simple process, and judging by the large number of applications made by the unions for conciliation committees it appears as though the unions are out to prevent at all costs any application being made to the Federal Court for reduced wages or increased hours' (30/9/30).

Conciliation Committees delayed, rather than prevented, the basic wage reductions. On appeal to the High Court, section 33 and parts of section 34 of the amended Act were found to be *ultra vires*, since a Committee decision 'amounted to neither conciliation nor to arbitration' (44 *CLR* 319). The government sought to overcome this constitutional difficulty by converting the Committees into tribunals required to hear the actual disputants before reaching a decision. In May 1931 a hostile Senate, which had been strenuously lobbied by employer organisations, refused to pass the Bill.

The Senate also rejected the Constitution Alteration (Industrial Powers) Bill, which provided for a referendum to increase the Commonwealth's industrial powers. Despite these setbacks, an important feature of the short-lived Scullin Government was that it frustrated the Bruce and employer attempts to remove federal arbitration. Any plans for economic recovery had to incorporate the retention of federal arbitration.

By 1930 the federal basic wage had been adjusted to changes in the Retail Price Index on a quarterly and automatic basis for nearly a decade. Thus, when prices began to fall from 1927 on, nominal wages also fell. Employers pressed for further wage reductions so as to depress real wages by 30 per cent. The level of reduction granted by the Arbitration Court, that of 10 per cent, seems to have been influenced by Professor Copland's evidence, which demonstrated that there had been a loss in real spending power of about 10 per cent as the result of falling export prices and a cessation of capital inflow (Foenander 1937: 100–18; Copland 1930:182–4). By the automatic adjustment of the basic wage to price decreases, and by the super-imposition of the 10 per cent reduction in real wages, the CCEA was able to bring the nominal basic wage for the first quarter of 1933 to about 30 per cent below the level prevailing in 1928.

Perhaps because it had accepted and acted on his advice, Copland credits the CCCA with giving policy makers a major lead in the direction of economic recovery. The Labor Government, he notes,

> was powerless to prevent the Court from ordering a reduction in wages . . . The award of the Court was a survey of the general economic situation at the end of 1930, and it is of more than passing interest to note that the first pronouncement on the crisis from a responsible authority was this award of the Arbitration Court . . . The Court with its independent position and known sympathy in the past with the demands for as high a standard of living as the economy could afford, was well fitted to call attention to the economic position and to the need for general adjustment. (Copland 1932:89–90)

The 'need for general adjustment' was taken up by the Premiers' Plan adopted in June 1931. This agreed to extend the 10 per cent wage cuts to other sections of the community including interest rates on mortgages, public service salaries, government loans and pensions. This plan, however, divided the Labor Party, which was brought down in November 1931. The United Australia Party, with former Labor Minister Lyons at its head, won the elections of December 1931.

From 1932 on, unions sought the rescission of the 1931 order. This was finally granted in April 1934. In May 1937 unions pressed for further adjustments of the basic wage on account of economic prosperity. After consideration of the 'mass of spoken and quoted economic material submitted in evidence' the basic wage was increased by, on average 5 shillings (50 cents) per week (Foenander 1947:27). A further application in 1939 was unsuccessful (61 *CAR* 527).

In addition to these basic wage test cases, both employers and unions were active on the hours front. Following the February 1927 decision in the Main Hours case the 44-hour week became the federal standard in several industries (Foenander 1937:151–62). This trend was halted at the end of 1927 because of economic recession (ibid:162). With the removal of the basic wage reduction in 1934, award variations again began to provide for the 44-hour week and by the end of 1935 the CCCA 'was showing an anxiety to concede 44 hours in all possible cases'. In 1936 Australia supported the International Labour Organisation's Convention for the 40-hour week and unions began pressing for this as the federal standard. The CCCA was not persuaded and as late as October 1939 determined 44 hours as the federal standard (*Employers' Review* 30/11/39).

Economic recovery and the conversion to arbitration

Economic recovery was accompanied by remarkable policy transformations on the part of employers — initially a reluctant acceptance 'that the arbitration tree is rooted into the community'; then qualified support for uniform industrial standards regulated by the CCCA; and finally a championing of arbitration as the appropriate mechanism for dispute handling.

The acceptance of arbitration was little more than a pragmatic realisation that if the system could survive under Bruce it had little to fear from Lyons. Acceptance of arbitration necessitated consideration as to 'how it can be controlled or kept in some sort of order. Should each state look after its own industrial disputes, or should one court alone deal with all the industrial affairs of Australia?' (CCEA Conference 1932, President's Address:7). Qualified support for uniform federal regulation was a compromise between the divergent federations' views. These were relatively minor adjustments compared with the total support for arbitration that became evident from 1937 on. In a period of increased collective bargaining, of prominent communist union leadership, of imminent war, and of increased government regulation employers saw arbitration in a new light:

> We Australians, employers and employees alike, are a type — we should know how to work together, and if differences do arrive, we have an Arbitration Court to settle them. In our arbitration system we have machinery for settling disputes. This machinery has been built up over the past 30 years. It had stood the test of the Great War and the Great Depression. It had become part of the life of our democratic country . . . If employers cannot get on without having strikes, they should question the ability of their managers. If employees cannot get on without strikes they should change their leaders. Disputes should always be settled by Arbitration. (*Employers' Review* 31/12/38)

These sentiments, which overturned three decades of CCEA hostility towards arbitration, were endorsed by other employer groups. Thus J. Heine, President of the Metal Trades Employers' Association (MTEA), who in 1928 had called for a return 'to the clear, open economic rings', commented in his 1937 Presidential Address: 'As far as the Arbitration

Court is concerned . . . The Association's view was that the Arbitration system was a sound one and that it would be a permanent feature of the Australian legal system' (*Metal Trades Journal* 25/4/37).

One reason for this conversion was easy enough to find. The economic recovery and buoyancy had altered bargaining relationships. 'What this country needs', claimed the EFNSW Vice-President at the Federation Dinner of 1937, 'is not a job for every man, but a man for every job' (*Employer's Review* 30/10/37:9). In his speech at that dinner the Minister for Labour dwelt at length on the shortage of skilled workmen, particularly in the building trades. He noted that advertisements in the Press offering as much as $4.00 per week in over-award payments (about 60 per cent of the basic wage at that time) were common (ibid.). In times of prosperity the delays and formalism that characterised the arbitration processes were to the advantage of employers. Other factors also influenced employers' new-found faith in arbitration. Hagan notes that employer organisations:

> were interested in having the Court hold down wages which shortages would have forced higher. But probably there was more to it than that. With shortages of craftsmen, some unions at least were in a stronger position to enforce demands which they believed were related to the prevention of unemployment among their members. Thus employer organisations began to look to the Commonwealth Court of Conciliation and Arbitration as their defender against claims for a 40-hour week and equal pay. (Hagan 1981:67–8)

Employer associations, which earlier had been pressing for reduced wages, now sought to have their members hold the line against sectional attempts by unions to exploit changed circumstances. With little success, associations sought methods of disciplining members who gave in to union pressure but had to admit that no 'practical solution of the difficulty' seemed available (VCM Council Meeting 1/4/39).

In addition to these compelling reasons was the association by many employer groups of collective bargaining with communist influence over unions. Arbitration provided some defence against such extremism and had thus become a 'part of the life of our democratic country', a factor given added emphasis by international developments. As the economy was increasingly placed on a war-time footing by way of government regulations against which employers had little redress, arbitration was further seen as a mechanism for making labour adjustments that permitted greater employer involvement.

War was declared on 3 September 1939. It was to be accompanied by the greatest centralisation of industrial regulation ever exercised in Australia.

The fact that much of this regulation emanated from Labor administrations only served to make the arbitration system, so long condemned, more attractive to employers.

THE CENTRAL COUNCIL AND INDUSTRIAL UNIFORMITY

The CCEA split

The 1920s had been years of instability for the CCEA. This instability arose from the deep divisions between the two major Federations over the question of administration. During that period the EFNSW tendered its resignation on two occasions. Its discontent arose from the fact that it paid an inordinate share of CCEA finances (45 per cent) and yet could be outvoted on policy decisions. During the 1930s, as New South Wales employers suffered a second bout of the 'blight of Langism', this discontent again emerged as the EFNSW strove to get other federations to accept the policy of industrial uniformity by way of federal regulation. The federations from the smaller states resisted these attempts but, through a strange turn of events, the EFNSW found itself allied with its former adversary — the VEF. After 3 years of trying to get other federations to change policy, these two federations resigned from the CCEA in 1935 and did not rejoin until 1937. Thus the 1930s were years of great stress within the CCEA.

A Special Conference was held in June 1932 to deliberate on the matter of exclusive federal industrial powers. It proved a stormy affair. In his presidential address E. H. Bakewell (SAEF) had directed attention to the subject matter of the Conference and noted:

> Having realised that the Arbitration tree is rooted into the community, we have to consider how it can be controlled or kept in some sort of order. Should each State look after its own industrial disputes, or should one Court alone deal with all the industrial affairs of Australia? . . . Some of the States appear to be satisfied with their own position, so far as one can judge, without putting the question to a vital test; others think differently. So much depends on the personality of the Courts, and that varies from time to time as fresh appointments are made. Some are of the opinion that local disputes can be better settled on the spot where the parties are, rather than 500 or 1000 miles away. Rates and conditions that suit Brisbane probably will not suit Perth, and even Sydney and Melbourne conditions may not always be the same. The cost of various necessities of life vary much in the different States. In one town or city meat may be cheap and most other things dear, and in another city the manufactured goods cost much less than when transported 1000 miles or more. Australia is a country of great areas and varied climate and conditions. The habits and customs and standard of life vary very much, and we must be cautious in trying to put ourselves all on one level.

VEF President Ashworth took objection to the address and accused Bakewell of arguing 'for State Courts as against the Commonwealth Court'. 'That', he added, 'is a subject upon which even you are hardly competent to speak for the Central Council as a whole'. It had been customary to publish the President's address in pamphlet form. With EFNSW support, Ashworth protested against such publication. After a long and heated debate a compromise position was reached whereby the address was left in the hands of a Publicity Committee to make alterations. Bakewell intimated his feelings by noting that he had been 'giving remarks for 30 years and had never been pulled up before' and by adjourning the meeting (CCEA Special General Conference 27–29/6/32).

Both the EFNSW and VEF circulated material in support of federal regulation. The former's circular noted that for many years 'the New South Wales Federation has taken an all-Australian view in regard to Industrial Powers . . . in order to maintain all the Australian industries in a fair competitive position'. It claimed that 'Langism' had placed employers in New South Wales in an intolerable position and the federation had sent a deputation to Canberra seeking relief. The Prime Minister and all the political parties had agreed that industrial conditions ought to be uniform. 'It was', the federation claimed, 'imperative to strike now, when the people were favourable to the Federal view in order that our industries will be free from State misgovernment, and only subjected, each and all alike, to the common Federal law' (EFNSW 'Industrial Conciliation and Arbitration', circular to Federations 18/4/32).

The VEF claimed industrial powers should be vested in one authority. This would reduce 'pace-making between authorities' and would enable employers to be more successful in the fight to remove compulsory arbitration:

> With one authority only to deal with, employers could concentrate their efforts upon influencing the legislation of that authority. At present they are divided, some States favouring legislation by the States, others legislation by the Commonwealth. The vital issue — the question as to whether or not we should have compulsory arbitration at all — is obscured. (VEF Circular 'Industrial Conciliation and Arbitration' 18/4/32).

Ashworth dwelt on this second aspect at the Special Conference in which he declared: 'My advocacy that the whole should be brought under the one authority — the Federal authority — is because I regard it as the first essential step to put an end to the evils of compulsory arbitration'.

The other federations were not convinced. Exclusive federal power, in the SAEF view, would extend beyond merely hours of work and the basic wage.

It would come to include factory administration, closing times and other matters best regulated locally. Its Secretary noted that the 'matter has been discussed for the last twenty years . . . and on every occasion the proposal of Federal control has been turned down in a most emphatic manner'. The QEF was not particularly interested in debating the subject. Its President declared that the CCEA could 'go on talking till Doomsday as far as Queensland is concerned, for we will not abide by Federal industrial control'. Despite a veiled threat by Ashworth that 'if we are defeated, it is just possible we may have to take steps independently to see if we cannot bring about what we want', the EFNSW and VEF were outvoted by the other three federations.

Thus the Special Conference did not resolve the issue for which it was called and the questions of federal regulation and industrial uniformity continued to divide the CCEA (as well as the ACMA[1]) for the rest of the decade. Since the question of industrial uniformity had been a perennial one for the EFNSW from about 1915 on, and since the VEF had previously strongly opposed the EFNSW line, it is worth considering more fully the strong motivations leading these federations to take action that had the potential of putting the CCEA out of existence.

As already noted the EFNSW had equivocated in its desire for federal regulation with the entry and exit of Labor administrations in that state. The proclivity with which Labor administrations legislated for higher labour costs in New South Wales caused the federation to seek federal regulation. It reverted to a desire for state regulation under non-Labor Governments. This equivocation came to an end with the election of the Lang Government in 1925, after which the EFNSW briefly departed from its federal control quest to accommodate Bruce in 1929. Lang lost office in 1927 but was re-elected in October 1930 at a time when employers were seeking to reduce labour costs. The EFNSW's *Employers' Review* highlighted the relative disadvantage of New South Wales employers as shown in Table 4.1

Table 4.1 *Basic wage and standard hours of work in capital cities, 1932*

City	Basic wage*	Basis of assessment	Hours
Sydney	$8.26	Wife and 1 child	44
Melbourne	$6.80	Wife and 3 children	48
Adelaide	$6.36	Wife and 3 children	48
Brisbane	$7.40	Wife and 3 children	48
Perth	$7.20	Wife and 3 children	48

* Converted to decimal currency

In addition to the higher basic wage and shorter working week, New South Wales employers were also confronted with child endowment tax of 6 per cent (per employee). This tax was not levied on employers by other governments. New South Wales employers were also concerned by Labor's reconstitution of the Industrial Commission in 1931 and the appointment of Mr Justice Piddington — a man of known Labor sympathies whose Basic Wage Commission had advocated considerable increases in the basic wage — as sole judge of the Industrial Commission. All but one of the newly appointed Conciliation Commissioners were ex-union officials (*Employers' Review* 30/5/31).

The experience at this time reinforced the federation's desire for federal regulation. The editorial of its journal greeted the election of the Lyons Government, with its declared policy of federal regulation, as 'A Light in the Sky'. 'All parties', the editorial noted, 'including the Lang Section, are agreed that the function of wage fixation in Australia should be confined to the Federal Court' (*Employers' Review* 31/12/31). Three months later 'A Cloud in the Sky' summed up the federation's impatience at the lack of any government action on the legislation front. Representatives were sent to Canberra and these returned convinced that all parties still supported federal regulation, and that this consensus provided a rare opportunity for concerted action in that direction. In these circumstances it was imperative to get the support of other employer bodies. After unsuccessfully trying to do so by way of the Interstate Conference of Employers (see below) the EFNSW attempted to press policy changes on the other federations.

The VEF position was more complicated and in time became entwined with its internal financial and membership problems. Its desire to reduce tribunal duality was understandable but begged the question as to why the VEF now sought to do so by federal, rather than state, regulation. One influencing factor was, no doubt, the flow-on of New South Wales conditions into federal awards and wages boards conditions. Yet another was that Victorian employers now thought themselves disadvantaged *vis-a-vis* their South Australian competitors (VCM Council Meeting 20/4/37). The major reason for the VEF's approach, however, seems to have been Ashworth's strategy of eliminating compulsory arbitration altogether. This, in his view, required the removal of state tribunals in the first instance. When Ashworth died in 1935 the VEF was left without the ability to formulate any new strategy. Thus the VEF persisted with the EFNSW line even though Victoria legislated in 1934 to impose federal arbitration standards on its wages boards, thus effectively removing many of the problems associated with dual regulation in that state.[2]

Thus for different reasons the EFNSW and VEF persisted with their demands for changed CCEA policy in relation to industrial uniformity. Despite numerous debates over this issue the smaller federations continued to outvote the two larger ones. This continued until January 1935 when both tendered their resignations. The CCEA effectively went out of existence until both organisations rejoined in 1937. By then legislation in both Victoria and New South Wales required the tribunals of those states to adopt the federal tribunals wages standards. To overcome the personality problems created by this major schism the CCEA returned to its previous practice of appointing an 'outsider' as President. Colonel E. F. Harrison, former Commandant of the Royal Military College Duntroon, was elected President in December 1937. He remained President until 1944 when he was recalled as Commandant of Duntroon.[3]

Industrial co-ordination

During the 1920s a Committee of Control had been established to help co-ordinate basic wage and standard hours cases and to raise the finance needed for such cases. In February 1930 the VCM sought the reconvening of this Committee 'on the question of approaching the [Arbitration Court] for re-adjusting the Basic Wage' (VCM Meeting 18/2/30). The Graziers' Federal Council had also written to the CCEA seeking the convening of the Committee 'with a view to making applications for a reduction in the basic wage' (CCEA Meeting 3/3/30).

The meeting took place in March. By then the question of basic wage reductions had become bound up with that of the Conciliation Committees established under recent amendments to the *Conciliation and Arbitration Act*. The meeting therefore took on a wider charter than that of merely controlling the conduct of any basic wage cases. It established an Employers' Committee to investigate and report on the Act and the proposed constitutional changes. Perhaps because of the wider frame of reference employed, the title 'Committee of Control re Basic Wage and Working Hours' fell out of use in favour of 'Interstate Conference of Employers'. The meeting approved of the Graziers' Federal Council, or some 'other suitable Employers' organisation', applying for a revision of the basic wage. In the event of the Court deciding 'to treat the application as one involving a general investigation, a further meeting was to be summoned to consider the question of financial and other assistance to the applicant in preparing and presenting the case' (CCEA Meeting 4/6/30).

Two further meetings, one in April and the other in May, discussed the Conciliation Committee developments and their effects on any basic wage applications. In September T. Maughan posted notices of a further meeting to receive the report of the Committee on the *Conciliation and Arbitration Amendment Act* 1930 and 'with the view of taking appropriate action, to consider the applications now before the Commonwealth Arbitration Court for review of the Federal Basic Wage, and the position that has developed through the appointment of Conciliation Committees with arbitral powers'.

At the September meeting Maughan, as Chairman of the Legislation Committee, reported on recent developments and referred to the 'unexpected and surprising change of front in the Senate in accepting the Government's compromise change in regard to the appointment of Conciliation Commissioners and Committees with arbitral powers, in face of previous assurances that the Senate would resolutely oppose such proposals'. Speakers 'expressed appreciation of the work of the Committee and the indebtedness of the Conference to the sub-committee which had made frequent visits to Canberra while the Arbitration Bill was before Parliament'. After debate a resolution calling for a 'united protest to the Nationalist Party against the manner in which employing interests have been treated in connection with the amending Bill' was amended to one protesting 'against the action of the Senate in respect of the appointment of Conciliation Commissioners and Committees with arbitral powers', and drawing this protest to the attention of Nationalist Party leaders in both Houses.

Mr H. W. Gepp, former Chairman of the Development and Migration Commission and who was acting in the capacity of industrial adviser and consultant to the Federal Government, had been invited to attend the Conference. With the approval and consent of the Acting Prime Minister he was to 'explain the Government's intentions with regard to desired assistance from employers in its endeavours to revive trade and industry and reduce unemployment'. Gepp 'emphasised the gravity of the financial situation and urged employers to respond sympathetically to the Government's invitation for their aid in the necessary economic reconstruction'.

In view of the strong feelings about perceived government activities to prevent any reduction in the basic wage, Gepp's pleas were not sympathetically responded to. The meeting resolved:

> The employers have been invited by the Government to assist them in restoring Australia to a sound industrial and economic position, but this meeting is of opinion that any proper rehabilitation of industry is impossible while the existing industrial legislation remains on the statute book. The meeting entirely deprecates the recent amendments of the *Conciliation and Arbitration Act* and the subsequent action of the Government in appointing

> Conciliation Committees to deal with industrial disputes already submitted to the Court of Arbitration. A condition precedent to any satisfactory adjustment of industrial conditions must be the immediate revocation of the appointment of Conciliation Committees and an assurance that the Government will refrain from making further appointments so that the way may be left open to the Court to deal at once with applications for review of the basic wage and standard hours. Further, that the Federal and State Governments be urged jointly to consider this aspect of the situation with a view to removing all statutory barriers to speedy reconstruction. (Meeting of Representatives of Employers' Organisations 9/9/30)

This resolution was conveyed in a letter to the Acting Prime Minister, J. E. Fenton, to which Maughan added: 'The employers are most willing and anxious to help the government in this time of national crisis, but they feel that action by the Government in the direction indicated in the Resolution is a necessary preliminary to any effective co-operation' (Circular CCEA Secretary Maughan to Federations 11/9/30).

Fenton considered the resolution as an 'arrogant demand and a threat' (*Advertiser* 23/9/30).

Another Meeting of the Interstate Conference of Employers was held on September 30 to consider the 'best way in which effect might be given to the resolution passed at the Conference on March 31 with regard to financial and/or other general support in any employers' application to the Commonwealth Arbitration Court for review of the Federal basic wage'. A committee consisting of J. W. Allen (Graziers), A. S. Elford (Ship Owners), W. Letcher (VCM), L. Mann (VEF), L. C. Meagher (Mines and Metals), T. Maughan (CCEA) and G. H. Boykett (SAEF) was appointed 'to consider and suggest an equitable basis of contribution by the various employers' organisations towards any costs that may be incurred in connection with any such application for revision of the Federal basic wage' (Conference of Representatives of Employers' Organisations 30/9/30).

The Employers' Committee appointed by the Interstate Conference met on six occasions between December 1930 and February 1931 to map out a strategy for a general basic wage reduction case. By the latter date the name of the Committee had been changed to that of Executive Committee, the High Court had declared section 33 of the Act *ultra vires*, and the Senate was making it difficult for the government to reconstitute Conciliation Committees to conform with the requirements of the Constitution (CCEA Meeting 13/3/31). The CCEA meeting of March 1931 'placed on record its recognition of the valuable services rendered by the Executive Committee appointed by the Interstate Conferences convened by this Council'. This recognition, however was somewhat qualified. The EFNSW, in its quest for employer support for federal regulation, had attempted to bypass the obstructionist smaller federations by having the Interstate Conference declare a policy supportive of federal regulation. The Executive Committee had been directed to make recommendations on this matter. This led the smaller federations to argue that the Committee should not have executive powers and should function only as an advisory and consultative body. Otherwise 'it might encroach on the rights and prerogatives of the Central Council' (ibid.). However, the CCEA gave full support for the central task of the Committee, countering actions by the Government to overcome the High Court invalidation of section 33 of the Act, and it resolved:

> That this Council is prepared to leave in the hands of the Executive Committee of the Interstate Conference of Employers, the matter of dealing with the amending Bill when introduced, relying upon that Committee to take such steps as they deem necessary to protect the employers' interests. (ibid.)

The smaller federations, still concerned by the EFNSW attempts to convert the Interstate Conference to a policy of federal regulation, had the SAEF Secretary write to Maughan about equal representation of the states on the ICE Committee.[4] 'In view of the important powers vested in this Committee especially in connection with Federal industrial matters', he wrote, 'this matter should be considered by the Council' (Boykett to Maughan 17/4/31). Only one member of the Committee at this time was not domiciled in Melbourne. In its meeting on 4 June, the Executive Committee considered the SAEF request to be impractical and pointed out that the 'appointments to the Committee by the Interstate Conference were made with regard to industries rather than States'. As the Committee had power to co-opt other members it invited the SAEF to nominate a person to its ranks (Meeting of Executive Committee of ICE 18/6/31).

The Interstate Conference of Employers was again convened in September 1931 following the rejection by the Senate of new amendments to the *Act*. The conference was convened by the CCEA at the request of the EFNSW 'for the purpose of discussing means of obtaining relief from Federal and State legislation with a view to the rehabilitation of industry and the reabsorption of the unemployed'. The meeting, in which 27 organisations were represented, confirmed the fears of the smaller federations that the EFNSW was using Conference for its own policy designs. The meeting resolved:

> (1) THAT in order to meet the grave problems confronting industry, and having regard to the serious growth of unemployment, immediate steps be taken to bring together the parties to industry for consultation, and that the Prime Minister be approached in the first instance with the view of

making arrangements for representatives of employers to meet (a) him and the State Premiers in conference and (b) subsequently the representatives of workers, so as to deal earnestly with the question of Federal and State industrial legislation and means for the restoration of industry and the re-absorption of the unemployed.

(2) THAT the matter be left in the hands of the Executive Committee to give effect to the foregoing resolution.

(3) THAT the Executive Committee be requested to prepare proposals to submit to any conference that may ultimately be arranged with representatives of the Unions, embodying a plan to be put into operation in the event of a temporary suspension of awards and determination being mutually agreed upon.

It is evident that many other associations shared the smaller federations' apprehensions concerning the Committee's expanded role. The Metal Trades Employers' Association wrote that 'whilst they appreciated and desired to encourage any effort to restore a better understanding in industry and reduce unemployment, they did not think that collective conference would achieve that object and did not therefore desire to support the proposals'. The Interim Report 'containing the outlines of a proposed scheme to be substituted for the existing system of compulsory arbitration' was received coolly. The meeting agreed not to divulge the contents of the Report until it had been referred 'confidentially to the President of each organisation represented for consideration and report as soon as possible' (Conference of Representatives of Employers' Organisations 4/11/31).

The CCEA considered this Interim Report in February 1931. Its approach reflected the sectional interests between the federations: 'Owing to divergent views held in the different States it was found impracticable to present to the Conference any united opinion from this Council and it was left to individual members to voice the independent views of their Federations at the Conference' (CCEA Meeting 8/2/32). Other associations avoided similar confrontation by quietly shelving the Report.

The Executive Committee of the Interstate Conference, while trying to formulate an employer offensive in which it had difficulty in getting general agreement from delegates, also had to contend with the counter-offensive from unions. In February 1932 it resolved:

THAT in view of the uncertainty prevailing as to the procedure that the Federal Arbitration Court will adopt on the 7th March in connexion with the applications for a restoration of the 10% reduction ordered last year, a meeting of the Interstate Conference be summoned for 8th March in order that the Committee may obtain instructions in the light of what occurs on the 7th as to the best means of presenting the case on behalf of employers generally, including the question of briefing counsel. (Circular, CCEA Secretary Maughan to Employers' Organisations 23/2/32)

The Executive thus retreated to a more reactive role. There was greater support for such a role by the general body of associations.

The smaller federations, still smarting from the resolutions of September 1931, now argued for the CCEA to move out of the Interstate Conference on the grounds that it was performing the work of the Central Council. The WAEF contended that the unions' applications to cancel the basic wage reductions must be combated but that this ought to be done through the CCEA. 'After their exhibition of want of ordinary knowledge of State affairs as exhibited at the last Melbourne Conference', the WAEF objected to the CCEA delegating its powers 'to the other crowd' (Letter, WAEF President Hedges to CCEA President Bakewell 25/2/32).

The CCEA Secretary and ICE Deputy Chairman, Maughan, replied that it was the ICE that considered the application resulting in the 10 per cent reductions and that 'the pending applications for restoration of that reduction are obviously a matter for the same Conference, which represents some 34 organisations, including the five federations. You will therefore see that the Conference covers a much wider field than that represented by the Central Council, and any costs incurred would be spread over a broader basis' (letter, Maughan to Carter 29/2/32).

The WAEF was not moved and considered that 'it would be much wiser to keep the control of matters of this description in the hands of the Central Council, which has had so much experience in past years in such important cases' (letter, Carter to Maughan 1/3/32). The CCEA experience, in fact, had been limited to convening, and being involved with, the former Committee of Control, a task not dissimilar to that under the Executive Committee of the ICE.

The EFNSW, peeved by the Interstate Conference rejection of its proposals 'to appoint a deputation to urge the government that a referendum be taken at the earliest possible moment with a view to getting exclusive industrial powers in the Commonwealth authority', also objected to the 'communications of the Executive Committee being circulated on the paper of the CCEA'. This federation informed Maughan that 'some of the proposals of the Executive Committee are unacceptable to the members of the Central Council and the circularising of the material as now done is apt to create a wrong impression to those not directly familiar with the position' (letter, EFNSW Secretary Schwilk to Maughan and CCEA Meeting 11/4/32).

The Executive Committee did handle the basic wage case in which the union applications were rejected. 'With the conclusion of these proceedings', Maughan wrote to the federations, 'the work of the Interstate

Conference would be completed, and it was doubtful that, in the changed circumstances, any further action would be taken with respect to the interim report furnished by the Executive Committee of the Conference on the question of industrial arbitration and means for rehabilitating industry and re-absorbing the unemployed' (CCEA Meeting 11/4/32). Thereafter the EFNSW sought the implementation of policy changes through the CCEA rather than through the Interstate Conference. As already noted, this caused considerable difficulties for the CCEA but had the effect of making the Conference more acceptable to the smaller federations. In the wake of repeated demands by unions for the restoration of the basic wage reduction it was agreed that the CCEA continue as the 'medium through which the interstate conference would be convened' and that it would be a matter for the Conference 'to decide on the appropriate procedure to follow' (CCEA Meeting 6/3/33).

Two such conferences were convened in 1933, one in March and the other in November. The first meeting discussed the Arbitration Court's decision against a further general inquiry and its proposal to deal with 'individual industries according to their financial position'. Associations were concerned that 'even in the individual cases the employers should not lose sight of the broad national aspect of the position and emphasise that phase of it before the Court' (ibid.). The November meeting considered the unions' applications for a restoration of the 10 per cent basic wage reduction and for a shorter working week. The CCEA decided to 'inform the Interstate Conference of Employers that in its opinion it would be unnecessary to incur the expense of briefing Counsel to act on behalf of the employers'. It also expressed its satisfaction with the services rendered by Messrs Mann and Grant in the previous case. L. Mann (VEF) and C. H. Grant (VCM) were appointed advocates to present the case on behalf of employers generally, and were given 'full authority to collect and prepare the necessary data to support their case, and power to obtain evidence from expert witnesses' (CCEA 'Report of Executive Committee', Annual Conference 14/11/34). At a time when the Arbitration Court was looking at industry as well as general capacity to pay, many associations indicated they would seek separate representation of their industries. This included the VCM, which, notwithstanding the fact that Grant was its industrial advocate, gave notice that 'consideration was being given to the question of preparing a special case as from the Manufacturing interests' (VCM Council Meeting 27/11/33). The Court delivered judgement in April 1934 and restored the wage reduction.

The Interstate Conference did not meet again until February 1936 when it considered Government proposals to establish a Committee of Enquiry into Hours of Work. A sub-committee was appointed to 'collect data and draw up methods of its collation in preparation for a possible case before the Arbitration Court' (VCM Report of Executive Committee to Council 2/3/36). Neither the Government's Working Hours Conference, Australia's endorsement of the ILO 40-Hour Week resolution, nor union applications for a reduction in working hours caused the Court to alter its 44-hour standard.

The Conference was reconvened in April 1937 following applications by 17 unions for a $1.20 increase in the basic wage and a decision by the Arbitration Court to treat these applications as a general enquiry. A committee was appointed to handle the case for employers generally, 'leaving it open to any individual respondent to appear separately by Counsel at his own expense if he so desired' (CCEA Meeting 13/4/37). Grant and Mann were again selected as advocates.

Following this case, in which the Court awarded a non-indexed 'prosperity loading', the sub-committee considered that it was desirable for employers to 'take a long-range view of industrial matters and make preliminary arrangements for the handling of future cases'. It suggested the appointment of a small committee to 'watch proceedings in the industrial field generally and act in an advisory capacity to the employers' organisations'. The sub-committee also suggested that employers 'should permanently retain an economist and/or statistician whom they could consult at all times on economic problems affecting industry' (CCEA Meeting 30/6/37).

The CCEA considered, but did not support, this proposal. In its opinion, 'the principal employers' organisations would not be willing to render the necessary financial assistance, and some of them were disinclined to recognise the need for any outside body to deal with cases which their own organisation was competent to handle' (CCEA Meeting 14/3/38). The VCM's reaction to the proposals affirmed the CCEA view. It agreed to co-operate with other organisations on general cases but was not agreeable to the 'setting up of a permanent organisation, which would practically mean the dictation of our policy by another organisation'. The chamber further considered that in the final analysis it did the bulk of the work anyway (VCM Meeting 21/9/37). It was subsequently critical of the CCEA's role as convenor of Interstate Conference (VCM Meeting 21/2/39).

The proposal was considered by the Interstate Conference at its September Meeting, when a sub-committee met to make a further examination of the matter (VCM Council Meeting 28/9/37).[5] Important associations refused to consider any permanent organisation, the VCM claiming:

> previous experience of such committees forced it to the conclusion that the one proposed would be unnecessary and not in the best interests of manufacturers. The VCM has a staff able to handle efficiently such enquiries to the best advantage of its members and while prepared to co-operate to the fullest extent possible with other organisations, it was felt that we should retain our complete independence and individuality. (VCM *Annual Report 1938*:6)

After a break of 2 years the Interstate Conference was convened for the last time in September 1939 'for the purpose of discussing what action, if any, should be taken in an approach to the Arbitration Court for a review of the prosperity loading'. In view of the international situation existing at that time the Court adjourned the matter indefinitely (*Employers' Review* 30/11/39).

Co-ordination barriers

The activities of the Interstate Conference of Employers tried to build on those of the previous Committee of Control and, for a while, extended the range of matters considered to include, not only basic wage and standard hours enquiries, but also industrial legislation, industrial uniformity and economic recovery. Though the Conference experienced a high degree of success in co-ordinating its 35 members, co-operation between members was regarded by them as necessary rather than desirable. The CCEA, which had charge of convening Conference meetings, had difficulties in its dealings with its own affiliates, while its relations with the ACMA remained distant. Two major reasons accounted for this. As with the CCEA , so too ACMA suffered internal instability on the question of federal regulation and had to stave off actions by its New South Wales affiliate to disband the ACMA. Further, while in New South Wales both the Chamber of Manufactures and the Employers' Federation were in harmony on this question, such was not the case in Victoria. The VEF's support and espousal of federal regulation irked the VCM, which was attempting to counter the New South Wales chamber's activities within the ACMA. Internal problems resulted in both the ACMA and the CCEA being inward looking, a situation that did not facilitate improved relationships between the two organisations.

The second major issue concerned the perennial differences over tariff protection — differences that increased under the stress of economic depression. The 1931 ACMA plan for rehabilitation proposed the alteration of existing arbitration systems 'so that the basic wage throughout the Commonwealth for a 48 hour week for the next 12 months shall be the federal basic wage average of the six Capital Cities, adjusted quarterly on the ascertained cost of living'. The plan proposed that margins for skill, overtime and other industrial matters be dealt with 'by committees acting upon the principle of conciliation and appointed in equal numbers by employers and employees in each industry with an independent chairman (without vote) to be appointed by the Committee'. The plan further proposed that to achieve a measure of permanency there ought to be a referendum on 'industrial matters to the extent of fixing a uniform basic wage for a standard 48 hour working week' (Hall 1971:455). This conciliatory approach, with its provisions for wage increases as early as 1931 and its greater accommodation of Conciliation Committees, contrasted sharply with that of the CCEA and other employer groups. It was also ahead of other associations in calling for the centralising of the basic wage and standard hours, a call that it repudiated 2 years later. The ACMA's more conciliatory approach, and its less restrictive wages policy, were derived from a different foundation of economic well-being from that of commercial and primary producers, a foundation based on tariff protection. While commercial and primary interests saw tariffs as adding to costs of production and sought their removal as a mechanism for rehabilitation, manufacturers took a contrary approach and saw tariffs as a means of stimulating production of local goods and employment.

The First World War had stimulated a diverse range of local manufacturing because of the lack of foreign competition and a domestic inflation that helped lower real labour costs. For a year or so at the end of the War the shortage of shipping continued to give local manufacturers a competitive advantage. Anticipating the re-entry of foreign competition, the Australian Industries Protection League, within which the ACMA was active, was formed to press for increased tariffs and in 1920 the Hughes Government established the Tariff Board. In the following year, the *Customs Tariff Act* set higher levels of protection and extended the range of goods protected. This Act also provided for the preferential treatment of British goods. Together with the active lobbying of British firms, the Country Party (which held the balance of power in the 1920s and which refused to serve under Hughes because of his protectionist policies) ensured that the 'Bruce–Page Government was never likely to set tariffs high enough to provide what the ACMA . . . considered an adequate level of protection' (Hagan 1981:28). With the fall of this government in 1929 the ACMA lobbied for increased protection. On the day when Scullin took office, the CMNSW wrote advising that the first step to economic recovery was to put 'the tariff upon an impregnable basis'. The ACMA plan was simple enough:

> The new tariff levels would protect Australian industry from countries which manufactured their exports 'under conditions with which Australia cannot fairly compete' – be these, presumably, either of superior efficiency or 'low wages and excessive hours'. Safe behind the tariff wall, Australian industries could employ those presumably unemployed because of the 'unnecessary importations'. Reduction of costs could then be effected — and that achieved, the tariffs could start to come down again. (Hall 1971:445)

Other employer groups strongly disagreed with this approach and claimed that the existing level of tariffs, which they saw as a twin evil accompanying the arbitration systems they were trying to remove, was a major source of economic depression. Thus the EFNSW reported that depression was the 'inevitable reaction' to the 'Arbitration Court fixation of wages and hours, and constantly rising tariffs'. In its view, economic recovery was only achievable by policy based on the 'realisation that a tariff which is constantly playing circles with an Arbitration Court, each running the other higher as the race proceeds' was pernicious, and that it resulted in 'a levy on the whole community, not only for the cost of protection of the secondary industries . . . but also the necessary concessions in the way of railway freights, pools, bounties, and other expensive schemes that must be given to the primary producer to enable him to live, and which, in their final incidence, only results in increased internal costs that defeat us in the overseas markets where our surplus products must be sold' (*Employers' Review* 31/3/30).

In opposition to the ACMA's lobbying activities, the Chambers of Commerce established a Joint Committee for Tariff Revision whose purpose was to press for tariff reductions (Hagan 1971:60).

Manufacturers won the day. Scullin asked the ACMA to appoint a 'small committee to enable him to confer at short notice with manufacturers on tariffs and other policies relating to industrial rehabilitation' (Hall 1971:452). Revisions to the tariff schedule had by the end of 1931 effectively doubled the tariff levels of 1929. Devaluation against the British pound conferred further additional protection against British goods. In 1932 the Lyons Government signed the Ottawa Agreement, by which tariffs were to be set at levels that would enable British producers to compete. Despite ACMA qualms about this Agreement, and the fall in nominal tariff rates after 1932 because of continued devaluation, 'protective measures as a whole were very much higher after 1932 than before it, and Australian manufacturers, despite their protests, generally continued to enjoy very substantial protection against products of the United Kingdom and those of other countries' (Hagan 1981:64).

This major policy issue naturally divided employer organisations. Thus, despite the close affinity of the CMNSW and the EFNSW in relation to federal regulation, the latter told the CCEA Conference of 1932 that 'you cannot get the Chamber of Manufactures to come near us; . . . it would be impossible to bring together the Chamber of Commerce and the Chamber of Manufactures to discuss either free trade or protection and to allow it to continue in an Employers' Federation Council' (CCEA Conference 1932:56) The MTEA's boycotting of the Interstate Conference seems to have been triggered by the perceived domination of conferences by the CCEA and the Mines and Metals Association. Both were regarded as free trade organisations. Further, the ACMA objected strongly to the EFNSW's calls for federal industrial regulation on the grounds that the tariff was federal and uniform.

In view of the organisational differences, an *ad hoc* body to co-ordinate major test cases was as much as could be expected. In this context, the ICE's major role was to organise the finances necessary for major cases, to decide on general policy to be pursued during cases, to try to temper the activities of those groups seeking to oppose the general policy, and to select a sub-committee to prepare the case and, if used, to brief counsel. Broader policy issues, such as the question of federal regulation, were areas that the Interstate Conference had difficulty in handling and eventually resiled from.

Even in the limited area of industrial co-ordination the conference was not problem-free. Organisations refused to give *carte blanche* authority to the Executive Committee to formulate the appropriate strategy. Further, the situation evolved in which no association or company was required to support the conference general policy and any could be separately represented. Though L. C. Mann and C. H. Grant appeared for 'employers in general' at many of the post-1930 test cases, multiple representation of private and public sector employers was a feature of these cases. Some 22 advocates appeared on behalf of employer groups at the 1930 basic wage hearing; 24 at that of 1931 and 7 in 1932. At the 1933 hearing 24 employer advocates appeared and in the following year this number increased to 37. The 1937 and 1939 cases saw employer interests represented by 33 and 17 advocates respectively.[6] Under the auspices of the Interstate Conference, individual federations, particularly the EFNSW, were able to seek separate representation and to make submissions not in harmony with CCEA policy. A situation arose in which competing federations sought separate representation so as to counter each others' submissions. The Chambers of Manufactures from different states also appeared separately, and with competing views (e.g. VCM Meeting 18/5/37). Under such circumstances, the conference was forced to restrict its role to that of reactor, which necessarily reduced co-operative initiatives. Though in 1930 it met on five separate occasions and on a further six occasions between 1931 and 1933, by 1934 reduced industrial demands had brought the conference to a state of dormancy. It met on only four occasions after 1933 and the efforts of its Committee to form a permanent organisation met with little support.

Summary and conclusion

The early years of the 1930s were years in which the CCEA and other employer groups continued to show their antipathy towards arbitration. This situation changed, however, in the late 1930s as full employment became the order of the day and employers sought to use tribunals to retard union gains. Whereas in the depression period associations had sought wage reductions and the introduction of payments-by-results, in the latter half of the decade they were concerned with having members hold the line and not concede above-award rates.

Having come to support arbitration, in the case of the CCEA after three decades of active opposition, associations were divided on the question of federal uniform standards. This question resulted in the near demise of the CCEA and its effective disbandment during 1935–37. The same problem plagued the ACMA. It also militated against any expansion of the role of the Interstate Conference of Employers and the establishment of any permanent co-ordination machinery. Despite this, the frequency of basic wage cases, the importance of defeating Labor Government legislation, and developments on the hours front, resulted in a higher degree of industrial co-ordination than had ever been experienced in the past, albeit on an *ad hoc* and impermanent basis. With the restoration of economic well-being, however, deep divisions became manifest. The program for economic recovery, and the role to be played by tariffs in such a program, resulted in the two major organisations capable of bringing about employer solidarity, the CCEA and the ACMA, maintaining their historic antagonism towards each other.

Notes

1 Conflicts within the ACMA over the question of federal industrial regulation were sufficiently intense for the CMNSW to seek to disband the ACMA, for sections of this chamber to defy ACMA policy and seek federal awards, for chambers in different states to contest the extension of federal awards and for the CMNSW to alter ACMA policy enabling state affiliates to repudiate national policies they did not support. These conflicts are outlined by Hall (1971), pages 418–9, 427–8, 457–8, 492–3 and 533–6. See also VCM Meetings 20/4/37 and 19/7/38.

2 The Victorian legislation provided that 'Where under the Commonwealth Act the Commonwealth Court of Conciliation and Arbitration makes or has made an award with respect to

employers and employees in any industry, the Wages Board for every trade concerned as soon as may be shall, so far as the provisions of such award are provisions proper to be included in a determination of a Wages Board, incorporate such provisions, as varied from time to time, in any determination of that Wages Board, and thereupon the provisions so incorporated shall be deemed to apply as if they were included in a determination of a Wages Board made in accordance with the provisions of the Factories and Shops Act (*Employers' Review* 31/12/34).

[3] Brigadier Harrison was again elected President of the ACEF in 1948. He died in office in that year.

[4] The Executive Committee consisted of S. McKay (VCM) who was chairman, T. Maughan (AMMA/CCEA) who was Deputy Chairman, L. Mann (VEF) and C. H. Grant (VCM) who acted as industrial advocates in the basic wage cases, and A. S. Elford (CSOA), W. Letcher (VCM), S. L. Officer (GFCA), L. C. Meagher (AMMA) and W. R. Schwilk (EFNSW). Only the last named was not domiciled in Melbourne.

[5] The sub-committee consisted of W. Letcher (VCM), C. H. Grant (VCM), L. Mann (VEF), S. L. Officer (GFCA) and W. Tyack (AMMA).

[6] These figures have been derived from the appropriate *CARs*.

5

WAR AND GOVERNMENT EXECUTIVE ACTION 1940–1949

By the time Britain declared war on Germany in September 1939 developments in federal arbitration had created the need for employer cohesion. Such cohesion was not easy to arrive at and attempts, emanating largely from the CCEA, to create a permanent national peak council of employers were never seriously pursued by other employer groups. Instead, a loose *ad hoc* Interstate Conference of Employers had been established for the purpose of co-ordinating the increasing number of national 'test cases'. Also, by the end of the 1930s, the major national umbrella organisations — the CCEA, and the ACMA — had both experienced internal schisms over the issue of uniform federal regulation of wages and hours of work. The Chamber of Manufactures of New South Wales, and the federations in that state and in Victoria, actively sought federal regulation. The other chambers and federations continued to support state regulation.

Developments during the war and immediate post-war periods, which are examined in the first part of this chapter, generated added reasons for employer solidarity and cohesion. Wartime regulation created the need for unified political activities to ensure that employers' long-term prospects were not jeopardised. Of great importance in this context was the return to government of Labor in 1941, during a period in which it was not constrained by the limiting industrial powers of the Constitution. The longevity of the Curtin and Chifley Governments, Labor control of the Senate in 1943 (the first time since 1915), concern with the thrust of wartime controls, and apprehension concerning the socialistic 'New Order' to be imposed in the post-war period, all contributed to greater cohesion between employer bodies than had existed in previous periods. War was accompanied by a high degree of centralism and the imposition of uniform federal regulation. This wartime experience conditioned employers to accept such regulation in the post-war period.

The second part of the chapter focuses on the organisational responses to the economic and political developments. Because of the challenges confronting employers their organisations experienced an influx of members and resources. In the case of the CCEA, these new-found resources were directed at political lobbying by way of a Canberra Secretariat, at free enterprise propaganda by way of a Sydney-based Bureau of Public Relations, and at national industrial services by way of the VEF. This part also examines employer co-ordination and the CCEA's major preoccupation of the period — the establishment of a national employer council to coordinate industrial activities.

The New Order

'From 1939 on', writes Sawer, 'the defence power rapidly came to replace practically all other powers as the basis of government' (Sawer 1963:104–5). Legislation passed within a week of the declaration of war 'bound Australians as one, as with hoops of steel for the purpose of defence' (Hall 1971:569). The *National Security Act* 1939 provided for the procurement and manufacture of war equipment whether by purchase, manufacture in government-owned factories or private enterprise in 'annexes' built with government assistance. Following the collapse of France in 1940 and the entry of Japan into the war in 1941, amendments to this Act gave the Governor-General power to make regulations 'requiring persons to place themselves, their services and their property at the disposal of the Commonwealth as appears necessary and expedient'. The amendments effectively authorised full military and industrial conscription of persons and property. In time the Act came to regulate all aspects of economic activity.

The general system of regulation instituted in late 1939 was accepted with little debate or strong objection. Employers, though apprehensive about some of the measures introduced, recognised the need and adapted quickly to the changed circumstances. Thus, concerning price fixing, an area in which its own President had been fined under the Regulations, the EFNSW's *Annual Report* for 1940 noted:

> The adoption of price control by the Government was viewed with apprehension when introduced. The wide powers conferred upon the Prices Commissioner and the immunity given to him and his officers in any proceedings for a breach of the Regulations was the subject of joint action with the Sydney Chamber of Commerce.

> Experience has shown that the power conferred on the officials is being used fairly and with discretion. (*Employers' Review* 31/10/49:26)

Other wartime measures were also accepted as necessary, with any attendant difficulties capable of redress 'through representations' (ibid.).

Developments on the political front soon led to employers taking a less accommodative approach. In August 1941, R. Menzies resigned as Prime Minister and A. Fadden, leader of the United Country Party, formed a new ministry. Within 2 months, however, he was forced to resign and the Curtin Labor Government was sworn into office. Thereafter employers became increasingly apprehensive and came to consider themselves as being under siege from a hostile government. 'Under the National Security Act', the CMNSW reported, 'the government can take sufficient powers to almost socialise Australia and make us a totalitarian State' (CMNSW *Annual Report 1940*:3). Within a short time of Labor gaining power the same organisation claimed that the emergency powers were being used to introduce 'socialism by stealth and regulation' (Hall 1971:592). The strained relationships between employers and the Government, and the siege mentality of the former, are illustrated by the events surrounding the institution and operations of the Industrial Relations Council (IRC) and the Women's Employment Board.

In January 1942 the Government gazetted regulations establishing the IRC 'for the purpose of assisting the Government in its objective, that of achieving the continuous production at the highest possible level in all branches of industry throughout Australia, for the duration of the war' (*Manufacturers' Bulletin* 1/1/42:1). Employers considered the IRC an advisory body but soon discovered otherwise:

> At the initial meeting it became obvious that instead of the Council being purely advisory, it was proposed to invest it with executive powers comparable with those of Arbitration Courts, and that the decision of the Chairman was to prevail.
>
> The first matters discussed were such controversial subjects as Equal Pay for Males and Females and Preference to Unionists. As the result of discussion it became only too evident that on both these matters the Chairman's vote would be cast in their favour, and that a decision given on a casting vote would go to the Government as a joint recommendation from both sides of industry.
>
> The employers' representatives felt that they could only advise the Government on industrial problems on which they and the employees' representatives could reach agreement. As experience showed in the very early stages that this would not be so, the employers' representatives had no option but to sever their association with the Council. (*Employers' Review* 30/11/42:48).

F. T. Perry, ACMA President, telegraphed the Prime Minister asking for a suspension of the IRC until discussions had been held with himself, the Minister for Labour and the Minister for Production. The Prime Minister declined to intervene. Following a further IRC deadlock and unsuccessful attempts to have the appropriate Ministers intervene, employer representatives, 'rather than be used to record trade union decisions camouflaged as joint recommendations', resigned from the Council (*Employers' Review* 30/11/42:48; Hall 1971:639–41). The Minister abolished the IRC shortly afterwards.

These developments deepened employers' mistrust (*Manufacturers' Bulletin* 1/2/42:1). They claimed to have been 'misled from the start' and that the IRC had been converted into 'a mere instrument of left-wing industrial policy under the cloak of war emergency' (*SMH* 20/1/41). The Attorney-General's defence of the Government's actions, in which he claimed that the employer representatives' opinions were 'unsound', that their complaints were 'trivial and frivolous', that they 'had completely misunderstood the advisory character of the Council' and that their objections were an attack on 'an outstanding Australian jurist' (i.e. Webb J, the Chairman) did little to heal the rift (*SMH* 2/2/42).

Government–employer relations were further estranged by the creation of special tribunals to deal with employment conditions in a number of areas. Employers deplored these as tribunals of 'mere expediency' and freely quoted Justice Higgins' observation that a 'tribunal of reason cannot do its work side by side with executive tribunals of panic' (*Employers' Review* 31/5/46:33). They were particularly critical of, and incensed by, the bias displayed in the establishment of the Women's Employment Board (WEB). The WEB arose out of the Government's desire to attract female labour into the munition and armaments industries, as well as the need to assuage union anxiety that, unless given greater wage parity, females might permanently displace men from these industries. The WEB was ostensibly set up to regulate the employment of females in occupations in which they had not previously been employed. When gazetted, however, the Regulations were less permissive than expected by employers and made it mandatory for the WEB to determine wage rates of between 60 per cent and 100 per cent of the appropriate male rate. Female award rates at that time were about 54 per cent of the male rate (VCM *Annual Report* 1944:8). Worried by the potential problems of anomalies and flow-ons resulting from the new tribunal, employers strenuously opposed its establishment. They claimed 'that, not only is the Arbitration Court quite capable of handling this question, but is the proper authority to do so and that any separate tribunal would be subversive to the principle upon which the Commonwealth Arbitration System is founded' (VCM *Annual Report* 1942:9).

Regulations empowering the Minister for Labour and National Service to institute the WEB were issued in March 1942. The Board was to consist of a permanent Chairman and one permanent representative each of employers and employees. The Minister requested the ACMA to nominate an employers' representative and a similar request was made to the Canberra Secretariat, which acted as a joint secretariat for the CCEA, the Associated Chamber of Commerce and three other employer bodies. The ACMA refused to make a nomination and instead wrote to the Prime Minister condemning the new tribunal (VCM 1942:9). The Canberra Secretariat nominated Mr. H. J. Johnstone, Secretary of the Boot and Shoe Manufacturers' Association of New South Wales, but also wrote to the Prime Minister supporting the ACMA's condemnation (VEF Meeting 14/4/42). The Minister responded by appointing his own nominee, Miss Ellen Imelda Cashman, as the Special Employers' Representative. Miss Cashman was employed in the Attorney General's Department and had previously been the Secretary of the Women's Section of the Printing Industry Employees' Union for many years. Needless to say, she was not an acceptable representative to employers (*Employers' Review* 30/11/42:49).

Until the WEB functions were reabsorbed by the Arbitration Court in 1944 employers continued to oppose and obstruct it, and to make representations to governments. They greeted the Government's announcement of the dissolution of the WEB in October 1944 as a vindication of the correctness of their position (VCM Annual Report 1945:7). Their expectations of untrammelled Court regulation of female rates quickly evaporated, however, as the Government chose to overturn the Court's judgement in relation to the Minimum Rates for Females by executive action. By way of amendments to the National Security (Female Minimum Rates) Regulations the Government provided for rates of 'not less than 75 per cent of the corresponding [male] minimum rate'. Employers were highly critical of this 'arbitrary interference' by the Government. If the actions of special tribunals were seen as threatening to industrial peace, interference by government executive action was seen in a more sinister light:

> It is evident that the mass of regulations and Orders, enacted by the Commonwealth Government on the plea that they are necessary for the successful prosecution of the war, are directed more and more at the gradual, but complete elimination of free enterprise . . . The time has assuredly arrived when employers must ask themselves whether all the restrictions imposed on them are really necessary for the successful prosecution of the war and affirm

as their policy that encroachment upon the liberties, rights and freedom of enterprise can only be justified by the exigencies of war. (*Employers' Review* 31/12/43:1)

According to employers, a 'New Social Order' was being implemented under the guise of wartime controls.

The notion that the war would help to establish some sort of New Order was not a particularly Labor one. Indeed Menzies himself made play of such a notion in a radio broadcast explaining the Parliamentary Committees established in 1941 to help in the prosecution of the war effort. 'I am not', he said, 'looking for a restoration of old privileges and old possessions. There must be no looking back to what was, in many ways, an unjust society . . . we must all look forward. We must be prepared to put our privileges into the melting-pot and strive only for common rights and equal opportunities' *SMH* 19/6/41). In an address to employer associations shortly afterwards Menzies added: 'A great deal is being said today about the New Order which is to come out of the war. People talk about it, dream about, it, and converse philosophically about it. I do not believe in nicely docketed ideas. I believe the New Order is being built now' (*SMH* 20/8/41).

Though the United Australia Party (and after 1945 the Liberal Party) notion of the 'New Order' does not seem to have been made explicit, that of other groups was. These ranged from the Catholic Church's *Pattern for Peace* (NSCA 1948), to the Communist blueprint outlined in L. L. Sharkey's *The Communist Theory and Practice of Trade Unionism* (1942). On behalf of employers CCEA President O. D. A. Oberg formulated a *Declaration of Policy*, which was adopted at a Special CCEA Meeting in May 1945 (Appendix 2). The 10-part Declaration attempted to counter Labor's regulatory full employment policy by declaring that full employment could best be achieved 'by encouraging the initiative of the individual', which implied 'freedom for employers in the investment of funds, management's inherent right to run its business and the placing and disposal of resources, and for employees in choosing their careers and living their own way of life'. The Declaration supported private ownership of enterprise, the right to profits, and the responsibility of employers to provide 'reasonable and adequate remuneration' and of employees to provide 'efficient service'. It called for a voluntary system of unionism, and 'the appointment of Staff Relations Officers and Committees to encourage such matters as discussion groups, merit-reward systems for suggestions and skill, and general facilities for the improvement of employer–employee relations including sports clubs and recreation areas'. It supported the establishment of subsidised superannuation schemes, sickness, accident and general welfare funds. The principle of industrial conciliation and arbitration was supported as the 'only satisfactory method for determining the just rights of employers and employees'. It deprecated 'all acts of lawlessness in the shape of strikes and lockouts'. The Declaration supported community education designed to 'resist any false ideology'. It also endorsed the principle of contributory National Social Security and, as a 'necessary prerequisite, urged the immediate acceleration of all matters affecting the rehabilitation of ex-servicemen and women' (ACEF Special Conference 1/5/45).

Labor's New Order entailed a continuation of many of the controls that employers considered to be of a wartime nature. 'The Prime Minister and Treasurer', in the view of the CMNSW's Secretary, were but 'the apostles of the Welfare State as a compact, unified and planned economic national policy' (Hall 1971:658). Employers interpreted many of the wartime regulations as little more than a process of conditioning the community into accepting centralised control in the post-war period. In an attempt to obtain greater powers the Government convened a Constitutional Convention in 1944. 'It was hoped', writes Hall, 'that a convention would achieve the agreement of the States to refer the powers sought, and thus avoid holding a referendum' (ibid.). When this Convention did not produce the desired results a 14-point referendum was submitted to voters in August 1944. Two other referenda followed in September 1946 and May 1948. For all its efforts the Government was only successful in gaining control over social services and pensions.

Employers considered that other government activities and policies were attempts to gain those controls sought and rejected in these referenda. Thus, the ACMA President commented on the White Paper on Full Employment: 'The White Paper is disappointing because its policies could contribute to full employment only under complete regulation. The gradual removal of emergency war time controls is promised but in their place new and permanent controls are proposed' (Hall 1971:716). The *Sydney Morning Herald* supported this view. 'The White Paper', it claimed, 'is a great deal more than a design for averting unemployment. It is Labor's manifesto for an entire post-war economic policy, the essence whereof would be highly centralised government control of production and spending by the States and local authorities, private firms and individuals' (*SMH* 9/6/45).

Employers' fears about the socialising objectives of Labor were compounded by the activities of Communist union leaders. By 1945 the Communist Party of Australia had reached the zenith of its influence over unions and controlled between one-quarter and one-half of all unions.

Communists also controlled unions in key sectors of the economy such as engineering; rail, maritime and road transport; and the stevedoring, electricity generating, coal mining, metal trades, iron and steel, building, textiles and clothing industries (Murray 1970, Rawson 1967).

Until Russia joined the war Communists disrupted the war effort. Following Russia's entry into the war they adopted the 'united front' policy of co-operating Labor. With the end of hostilities, however, there was a further resurgence of Communist-led strikes, including the coal miners' strike of 1948.[1] In his Presidential address to the VCM in May 1947, Captain L. Robinson summed up the employers' mood:

> This Chamber has always been a non-political body, and still is, so far as legitimate politics are concerned. We have always, and will always, abide by the dictates of the national appointed Government . . . but this present danger, although found within Government, and with suckers invading practically every other phase of our industrial and civil life, is no more a true part of our national politics than is cancer a true part of the human body; and, as a cancer must be cut from our national life – and just as ruthlessly if Australia is to survive . . . We have come to the very edge of revolution. (VCM President's Address 1947)

Though Robinson and other employer representatives scarcely distinguished between the Labor Government and Communists, the Labor Party did set out to regain control over Communist-dominated unions. This it did by establishing the Industrial Groups in 1945 with a charter of removing Communist leadership from unions. Aided by amendments to the *Conciliation and Arbitration Act* in relation to union elections and the activities of the Catholic National Rural Movement (later renamed the National Civic Council), the Industrial Groups had a high degree of success in removing the Communist leadership in a number of unions (Murray 1970:3–44). The activity of these Industrial Groups, however, did little to allay employers' fears. Menzies capitalised on the 'Red menace' in winning the 1949 elections.

The Arbitration Court and executive action

Under the emergency conditions the Commonwealth Conciliation and Arbitration Court was called on to play a wider role than had come to be expected of it. The National Security (Industrial Peace) Regulations conferred additional powers on the Court for the duration of hostilities. It was empowered to declare a common rule for any industry or calling; its jurisdiction was not limited to the ambit of the matter in dispute; it was empowered to settle intrastate disputes and non-'industrial' disputes; and the Court's orders could not be challenged because it had not engaged in 'conciliation' and 'arbitration'. In short, these Regulations sought to remove those limitations on the Court that High Court challenges had demonstrated to exist. This resulted, among other things, in the dominance of the Court over state tribunals even in relation to state awards, and thus the removal of many of the difficulties arising out of the dual tribunal system. The Regulations also increased the Court's scope by the appointment of additional Conciliation Commissioners and the creation of Conciliation Officers. The latter had the powers of Conciliation Commissioners but were appointed to deal with specific issues.

As detailed in the previous chapter, by 1939 the federations in the two major industrial states, as well as the CMNSW, were committed to the Arbitration Court determining standard hours of work as well as the basic wage. Thus the usurping of state tribunal functions by the Court caused no great concern to these bodies. Other organisations saw this as a wartime necessity. Complications soon arose, however, not as in previous years because of federal–state tribunal incompatibilities, but from a new source of dualism. This resulted from executive action of the Government, which, in many instances, over-rode determinations of the Court and created wage comparability problems. To this form of dualism was added that resulting from the operation of special industry tribunals and the WEB.

As part of the efforts to mobilise the war industries, governments, by executive action, fixed employment standards and wages. These standards were superior to those in other industries. This necessarily conflicted with the Court's approach, based on the criteria of uniformity and comparability. Margins were fixed by the Minister for tradesmen in the munitions industry, which quickly led to metal unions applying for flow-ons. The subsequent freezing of wages compounded comparability problems. 'The entry of the Executive into the field of industrial relations', Foenander wrote, 'was creating in a new form the very evil from which the country was, in such great measure, contriving to escape' (1943:9). A major problem associated with executive action, this author noted, was the uncertainty surrounding it (ibid.).

Employers were quick to condemn this government interference and to register support for the Court, an institution they had derided for three decades. Under the caption 'Arbitration — Not Regulation' the *Employers' Review* voiced employers' concerns:

> Government by Regulation has been accepted as an inevitable method of control in time of war of matters which it has not been found necessary to regulate in normal times. Recently there has been a tendency to extend this method of control to the field of industrial arbitration. . . . There is no cause

> for interference with the Courts by regulation. On the contrary, such actions must only result in impairing their efficiency and destroying the confidence in which they are held and which they richly deserve. (*Employers' Review* 31/10/40:1)

Executive action increasingly came to restrict the Court's competence in many areas. Award conditions regulating employers' powers of dismissal were over-ridden, as were apprenticeship requirements. Maximum hours of work were fixed (56 hours for male adults) and wages pegged at their February 1942 levels. These and other Regulations that the government considered necessary to the most effective use of manpower for war purposes were poorly received by both unions and employers. The latter's usual support for wage restrictions was absent as the Regulations prevented them from competing for scarce labour. Restrictions on overtime further hampered their ability to capitalise fully on demand conditions. A major cause of complaint was that the Government itself was not prepared to accept its own standards.

With the end of hostilities, and Labor's failure to gain added Commonwealth industrial powers, government determination of employment standards came to an end. With the ending of emergency powers, however, Labor set about one of its major industrial reforms —that of the Arbitration Court.

During the period of war no amendments were made to the *Conciliation and Arbitration Act*, governments at that time having more direct powers of regulating employment relations. From 1944 on, unions pressed for amendments to the Act. These amendments sought to 'streamline' the system by removing legal technicalities, making the system more flexible, reducing the role of arbitration and making arbitral proceedings less lengthy. Employers reacted from a deep-seated suspicion of Labor's 'New Order' designs rather than on the merits of the changes proposed. They themselves had criticised the federal tribunal system during the war. In July 1940, for example, the *Employers' Review* (31/7/40:1) claimed that under the Act 'Conciliation was starved and arbitration fed until it grew out of its industrial disputes clothes and came to dominate all industry . . . It has sapped Australian industry of its rugged strength to make its own agreements, and has encouraged the attitude of agreeing to nothing and "passing the buck" on to the Court to make the decision'. Even as late as September 1943 the same organ claimed conciliation was 'very much in the background' and that the 'technicalities and difficulties inherent in arbitration are such that only union officials have any hope of mastering them' (30/9/43:1).

Many of Labor's proposals aimed at removing some of the weaknesses that employers themselves claimed to exist. Employers had little confidence in Labor's ability to implement needed changes in a fair manner. Thus, they strongly advocated no amendments to the existing Act other than to strengthen the Court's powers to enforce its awards and orders. The *Review* claimed that though 'the system may not be perfect, and frequently either side or the other may be disappointed with the result. The fact remains that it has worked' (*Employers' Review* 31/7/40:1).

The Act was amended in October 1947, providing for the appointment of 16 Conciliation Commissioners and restricting the functions of members of the Court to judicial matters such as interpretation of awards and appeals from the decisions of the Registrar in relation to organisations. The judges' industrial role was limited to Full Bench matters. The 1947 Annual Report of the EFNSW noted that 11 new Conciliation Commissioners had been appointed and 'with one exception, were all Union Officials or known adherents of the Labour [sic] Party' (*Employers' Review* 31/10/47:21). The Commissioners who had been appointed under the old Act were retained in that position. As well as concern over the appointments, employers were concerned at the potential pace-setting role of Commissioners acting independently of each other. With the election of the Menzies Government in December 1949 employers sought the 'general strengthening and restoration of the powers and functions of the Judges of the Court' (*ACMA Canberra Newsletter* 16/12/50). Amendments to the Act in 1952 did not remove award matters from Commissioners. They did, however, provide for a limited appeals mechanism from decisions of Commissioners to Full Benches composed of judges.

Test cases

Three Basic Wage cases were conducted during the period, namely those of 1940, 1946, and 1949–50. A major Standard Hours case was held in 1946–47. During the period the Metal Trades Margins cases increasingly came to take on the characteristics of national test cases, which required a co-ordinated employer response.

There was only one Basic Wage case during the war. In August 1940 the Full Court began hearing a combined union application for an increase in the basic wage as well as the indexing of the 'Prosperity' loading awarded in 1937. In a judgement delivered in February 1941, the Bench refused to grant any increase on the grounds of 'the uncertainty of the economic outlook' (44 *CAR* 41). The Bench decided, however, that the application should be stood over rather than dismissed. Because of this decision, several applications were made by unions for a reopening of the case and the ACMA and the CCEA were ever alert to this possibility. It was not until 1946 that the case was reopened as the result of an application by the Attorney-General during the Standard Hours case. In order not to delay unnecessarily what was already a marathon Hours case, in December 1946 the Bench decided to award an 'interim' increase of 70 cents per week (57 *CAR* 698). This case was eventually finalised in the Inquiry of 1949–50 when the basic wage was increased by a further $2.00 per week (68 *CAR* 842).

Hours of work

The actions of federal and state Labor Governments on the hours front added to the beleaguered mentality of employers. Towards the end of 1942 National Security Regulations were introduced governing the hours of work for manual workers. These set ceilings of 56, 52 and 48 hours per week for males, females and juniors respectively. Though employers were not in agreement with these regulations, they could see that they were motivated by non-sectional interests. Activities by state governments, particularly those of New South Wales and Queensland, that increased labour costs by reducing standard hours of work or by increasing paid annual leave were construed in a different light.

In December 1944 the New South Wales Parliament amended the *Annual Holidays Act*, which, at that time, provided for 1 week's paid annual leave. The major amendment, to become operative from 1 January 1945, provided for an additional week of paid annual leave for state award employees. This generated a movement for increased paid leave in other jurisdictions and in February 1947 the Metal Trades Award was varied to provide for 2 weeks' annual leave. Other federal awards quickly adopted this standard.

State legislation also influenced the reduction of standard hours of work. In 1942 building trades unions had sought the introduction of a 40-hour week in the industry. In a brief hearing the Arbitration Court stated that 'the matter was not exclusive to the Building trades, and a proper examination of the reasons in support would involve a complete review of hours of work in industry generally'. The Court did not consider that the period of national emergency was one in which such a review ought to be conducted (VCM *Annual Report 1942*:12). In 1946 printing unions sought an award variation providing for a 40-hour working week, which resulted in this claim being converted into a Standard Hours case and in Government support for the adoption of the 40-hour standard during the case. The case was to prove a long and expensive one for both employer organisations and the ACTU. The former expended over $71 000 and the ACTU an estimated $30 000 (ACEF *Annual Report 1947*:2). The case opened in November 1945 and concluded 22 months later. It required some 158 sitting days by the Full Court and nearly 9000 pages of transcript. Evidence was heard from 225 witnesses and almost 500 exhibits were tabled (59 *CAR* 586). In the final analysis, however, the Arbitration Court was presented with a *fait accompli* by legislation in New South Wales providing for a 40-hour week from July 1 1947 and a Bill to provide for the 40-hour week in Queensland. In its judgement the Bench noted:

> There is no doubt of the constitutional authority of the States to make industrial laws and to pass Standard Hours Acts . . . New South Wales did exercise that authority . . . [and] the Queensland Government proposes to pass a similar Act during the year. It would, in the constitutional circumstances, be wrong for this Court to criticise the exercise by a sovereign State of its powers, and we do not do so. But it is of course very obvious that the New South Wales Act did alter very material economic and political factors and did, during the hearing of the case, present this Court with a *fait accompli* in relation to a substantial section of its industry, and to that extent did affect the freedom with which the Court might have acted. We have, as is proper, weighed these facts and they form part of the bases of our judgement. (59 *CAR* 589)

During 1946 and 1947 metal unions and employers became embroiled in a massive conflict over wage rates notwithstanding the existence of the wage-pegging regulations. A strike-cum-lockout situation developed of sufficient proportions for the Industrial Registrar to seek the deregistration of the VCM and four unions (VCM Annual Report 1947:1–3). The relaxation of the wage-pegging regulations to help bring about a solution to the dispute enabled Commissioner Mooney to attempt a solution. He handed down his decision in March 1947. This increased the margins of tradesmen from $3.60 to $4.50 per week, an increase of 25 per cent (58 *CAR* 553). However, the awarding of even higher proportionate increases in the margins of less skilled employees (56 per cent in the case of tradesmen's assistants), led to a continuation of strike action by tradesmen who were seeking a restoration of lost relativities. The matter was then handled by the Full Court, which increased the margins of tradesmen by a further 70 cents per week and those of tradesmen's assistants by a further 33 cents per week (58 *CAR* 1093). The effect of this judgement was to approximate previous relativities, the fitters' rate having increased from $3.60 to $5.20 (100 per cent) per week as the result of the combined judgements, and the assistants' rate having increased from 90 cents to

$1.76 (94 per cent). Non-tradesmen now pressed for a restoration of the earlier relativities established by Mooney. In the meantime the Act had been amended to place Commissioners in charge of industries and the dispute reverted back to Mooney. The final settlement, in which the margins of tradesmen were not increased while those of tradesmen's assistants were increased by 55 cents, was arrived at by agreement between the parties. Though the tradesmen's relativities had again been upset, both tradesmen and non-tradesmen had done well:

> It gave the Fitter the highest relativity to the basic wage he had ever received of 48.6%, as compared with the previous highest of 42.8% of the Harvester Judgement, and gave the non-tradesmen the most favourable marginal relativity to the Fitter that they had ever achieved. (Hutson 1971:156)

Despite the Bench's earlier ruling that the decision in the metal case 'was in settlement of a specific industrial dispute and was of little value as a precedent' (58 *CAR* 1092), within a short time the Court was forced to concede that 'by consent and by adjudication, the Metal Trades marginal increases are beginning to percolate into other industries' (59 *CAR* 959). The next metal margins case, that of 1952, was conducted 'in the nature of an economic inquiry in miniature' (73 *CAR* 340).

ASSOCIATION GROWTH AND COHESION

The ACEF

Wartime regulations and the defensive measures necessitated by Labor Government activities proved a fertile ground for the growth and development of employer organisations. The VEF, which until the beginning of the War had perennial financial difficulties, experienced an influx of new members and resources. The number of affiliated associations increased from 37 to 57 between 1940 and 1944. Other federations experienced a similar growth. The EFNSW accepted over 70 new members in the first half of 1944, a situation that contrasted with earlier periods, when the number of resignations often exceeded new applications. This federation added a third industrial officer to its staff at this time.

The Central Council's lot prospered with these developments. In May 1942 it decided on a name change since the existing 'designation of the Central Council did not properly describe the affiliations of the Employers' Federations in each state'. The new name chosen was that of the Australian Council of Employers' Federations (ACEF) (CCEA Meeting 13/5/42). The ACEF's new-found resources were directed at immediate needs. During the war period and its accompanying 'Government by Regulation', representation in Canberra and the ability to lobby governments were accorded high priority. As Labor sought constitutional changes and a 'New Order', resources were devoted to publicity and propaganda. With the lifting of wartime regulations and the resurgence of industrial tribunal activity, the need to provide a nation-wide industrial service competed for resources with the political and public relations functions.

In 1941 the CCEA, the Associated Chambers of Commerce of Australia (ACCA), the Graziers' Federal Council, the Australian Council of Retailers and the Fire and Accident Underwriters' Association formed a Joint Secretariat, located in Canberra. The ACMA and the MTEA entered into a similar arrangement at about the same time. Mr P. R. Wilkins, the Secretary of the New South Wales Master Printers' and Allied Trades Association, was appointed Secretary. He was also appointed ACEF Secretary. The cost of maintaining the Secretariat was estimated at $6000 per year, of which the ACEF was expected to contribute a quarter (ACEF Meeting 2/7/41).

Under Wilkins, the Secretariat soon showed its value and gave the ACEF a high national profile. 'The standing which Mr Wilkins enjoys, from the Prime Minister right down to officers in Departments', claimed the ACEF President in 1947, 'has made possible the most effective presentation of matters concerning Employers' interests' (ACEF President's Report, p.8). Within a few weeks of its establishment the VEF anticipated that 'speedier information would be obtained on matters of current interest as had already been evidenced by the communications already received' (VEF Meeting 21/10/41). The QEF sought clarification concerning the application of the regulations applying to reinstatement in civilian employment and Wilkins was asked to 'consult with the appropriate authorities with a view to clarifying the rules and to advise the Federations' (ACEF Meeting 12/1/42). In 1941 Wilkins was asked to liaise on behalf of the SAEF regarding the 'acute shortage of charcoal in South Australia, suggesting that Italian war prisoners and/or refugees be employed in the cutting of timber and burning and grading of it' (ACEF Meeting 13/10/41).

The *Annual Report* of the EFNSW for 1943 indicated the scope of the Secretariat's work. Wilkins had been asked to address the annual meeting and the Report noted:

> In so doing he reviewed the principal matters dealt with since the inception of the secretariat. He referred to the expansion of interests which the secretariat represented. During the past year the major political and economic matters affecting employers had been of especial concern. Four per cent profit limitation; taxation of companies; ARP expenditure; Price Regulation Con-

> ferences with Treasury officials in respect to the scale of tax instalment deductions and drawing Government cheques; industrial legislation; post war reconstruction problems and contacts with Government leaders and officials on current matters had constituted some of the day to day work of the secretariat. (*Employers' Review* 20/10/43:5)

Despite the benefits to members of the Joint Secretariat's Canberra representation, relations between the ACCA and the ACEF became strained after 1945 over the question of control and finances. The ACCA, which provided the major financial contribution, had control over the Secretariat and resisted ACEF moves for a Joint Management Committee of control. The ACEF increasingly came to consider that its needs were subordinated to those of the ACCA and that its own identity was at risk. In 1947, at a time when 'Government by Regulation' was winding down and when the ACEF was becoming embroiled in expensive and drawn-out national test cases, the ACCA attempts to double the ACEF's contribution to the Secretariat caused most federations to favour disaffiliation. Despite the strong pleas by ACEF President O. D. A. Oberg, and the mediating role of Sir Robert Knox (a long-time member of the Executive Committee of both the ACEF and the ACCA), relations between the two organisations deteriorated. In October 1948 the ACEF gave notice of its intention to cease contributing to the Secretariat as from March 31 1949 (ACEF Meeting 6/7/48). In April 1949 it appointed Mr K. M. F. Powell as its first full-time Secretary.

In addition to establishing the Joint Secretariat, the ACEF had also become involved with the propaganda and public relations activities of the Sydney-based Bureau of Public Relations.[2] This body was the brainchild of the EFNSW, which was concerned 'to counteract what it perceived as the one-sided propaganda for "reform" and with the fact that the case for the suppression of free enterprise had been more actively presented than that for its retention' (*Employers' Review* 31/10/44:22). Membership of the Bureau came to include the members of the Joint Secretariat as well as a number of other organisations. In addition it received financial support from the Institute of Public Affairs. At its zenith, the Bureau consisted of 'two young University graduates trained in research and a secretary' (ACEF *Annual Report 1948*:3). In 1948 its Director, Mr S. Howard, summarised the Bureau's functions as:

> 1 To present through all possible channels in Metropolitan, Country and Suburban press and Radio News Sessions, a positive case for free enterprise.
> 2 To combat communism and socialist propaganda being circulated in Australia.

3 To present through the avenues available factual material of particular importance to subscribing members.
4 To conduct research and report on important trends in economic and social affairs, taxation and industrial matters.

By 1948 the ACEF was expending $4000 per year on the Bureau. In October of that year, however, the question of control, which had plagued the Secretariat, also affected the Bureau. It was intimated that Howard was 'preparing to place the Research Service on the basis of a private venture'. The meeting discussed the possibility of a 'situation arising where the Research Service might produce a survey which would be inimical to the employers' interests'. As if to confirm this fear the results of a survey commissioned by the ACEF in relation to the Basic Wage Inquiry arrived during the meeting. On examining the Survey, Acting Secretary Gibson claimed that 'as a survey it was a most excellent production, but as a document for publication on the eve of an important review of the basic wage structure . . . it represented "complete dynamite" from the employers' point of view'. Gibson feared that the survey, if published, would prove 'very prejudicial to the employers' case'. A telegram was dispatched claiming it was 'imperative every single copy of the report be recalled and impounded' and that the same could do 'irreparable damage'. The Executive decided to withdraw from the Research Service from October 1 1948 (ACEF Meeting 20/10/48).

As wartime regulations gradually wound down and industrial tribunal activities picked up, the federations and the ACEF were forced back into their traditional role and *raison d'etre*. The ending of emergency powers, the inability of Labor to extend the Commonwealth's industrial power, and the election of the Liberal–Country Party Coalition in 1949, all reduced the urgency of political liaison and public relations.

By 1947 Labor had directed its reforming zeal to the Arbitration Court, an area of concern to the ACEF but only marginal interest to the ACCA. Restrictions of wage-pegging regulations in that year and the Basic Wage and Standard Hours cases of 1946 and 1946–47 meant that the ACEF's industrial activities were again directed primarily at tribunal rather than governmental operations. Similar activities at the state level also meant that the federations' industrial activities came to demand added resources. From 1947 on, they sought the provision of an industrial service by the ACEF. This was a major testament to either the degree to which wartime regulation had acted as a catalyst to the centralisation trends identified in earlier chapters, or to the way in which it had helped break down the parochialism of state federations. The role of the Arbitration Court in setting national standards for the basic wage and hours of work, a role that had resulted in the near demise of the CCEA in earlier periods, was now accepted by all federations as either desirable or unavoidable. In such circumstances it was easier for federations to provide those resources needed to establish the appropriate mechanisms for handling test cases rather than relying on the *ad hoc* approach previously adopted. Further, as federations came to accept rather than fight their greater involvement in tribunal proceedings, the need for some national industrial service for 'routine', in addition to 'test case', matters was also found desirable. The process of building up such an industrial service began in 1948 when the VEF was contracted to provide a national industrial service for the federations on the ACEF's behalf. This supposedly temporary measure continued until Mr Polites became the ACEF's Executive Director 11 years later.

Employer cohesion

Industrial, legislative and political developments during the period necessitated continued employer co-ordination and co-operation. Indeed, the degree of interaction was sufficiently great for the ACEF to propose the establishment of a Confederation of Employers in 1943, and to pursue this proposal for much of the period. The ACEF's falling out with the ACCA over the Secretariat did not help in such a venture and the ACMA's support was imperative. Though the ACMA co-operated with the ACEF on many joint ventures, it was reluctant to surrender its independence and was not convinced of the need for a confederation.

The Basic Wage Inquiry of 1940 brought about employer co-operation early in the period. In March, delegates from 30 organisations and companies attended the Interstate Conference of Employers chaired by ACEF President E. F. Harrison. The Conference had been instituted in 1930 and had operated on an *ad hoc* basis since that time. The Conference resolved, *inter alia*, that 'an economist of repute' give evidence on behalf of employers. It also resolved that organisations that had already separately briefed counsel ought to collaborate 'for the purpose of avoiding divided councils and presenting a strong united case as a whole to the Court' (CCEA Meeting 19/3/40). The Conference also agreed to the formation of a Consultative and Co-ordinating Committee to manage the case. This *ad hoc* committee consisted of representatives of the Chambers of Manufactures and the Employers' Federations of Victoria, New South Wales and South Australia, together with nominees from the MTEA, the Graziers' Association of

Victoria and the Mines and Metals Association. Its role was taken over by the Basic Wage Steering Committee in 1947.

The Inquiry was still under way when, in June 1940, the Prime Minister's proposed tripartite conference brought the major employer groups together to formulate a united strategy (CCEA Meeting 19/11/40). By the end of 1940 wartime regulations had begun to affect Association activities and federations pressed on ACEF the need for 'closer collaboration between employer associations'. It was decided that the secretary, 'in notifying the other associations of the action taken in regard to industrial arbitration generally, should take the opportunity for urging closer organisation between the various bodies, particularly in war time, and to invite their views on the suggestion that it was desirable to arrange, if possible, for an employers' conference at an early date to discuss the subject' (ibid.).

ACEF co-operation in the establishment of the Canberra Secretariat in 1941 was viewed as part of a venture in the 'closer collaboration between employers' (ACEF Meeting 30/6/41). From October of that year, Labor Governments spurred on efforts at closer co-operation between a wider range of organisations. In May 1942 the ACEF's Executive resolved to initiate action to bring about 'the more complete organisation of employer cohesion'. Affiliates were asked to assist in this at the state level (ACEF Meeting 6/5/42). Activities towards this end were reviewed in October. Several meetings had been held 'between the central employers' organisations and possible means of securing unity had been explored'. A committee had been set up to draft proposals that were to be available for consideration at an early date. In New South Wales several organisations had examined ways of achieving unity, and in South Australia 'official action had been taken to integrate the SAEF and the SACM. Both bodies were working towards better relations and there was reasonable hope of achievement'. In Western Australia there existed 'excellent relationships between the central organisations and a clear demarcation of function of each'. In Victoria a joint committee had been established by the VCM, VEF and Melbourne Chambers of Commerce (MCC) to co-ordinate action against the proposed referendum to increase Commonwealth industrial powers (ACEF Meeting 12/10/42).

At the ACEF Executive meeting of March 1943, Sir Robert Knox congratulated 'the special committees and others who had worked in the various States to secure amendments to the measures for the transference of powers to the Commonwealth'. He added that as a result of the 'principal organisations in Victoria being brought together by this matter, a much better understanding had been developed, and a great deal of work . . .

done'. He considered that 'a stage had been reached where a wider Council of all employers' interests should be established. A confederation of employers appeared to be essential . . . and he would like to see steps taken to bring the central bodies together upon a permanent footing as soon as possible' (ACEF Meeting 3/2/41). O. D. A. Oberg (EFNSW) seconded a motion by Knox to this effect and the Chairman (Harrison) 'was requested to confer with the Federal Presidents of other appropriate Commonwealth organisations of Employers with the object of consolidating employers' interests through a confederation of employers'.

In April 1943 Brigadier Harrison reported on his meetings with his ACCA and ACMA counterparts. He was not particularly optimistic of a satisfactory outcome and 'in view of the difficulty at that stage of dealing with the question on an Australia-wide basis' had conferred with representatives of the VCM, MCC and VEF as to the 'possibility of unanimity in Victoria' (ACEF Meeting 30/4/43).

Activities again shifted to the national level in June 1943 when a conference of the ACMA, ACCA and ACEF was held to discuss 'nationalisation and socialism' (VEF Meeting 10/8/43). Harrison proposed the need for 'more effective liaison between all employers' organisations with the particular object of replying to labour propaganda on industrial matters'. Oberg supported this and claimed that 'there should be some counterpart to the ACTU for countering the activities of the labour organisations'. After lengthy discussion it was 'agreed to approve the suggestion in principle but to propose that before any further action were taken a conference of all Federal organisations should be convened to consider the proposals' (ACCA–ACMA–ACEF Conference 12/6/43). The referring of such proposals to a wider audience was one method by which any confederation moves came to be aborted. The other was to refer proposals back to state affiliates for discussion with their counterparts.

Nothing came of these initiatives. In his Presidential address of October 1943 Brigadier Harrison noted that the year 'was one in which ACEF watched with anxiety the attempt, first, by Trade Unions, and, subsequently by Labor Governments to filch more and more from the Employers'. He further noted that the 'fault lies, in part, with the Employers themselves, for what body can speak for *all* the Employers? Which voice can be raised as sole spokesman for all non-socialistic organisations? Which voice can speak unanimously for free enterprise as the ACTU speaks for Socialism?' (ACEF Meeting 20/10/43).

In March 1944 President Oberg reported on his discussions with the Presidents of the ACMA and the ACCA and the VCM, all of whom favoured his proposal in principle. He had submitted 'seven principles as the basis for closer collaboration between the principal employers' organisations'. Most of these were, consciously or otherwise, restatements of the original objectives of the newly founded CCEA in 1904, though the new support for arbitration contrasted with the 1904 position. The principles were:

1. To protect, improve and further the interests of employers collectively in Australia.
2. To affirm the principle of private enterprise as opposed to socialisation.
3. To develop understanding and recognition of the value of leadership in industry and its importance in post-war reconstruction.
4. To encourage unity of action among employers.
5. To encourage a better understanding between employers and employees.
6. To consider, originate, promote, support or oppose legislation or amendments affecting the interests of employers.
7. To maintain industrial arbitration and oppose political interference with Arbitration Courts.

Captain Derham, President of the ACMA, had undertaken to submit the principles to the next meeting of that body's Council. Concerned at the ACMA's apparent lack of interest, Sir Robert Knox argued that there 'should be established without delay a "Federation of Australian Industries", and even if all the main interests were not disposed to co-operate, then we should proceed to weld together those employers' organisations who were prepared to come together'. This move was not generally supported at the time (ACEF Meeting 16/3/44).

Perhaps because of the futility of attempting to form a national organisation that omitted the most dominant potential member, the ACEF did not push ahead with its 'closer linking' plans. It moved away from the confederation concept and in its place suggested the establishment of an Employers' Consultative Committee. The ACMA expressed initial interest in such a Committee and the Annual Meeting of its Council endorsed 'the proposals that a greater degree of co-ordination should exist among employing interests'. It sought a meeting with the ACEF to that end (VEF Meeting 23/1/45). Again, however, nothing came of these proposals. In February 1946 Oberg outlined 'in detail discussion with successive Presidents of the ACMA all aimed at achieving co-ordination of employers' interests'. As a result an Advisory Committee had been set up but 'had not served any purpose' and his considered opinion was that 'any further efforts to achieve real unity were doomed to failure'.

This proved the case. The ACMA had by now asserted itself not only as the dominant political body but also as the major national industrial organisation. It had become the linchpin in any unity moves. Though the

CCEA had been recognised as the appropriate organisation to convene meetings of national employer bodies to determine the conduct of test cases in the period to 1940, its successor found itself under increasing challenge from the ACMA, which emerged over the period as a more dominant organisation. The financial resources of the ACMA, derived in large measure from affiliates' previous decisions to establish insurance companies; its greater affinity with the Labor administration whose war efforts depended on a co-operative manufacturing sector; its added prominence during a period of manufacturing boom and diversification: all increased ACMA prominence at the expense of other employer bodies. The ACEF's eclipse was also a long-term heritage of the disintegration of the VEF in the 1930s. As Melbourne-based arbitration test cases began again after the war, the VCM proved the natural organisation from which to control such cases. Itself based in Melbourne until 1944, the CCEA had been able to fulfil this role. However, following the ACEF's move to Sydney under Oberg in 1945, national bodies preferred the VCM to the VEF as their test-case base. This preference was to elevate the VCM's and ACMA's industrial position for the next two decades. Thus, though the CCEA convened the 1940 Interstate Conference of Employers, the ACMA affiliates, and particularly the VCM, played the leading role thereafter.[3] P. C. Oakes of the VCM became Convenor of the Consultative and Co-ordinating Committee. In addition ACMA affiliates had three times as many representatives as the Federations on the Basic Wage Steering Committee, which replaced the Consultative and Co-ordinating Committee.[4] The VCM continued to act as Convenor of this Committee until the mid-1960s. The ACMA largely determined the distribution of expenses resulting from test cases (ACEF Meeting 25/2/47) and itself bore over half the costs for much of the period. It remained impervious to ACEF confederation and closer unity attempts. The ACMA's dominant role was, no doubt, a contributing factor to its independence and disinterest in a national co-ordinating body. Since this role required the ACMA to expend resources on activities that profited all employer groups, however, it is unlikely that this in itself would have prevented the ACMA from being interested in a Confederation, albeit one in which its influence was acknowledged. Such was the situation in relation to the Steering Committees that handled 'general cases'. A factor contributing to the ACMA's lack of co-operation may well have been its Constitution, which provided for an annual rotation of key office bearers among its affiliates. Thus, in attempting to negotiate a confederation with the ACMA over a number of years, ACEF President Oberg found himself dealing with a number of ACMA Presidents, many of whom may not have realised the need for a confederation. Other interested Presidents (Derham seems to have been genuinely interested in a confederation) lost office before anything permanent could be accomplished.

A more compelling reason for the ACMA's aloofness relates to its traditional insecurity about other organisations' designs concerning tariff protection. This may seem a paradoxical position at a time when war hostilities had sufficiently reduced imports to allow the Tariff Board to take on other war activities(Hall 1971:574). The chambers, however, never took a short-term view. Thus only 7 months after the declaration of war, and after commenting on the fall in applications for protective duties because of 'the temporary abatement of overseas competition', the VCM urged members 'to look ahead and be prepared for post-war conditions' (VCM *Annual Report* 1940:9). The early wartime preoccupation with the 'New Order' and with Post-War Reconstruction did not allow the ACMA to forget its long-term interests. The large number of 'infant industries' induced by wartime necessity heightened its apprehension. As Hall notes, 'it would be impossible for manufacturers to contemplate such a wide and diversified extension of factory production without asking an obvious question — "And when the war is won – What then?"' (Hall 1971:607). Annual Reports and Presidential Addresses of the chambers kept this question to the fore. Indeed, because of international developments to which Australia was a party, they could hardly have done otherwise.

In 1941 Roosevelt and Churchill signed the Atlantic Charter, a 'New Order' for international relations for the post-war era. Article 4 of this Charter bound signatories to 'endeavour with due respect for existing obligations to further enjoyment of all States, great and small, victor or vanquished, of access, on equal terms, to the trade and raw materials of the world which are needed for their economic prosperity'. The last shot of the war had scarcely been fired when, in October 1945, a Preparatory Committee for the ensuing International Tariff Conference of 1947 met in London. The 1947 Conference resulted in the General Agreement on Tariffs and Trade (GATT) 'which cut across one of the Chambers' first principles', namely that of 'high protection' (Hall 1971:803). GATT resulted in numerous conferences being held and took on the 'paraphernalia of a peripatetic parliament of nations as far as tariffs and trade were concerned' (ibid.). The Geneva negotiations of 1947 had resulted in multilateral agreement covering over 600 items on the Tariff Board's schedule. Subsequent conferences increased this list (ibid.).

In addition to the protracted lobbying, the ACMA was also concerned to ensure sufficient representation on the Australian delegations to international negotiations. The fact that it was forced to share representation with other national groups — the ACCA, ACEF and the Australian Exporters' Federation, which traditionally had been anti-protectionist — may have induced the ACMA to see its interests as being opposed to, rather than aligned with non-manufacturing employer bodies. The grouping of the ACMA and MTEA into a 'manufacturing' Secretariat and the ACEF and ACCA into a 'commercial' Secretariat may have increased any perception of opposing camps. If so, the ACEF's withdrawal from the Secretariat in 1949, and its apparent neutrality on the question of tariffs, may have contributed to a better accommodation of the two organisations in subsequent periods. During the 1940s, however, despite Labor rule and much test-case activity following the ending of wartime hostilities, employer co-ordination machinery did not advance beyond that which had been developed in the preceding decade.

Summary and conclusion

The necessities of war resulted in a greater degree of centralism of economic and industrial relations management than had previously been experienced in Australia. This was to prove a continuing feature of the economy. Though the federations had quarrelled with each other in previous years over a federal system of industrial regulation, war conditions conditioned them to such a situation and in the post-war period the standardisation of the basic wage and hours of work was not a major cause of division. The period was one in which employers felt under considerable threat because of the perceived socialisation activities of Labor Governments. This threat, and the pressures associated with wartime administration, resulted in an influx of members in most organisations and therefore a greater degree of resources than had previously been the case. Together with the reduced test-case activity in the period 1940 to 1946, they further resulted in the ACEF diversifying its activities and placing a high priority on public relations — something it had not done after the passing of the *Conciliation and Arbitration Act* in 1904. Political lobbying, a hallmark of ACEF activities since its inception, was also given greater impetus during the period. Further, with the establishment of the Canberra Secretariat, such lobbying involved a higher degree of collaboration with other organisations than had previously been the case. Industrial activities, which vied for resources with the political, research and public relations functions for much of the period, again emerged as the ACEF's dominant concern following the end of war hostilities.

The period, though one in which inter-organisational ructions did occur, was nevertheless one in which there was a higher degree of co-operation and collaboration between national employer groups than in previous periods. In contrast to test cases conducted in the 1930s, those held after 1945 witnessed few employer advocates, most being prepared to be represented by Counsel briefed by the Basic Wage Steering Committees on behalf of employers in general. No doubt pressures from wartime regulations and a perceived hostile Labor administration contributed to the greater readiness to co-operate, but these were not sufficiently great or sustained to bring about a permanent co-ordinating organisation. Thus, ACEF efforts to bring about a Confederation did not materialise. It may be argued, however, that the ACEF's distancing of itself from the ACCA following the demise of the Canberra Secretariat, and its greater enforced collaboration with the ACMA over test cases, were necessary pre-conditions for the eventual establishment of permanent co-ordinating machinery. If so, then this period laid the foundations for such a development.

Notes

1 It is surprising, in view of the economic and social dislocation of the 1948 coal strike, and the anti-Communist sentiments expressed by employers at that time, that this strike does not appear to be the subject of comment in the journals, Annual Reports or minutes of meetings of the ACEF, ACMA or their major affiliates.

2 The name of this Bureau was subsequently changed to that of the 'Economic Research Service'.

3 It should be noted, however, that, like the ACEF, the ACMA did not have its own Industrial Department. The VCM became the ACMA's *de facto* industrial department.

4 Three members of the Basic Wage Steering Committee were members of ACMA affiliates, and one a member of the VEF. One represented the MTEA, one the Master Printers' Association of Victoria and another the Commonwealth Jam Preserving and Condiment Manufacturers' Association. The last two organisations had strong links with the VCM.

6

CONSOLIDATION 1950–1959

The previous chapter outlined developments in the decade 1940–1949. During this decade the CCEA was renamed the 'Australian Council of Employers' Federations' (ACEF). Labor was in office for much of this period. Its use of wartime powers was a major factor in promoting the growth of employer organisations. The same consideration gave rise to both the ACEF and the ACMA joining different Canberra-based joint secretariats, to expenditure on research and propaganda, and to lobbying activities reminiscent of the period when the *Conciliation and Arbitration Act* was first introduced. In the final result, three lasting elements emerged from this experience: better resourced employer bodies, a high degree of centralism in relation to wage determination, and a restructured Commonwealth Court of Conciliation and Arbitration.

These factors conditioned national employer association developments in the 1950s, which are the subjects of this chapter. The first part reviews the operations of the Ministry of Labour Advisory Council. The activities of the Council provide a ready reference for the industrial context of the period. The chapter also reviews the important national test cases of the period, which induced a co-ordinated employer response. Its second part of the chapter reviews the organisational developments of the period.

Tripartism

A hallmark of the 1950s was the post-war economic boom that helped to increase the resources, both financial and human, of employer associations. The ACMA prospered during the manufacturing boom created by a protective environment. Its increased affluence and its special relationship with

Ministers made it more aloof from the ACEF and other potential competitors. In addition the absence of 'hostile' federal governments removed a compelling incentive of the earlier period for employer coalescence. 'Friendly' governments, however, did not result in associations obtaining industrial legislation that was completely to their liking. For example, they unsuccessfully lobbied to have the Labor reforms of 1947 repealed and to reduce the role of Commissioners. The major concessions they obtained were the appeals and referencing mechanism introduced in 1952. These removed the total autonomy of Commissioners in relation to award determination. The other significant legislative development of the period — that of 1956, the splitting up the Commonwealth Court of Conciliation and Arbitration into the Conciliation and Arbitration Commission to deal with arbitral matters, and the Industrial Court to deal with judicial matters — resulted from a successful union High Court challenge to the constitutional competence of the Arbitration Court to exercise both these functions.

The basic labour policy under H. Holt as Minister for Labour and National Service was one of tripartism. This was evidenced by the tripartite Conference on Inflation, Production and Industrial Relations of 1951, and in more permanent form by way of the Ministry of Labour Advisory Council (MLAC). The purpose of the Council was twofold:

> (1) To provide a means whereby employers' and workers' organisations may, at the highest level, have the opportunity of -
> (a) participating with the Government in the consideration of employment, industrial relations, employee welfare and related industrial economic matters;
> (b) consultation together and with the Minister for Labour and National Service and, as necessary, other representatives of the Government in free and frank discussion of such matters;
> (c) expressing to the Government through the Minister for Labour and National Service their considered opinion on such matters.
> (2) To assist with guidance, information and advice the Department of Labour and National Service in the discharge of its functions. (DL and NS 1953)

It was proposed that the MLAC consist of the Minister as Chairman and the Secretary of the Department of Labour and National Service (DL and NS) as the Deputy Chairman. There were to be seven employer representatives 'appointed in consultation with the employers' organisations concerned'. Each was to represent a 'major employing industry'. It was further proposed that the DL and NS provide the Secretariat. Other Ministers and senior officials were to attend 'as necessary to provide information and to assist the Council in its deliberations'. Representatives from other industries and organisations were to be co-opted as necessary and the Assistant Secretaries from the DL and NS were 'to attend as observers in order to obtain a proper understanding of the Council's work.' No votes were to be taken and meetings were to be confidential and 'without verbatim reporting'. No proceedings of Council were to be quoted against any member in any circumstances. Press information was to be given by the Minister only, and then only in relation to matter 'of an agreed character'. Ordinary meetings were to be held half-yearly and special meetings as necessary. An Executive Committee, consisting of the Chairman and/or Deputy Chairman and five members, was to 'handle emergent matters between Council meetings'. Sub-committees were to be appointed as required (ibid.).

After much procrastination, in July 1954 the ACTU announced its intention to join the Council. By then the Government had decided that there would be nine employer representatives: two each from the ACMA, ACEF and the Australian Metal Industry Association (AMIA), one each from the ACCA, the Graziers' Federal Council of Australia (GFCA) and 'Public Utilities'.

The first MLAC meeting was held in October by which time only the ACTU and the ACEF had formally accepted membership and had representatives appointed. Other employer organisations attended as observers (ACEF *Annual Report* 28/1/55). No doubt H. Bland (Secretary DL and NS) pressed on with this meeting as an inducement for other organisations to join. Not to do so would have left the ACEF as the employer mouthpiece. Under the circumstances, however, the first meeting was largely a ceremonial affair.

By the end of 1954 the other organisations had accepted membership of the MLAC. Eleven more 'official' meetings were held before the ACTU announced its withdrawal in 1958. Subsequent to its withdrawal, however, it was not averse to participating in *'ad hoc'* meetings composed of MLAC members. Three such meetings were held.

MLAC meetings discussed a range of issues. These included industrial safety, the shortage of skilled labour, apprenticeship and adult training, retirement age, technological change and automation, demarcation disputes, productivity councils, the operations of the Commonwealth Employment Service, basic wage developments, and industrial legislation. Under the auspices of the MLAC a Standing Committee on Productivity and the Australian Apprenticeship Advisory Council were established. Two publications — *Productivity* and *Automation* — were published under the

MLAC's name in 1956. The area most keenly debated related to changes to the Act. Following the Boilermakers' case, the MLAC deliberated on the merits of establishing two separate industrial tribunals, one of a judicial nature and the other to be concerned with the prevention and settlement of industrial disputes. (AMIA Report of MLAC Proceedings 19/3/56). Members favoured the establishment of the dual tribunal system. The implementation of the penal provisions of the Act by an Industrial Court, which was divorced from the industrial relations implications of its decisions, forced the MLAC to reconsider this situation on a number of occasions. It was this issue that finally resulted in the ACTU withdrawing from the Council.

By the time of the elections of November 1958 the penal question was a burning issue. Before the election the ACTU Interstate Executive decided by nine votes to seven to withdraw from the MLAC. Holt's press statement depicted the ideological and other pressures within the ACTU leading to its withdrawal:

> I would be disappointed if any of those representatives of the ACTU who have participated through the work of the Council lent their support to yesterday's decision to withdraw . . . To any one familiar with the work of the Council, the published reasons for the decision are patently absurd . . . The claim that the work of the Council has not brought direct material benefits to the trade union movement reveals a regrettable insularity and narrowness of view. . . . The plain fact is that the Communist members of the Interstate Executive who as a result of successful tactical manoeuvres at the last Biennial Trade Union Congress doubled their representation have been quick to capitalise on their gain. (Minister for L and NS, Press Statement 21/2/58)

The Coalition won the November elections and in the ministerial reshuffle Mr W. McMahon replaced Holt as Minister for Labour and National Service. The ACTU sounded him out regarding the penal provisions. It agreed with McMahon's suggestion of an '*ad hoc*' meeting of MLAC members. This was held in February and considered a document prepared by the DL and NS on sanctions. It outlined the legal developments to 1958, the use of contempt provisions under the Act, the attitudes of unions towards sanctions, the attitude of employers, and the attitude of the Government. The document advanced the view that 'it is probably true that some observers thought, when the 1956 Bill was under consideration, that the new Commonwealth Industrial Court would approach applications for orders under the new section 109 with a feeling for the industrial issues involved and exercise a broad discretion somewhat in the manner of an Equity Court and as the old Arbitration Court did'. It suggested consideration be given to the President of the Conciliation and Arbitration Commission, either personally or by delegation, attempting to settle the matter in dispute in the first instance. Only if this failed would a certificate be issued permitting recourse to the Industrial Court. Thus the document anticipated the legislative changes in this area by 10 years. The meeting broke up without any definite decisions being made (ACEF Circular 12/1959, 4/3/59).

A further *ad hoc* meeting took place in February 1960 when the penal provisions were again debated. ACTU President Monk reiterated that unions would not surrender the right to strike. He accused employers of 'taking action to prosecute the unions without recourse to conciliation'. Employers replied that the union claims were 'hollow and that the abolition of penalties was inspired by communists' who merely wanted 'freedom to embark on a policy contrary to industrial law and against the public interest for which they have no moral grounds' (AMIA Report of MLAC Ad Hoc Meeting 29/2/60).

Unable to make any headway on the sanctions issue the ACTU determined not to attend further MLAC meetings. It was not until 1967, when the National Labour Advisory Council (NLAC) was formed, that the ACTU returned to tripartite discussions. A major factor in forming the NLAC was the question of penal sanctions.

National test cases

In addition to six Basic Wage cases during the period employers were involved in test cases relating to standard hours of work (1953), uniform long-service-leave provisions (1958 onwards) and metal trades margins cases, which, after 1952, were heard by Full Benches in a way to afford general guidance for all federal awards. The Standard Hours case, which was combined with the 1952–53 basic Wage Inquiry, can be passed over quickly. In that case metal industry employers, with only token support from other employers who considered the application had little chance of success, applied for a restoration of the 44-hour working week. The Bench rejected the application.

Basic Wage determination during the period impacted considerably on employer associations' resources and was an important fact enabling the ACEF to induce other organisations to support the establishment of more permanent machinery for handling national test cases.

The most significant decision of the period was that the 1953 Basic Wage case led to the abandonment of the Automatic Quarterly Cost of Living Adjustment (AQCOLA) system, which had operated since 1922. This decision affected national employer association developments in different ways. In abandoning the AQCOLA mechanism, the Arbitration Court introduced a system of basic wage adjustment supposedly designed to ensure that the basic wage was maintained at the highest level sustainable by economic capacity to pay. In this schema the basic wage was to be adjusted in relation to seven economic indicators: employment, investment, production and productivity, overseas trade, overseas balance of payments, the competitive position of secondary industry and retail trade indices. Though the use of these (or similar) indicators is evident in earlier basic wage inquiries, the high degree of automaticity in basic wage determination to that time, and the infrequency of such inquiries (only eight between 1922 and 1950), resulted in a lack of expertise on the part of employer organisations even in relation to very basic economic terms and concepts (D'Alpuget 1975:140–6). The greater frequency of such inquiries, and the greater reliance on economic argumentation, necessitated a greater degree of sophistication in basic wage submissions. National organisations' interest in research facilities was rekindled. This interest was furthered by the 1956 decision which provided for annual reviews of the basic wage.

Another outcome of the 1953 case may have been an arrest to the momentum then under way to establish a Confederation of Employers. As noted below, the ACEF had been very active in the period 1951–53 in such a development and was sufficiently confident of success to take out Articles of Registration and of Association under the *Companies Ordinance* 1931. Employers' success in having AQCOLA removed without any formal Confederation may have reduced some organisations' interest in such a development. If so, then the periodicity of basic wage cases after 1956, the continuous need to oppose ACTU calls for the restoration of AQCOLA, and the growing economic sophistication of arguments at test cases, all made it necessary for employers to improve on the *ad hoc* Committee system that had operated since the 1930s. By the end of the period both the Basic Wage Steering Committee and its co-ordinator, the Policy and Consultative Committee, had been reconstructed on a permanent basis.

The need to develop better co-ordination machinery was emphasised by the need to increase the financial resources for national test cases. This, in turn, forced the three major organisations controlling the Committees responsible for such cases (ACMA, ACEF, and AMIA) to evolve machinery allowing for a greater input from contributing organisations. That development, in turn, led to the formation of the National Employers' Associations in 1960. The financial resources expended on such test cases are shown in Table 6.1.

Table 6.1 *Cost to Employers of National Test Cases, 1950–59*

Case	*Cost ($)*
1949–50 Basic Wage Inquiry	9 000
1952–53 Basic Wage and Standard Hours Inquiry	72 000
1956 Basic Wage Inquiry	20 400
1956 Boilermakers' case (High Court)	4 696
1956–57 Basic Wage Inquiry	18 800
1958 Basic Wage Inquiry	30 000
1958 Long Service Leave case	8 000
1959 Basic Wage Inquiry	33 000
1959 Margins case	18 000
TOTAL	213 896

Source: ACEF records.

It can be seen from the table that considerable sums were spent on test cases — on average nearly $22 000 per year. The large outlays involved in such cases were also the cause of a major rift between the ACEF and other organisations, particularly the ACMA. The ACEF favoured representation by lay advocates and considered that the industrial officers in the employ of federations were competent to handle such cases at a fraction of the cost incurred when Counsel was used (ACEF Meetings 19/11/51, 2/9/53, 6/8/55, 27/8/59). The ACMA was not persuaded by this argument.

Metal Trades Margins cases were conducted in 1952, 1954 and 1959. They had the effect of creating federal standards and by the end of the period margins were being determined by way of national test cases in a similar way to the basic wage. Thus in the first Margins case of the period some 20 unions, 8 employer associations, 11 state instrumentalities, 3 state governments and 6 large companies were given permission to intervene. Commissioner Galvin noted in his decision:

> It has been said on numerous occasions (and in the light of experience not without warrant) that, to an extent, the principles laid down in the Metal Trades Award, form the pattern for quite a large number of other awards. What transpired in the case of other awards subsequent to the then Full Court's decision of 1947 amply bears that out, and that being so it is evident that these proceedings do take on something in the nature of an economic inquiry in miniature. In brief, the ultimate determination of this dispute is, as has been said, one fraught with possible grave consequences not only to the metal industry but to all industries. (73 *CAR* 340)

According to the 1954 Metal Trades Margins Bench, decisions in such cases were explicitly designed 'to afford general guidance to all authorities' (80 *CAR* 531). The 'economic inquiry in miniature' quality of margins cases was furthered in 1959 when a Full Bench heard jointly margins applications for unions covering the metal trades, metalliferous mining, the banking industry and the aviation industry. The Basic Wage Steering Committee, whose charter was limited to basic wage matters, nevertheless undertook the case on behalf of employers generally, a further indication of the inter-industry or general nature of such margins applications.

CONFEDERATION GENESIS

ACEF developments

The first half of the 1950s was one in which the ACEF marked time rather than capitalised on economic circumstances. The QEF continued to suffer the financial difficulties that had beset it in the 1940s. In addition the SAEF, for decades a most stable and financial member of the ACEF, experienced organisational problems that led to its near extinction. Compounding these problems were differences between affiliates concerning the ACEF's role and identity. By 1953 these problems had led to two federations ceasing to be full members and a third federation threatening to disaffiliate.

The demise of the SAEF appears to have been largely the result of difficulties members experienced in dealing with G. H. Boykett. Appointed Secretary in 1907 (after an earlier period as Assistant Secretary), by the mid-1940s he increasingly alienated members by his arrogant and secretive manner. In 1936 the rival Chamber of Manufactures established an industrial division, which reduced the SAEF's monopoly over industrial matters. As members found Boykett more and more difficult to deal with they left the federation. By 1950 the SAEF was experiencing sufficient financial and membership problems to consider being absorbed by the Chamber of Manufactures, a move that would have left ACEF with no South Australian affiliate.

The SAEF's existence remained in the balance during 1950 and 1951. Its survival owed much to the VEF, which, following the forced resignation of Boykett, gave financial assistance and helped restructure the SAEF along VEF lines. By 1956 it had overcome many of its organisational problems. However, it never regained its former status and was not able to capitalise as fully as it might have done on the burgeoning post-war industrial developments in South Australia. In particular, the SAEF was never to regain membership of the engineering and metal industries, which had provided it with influential office bearers since its inception. By that time Western Australia was the only state in which the federation had exclusive control over industrial matters on behalf of employers.

In addition to the SAEF decline, the ACEF also suffered internal instability due to differences over the scope and functions of the national organisation. During the 1940s political developments had led to the ACEF placing a high priority on public relations and political liaison activities. By 1949 the changed political context and the greater degree of industrial activity had caused a reassessment of priorities and use of resources. A compromise solution formulated in October 1949 resulted in the Sydney-based full-time Secretary (Powell) handling the secretarial, public relations and liaison functions and supposedly 'initiating and directing' industrial services. As Powell was unable to provide such industrial services directly, the VEF was requested to provide these services on a contractual basis. Because of the lack of assurances concerning the permanency of its national industrial service, the VEF refrained from securing the staff needed to provide an efficient service.

In February 1951 the WAEF again pressed for an independent ACEF industrial service. It claimed that the ACEF's prime role ought to be the provision of a complete industrial service and that its political and public relations activities ought to be of a secondary and part-time nature. It considered the service provided by the VEF to be inadequate, a view supported by the EFNSW. It delivered an ultimatum. If the ACEF, or the VEF, were unable to provide an efficient service, the WAEF would set up its own branch office in Melbourne and would consider withdrawing from the ACEF. The VEF reciprocated with its own ultimatum. If the ACEF replicated the VEF services, VEF subscriptions would be reduced accordingly. The final decision was a compromise one: 'That the Federal industrial service be carried out on a contractual basis by the VEF to those states desiring that service and that such services be supplemented by each Federation keeping other federations fully advised on industrial matters' (ACEF Meeting 20/2/51).

The VEF's resentment at the attempted dilution of its control over the Industrial Service was compounded by ACEF elections at that time in which the VEF felt slighted. O. D. A. Oberg, who had been elected President in 1943 remained in office until the end of 1948 when D. Fell, also from New South Wales, was elected. In August 1952 Fell advised that 'for business and personal reasons' he wished to be relieved of office. Oberg was approached by some federations to take up the Presidency again. The VEF, which was burdened with the ACEF's industrial work, was not keen for Oberg to be re-elected President. He had been a prime mover in both the Canberra-based Joint Secretariat and the Sydney-based Public Relations Bureau. He had also strongly supported Canberra as the location for the

ACEF Secretariat. The VEF considered that under Oberg's leadership industrial services would continue to take a subordinate position in the allocation of finances. Thus, the VEF would continue to be the target of criticism by other federations.

Oberg's election, in preference to the VEF–SAEF nominee, L. C. Burne, resulted in a dramatic response from the defeated federations. In March 1953, they announced that they no longer considered themselves full members of the ACEF and would therefore make only a token financial contribution. The matter was settled in June when rule changes providing that no one state could hold the office of president for more than two consecutive years were passed. The federations also resolved that 'while confirming the desirability of rotating the position of President between member States, this meeting recommends that it is desirable that Federations should consider favourably a nomination to be made by the VEF for the year beginning 1955' (ACEF Meeting 30/6/53).

Despite this settlement it is clear that federations resented the VEF's tactics and the increasing difficulty experienced in having it provide its allocated share of ACEF costs to national cases levied by the Basic Wage Steering Committee. The federations did not honour the implied commitment to elect the next President from the VEF. Instead the QEF nominated A. L. Blake (EFNSW) who was seconded by his own federation. The VEF took strong exception to this nomination and claimed that the resolution of June 1953 entitled it to exclusive nomination. It was not until 1957, however, that L. C. Burne of the VEF was finally elected ACEF President. In addition to breaching the spirit of the 1953 resolution, federations voted to form a Standing Industrial Committee, which removed the VEF's control over the ACEF's industrial service. Further, in 1955 both the QEF and TEF contracted with the EFNSW for the provision of a federal industrial service (EFNSW Meeting 3/3/55).

By 1957 there was sufficient internal stability for the ACEF to direct its attention towards reorganisation and redevelopment. Its continual attempts at establishing a Confederation of Employers and at having the Steering Committee placed on a more permanent basis had met with little success. There was a general feeling among federations that the only way in which the ACEF could achieve greater co-ordination among employer groups was by establishing itself as the recognised organisation around which other employer groups could coalesce for industrial relations purposes. A number of approaches to achieve this end were considered, including the broadening of ACEF membership. In December of that year the EFNSW proposed that 'affiliated organisations with national characteristics — such as Graziers' associations — should be represented on the ACEF Executive'. Because of the existing method of appointing members of the Executive, the EFNSW noted that major industries were not represented on that Executive. 'These included graziers, shipping, oil, insurance, banking, retailing, wholesale distributing, coal, metalliferous mining and general manufacturing. This did not accord with federation affiliation in which all, with the exception of manufacturing, were generally well represented'. To support the latter contention the memorandum included a table showing industry affiliation with constituent federations (Table 6.2).

Table 6.2 *Industry affiliations, employers' federations, 1957*

Industry	Qld	NSW	Vic	SA	WA
Grazing	✓	✓	–	–	✓
Shipping	✓	✓ (a)	–	–	–
Oil (b)	✓	✓	–	–	✓
Insurance	✓ (b)	✓	–	–	✓
Banking (b)	✓ (b)	–	–	–	✓
Retailing	–	✓	–	✓	–
Wholesaling	✓	✓	–	–	✓
Coal	✓	✓	–	–	✓
Mining	✓	✓	–	–	✓
Metal trades	✓	–	–	–	✓
Building	–	✓	–	–	✓
Timber	✓	✓	–	✓	✓
Road transport	✓	✓	–	✓	✓

(a) Overseas Shipping Representatives Association.
(b) No formal association exists.

Source: EFNSW Memorandum 'Report re ACEF representation', 4/12/57.

The table is useful in showing the interests represented within federations as well as the relative strength of these federations. It indicates the QEF's apparent success in regaining ground lost as the result of earlier trade associations disaffiliation to form the Queensland Employers' Council in 1945. The SAEF's position may be compared with that of the WAEF. The latter had been able to maintain its industrial relations monopoly, a situation that had existed in South Australia until the decline of the SAEF in 1950. The table understates the industry representation within the VEF as the result of the federation not submitting the necessary information. Unlike other mainland federations, the VEF has been reluctant to give lists of affiliated associations, possibly because of its membership competition with the VCM.[2] As indicated in Table 6.3, the VEF had 73 affiliated trade associations at this time. It is therefore unlikely that it did not have representation from many of the industries itemised in Table 6.2.

Table 6.3 *Membership, employers' federations, 1957*

Federation	Direct members		Associations	
	Employers	Employees	Number	Employers
EFNSW	980	70 000	84	40 000
VEF	1 000	–	73	65 000
QEF	170	15 000	30	22 000
SAEF	–	–	23	8 150
WAEF	3 000	–	52	13 000

Source: EFNSW Memorandum 'Report re ACEF Representation', 4/12/57.

Table 6.3 indicates the relative size and strength of ACEF affiliates. It highlights the relative importance of the EFNSW and VEF in ACEF affairs, and thus the potential difficulties posed by either of these federations disaffiliating from or refusing to play a full role within the ACEF. The table further indicates the decline of the SAEF, which historically had been the third largest ACEF affiliate. It also indicates that the QEF's recovery was more apparent than real. Though it had representatives from most industries itemised in Table 6.2, relative to the WAEF its membership continued to be small. No information was provided by the TEF.

On the basis of the above information the EFNSW suggested that the ACEF should increase the number of state delegates from two to three, and 'that efforts be made to appoint the additional delegates from the following industries: graziers, shipping, mining, manufacturing with the following amongst the alternatives: oil, insurance, banking, merchants'.

At the next Executive Meeting (February 1958) EFNSW President Mullens argued the case for appointing Executive delegates from major industries. The ACEF, he argued, 'was the logical body to provide representation and to develop policies on behalf of all sections of employers'. He noted that many national groups had no central organisation to which they could belong, and he claimed consideration ought be given to the possibility of including such organisations within the ACEF. Following a long discussion it was resolved that a special sub-committee be appointed to examine three matters: Confederation developments, the scope and functions of the ACEF, and the ACEF secretariat (ACEF Meeting 14/2/58).

After much debate the sub-committee resolved to recommend the appointment of a full-time National Secretary but not that of an industrial advocate. The National Secretary 'should be capable of rendering some industrial services and providing industrial liaison for member Federations' and should be located in Melbourne. The question of Associate Members was left to a later time (ACEF Sub-Committee Meeting 11/3/58).

The Committee's recommendations were accepted. In April 1959 the ACEF advertised for an Executive Director in the following terms:

> The position calls for the appointment of an Executive with general business experience and a wide knowledge of Australian Industrial Arbitration Systems and procedures. The Executive Director will be responsible to the Federal President for the general co-ordination of the industrial and related services. He must be capable of representing the Council in its relations with Governments, Trade Unions, employers' organisations and the Press. The Secretariat will be located in Melbourne. Commencing salary will be at a minimum rate of [$6000] per annum according to qualifications and experience, plus appropriate expenses. (*Daily News* 18/4/59)

Mr George Polites, formerly an industrial officer with the VEF and Personnel Manager with Utah (Australia) Ltd was selected from a list of 19 applicants. He took up his duties from 1 January 1960.

Confederation attempts

Attempts to establish an employers' Confederation were to absorb ACEF energies for most of the decade. Two methods of implementing such a body were attempted: the enlargement of the Basic Wage Steering Committee (Steering Committee) into a permanent organisation with full-time research and advocate staff and the replacement of this Committee with a Confederation made up of major national employer organisations.

By 1950 the major vehicles for co-ordinating employers' submissions at national tribunal hearings were the Steering Committee and the Policy and Consultative Committee (Policy Committee). Both were *ad hoc* bodies. The former consisted of industrial officers, usually the Secretaries, of key affiliates of the ACMA, ACEF and AMIA, and was effectively under the management of the VCM. Its role was to assist and brief Counsel. This Committee was under the control and direction of the Policy Committee consisting of the Presidents of the ACMA, ACEF, and AMIA. National policy in relation to each case was formulated by general meetings of employer organisations called by the President of the

ACMA. By 1950 nearly 40 national organisations or major companies attended such meetings.

In September 1951 ACEF Secretary Power invited 30 Presidents of 'the most influential bodies representative as far as possible of the principal divisions of commerce and industry' to an informal dinner at which the Confederation moves were to be discussed. The letter noted that 'apart from the social aspect of the occasion, it is hoped to provide an opportunity for an exploratory discussion of the question of providing a united national voice of employers'. The letter called for the establishment of a 'National Confederation of Employers' Organisations'. Its members were to be 'all employers' organisations which are federal in character'. No organisation was to lose any autonomy and it therefore followed 'that the declared policy of the Confederation could only be the result of unanimous decisions'. It was proposed that the Confederation could function in one of two ways: either 'the form of a convention held at regular intervals or for specific purposes at which common policy would be determined' or 'the form of a permanent organisation under the control of a Council consisting of the Presidents of member organisations' and with the appropriate staff. The functions of the Confederation were to 'constitute a focal point of employer opinion and policy on matters having a general interest', 'to enable the full weight of employer opinion to be co-ordinated', 'to safeguard the common interests of employers', and to 'facilitate the representation of Australian employers in the international sphere'. In the industrial field 'it could promote closer co-ordination of employers' efforts in regard to such matters as amendments to Commonwealth industrial legislation, presentation of employers' viewpoints before inquiries into the basic wage, standard hours etc.'. In the 'economic field it could permit a concerted examination by all sections of employers of the economic problems facing the Commonwealth from time to time'. It was further proposed that the 'organisation could eventually include an Economic Research and Information Bureau equipped to carry out economic research, to interpret available statistics in the interests of employers and to carry out a skilfully directed campaign in support of the system of free and competitive enterprise' (ACEF 'Draft Proposal for Establishment of a National Confederation of Employers' Organisations', n.d. (September) 1951).

Nineteen organisations accepted the invitation to a dinner held on 19 November. Other organisations sent apologies with 'distance from Sydney' being 'the principal cause of non-attendance'. Both the ACMA and the ACCA were represented, together with representatives from the insurance, shipping, coal, newspaper, pastoral, wheat, automotive, meat slaughtering, metal trades and retailing industries. ACEF President, D. Fell, led the discussions during which he noted that although his organisation had taken the initiative in calling the meeting it 'had no desire to participate in the proposed confederation other than as a constituent member'. He reiterated the need for employer unity and referred to calls by the Prime Minister and Minister for Labour for a central employer body. There was a degree of support for the formation of a Confederation and a committee of eight was established 'to draw up a plan setting out the details of the proposed Confederation of Employers to be submitted in writing to all organisations represented at or invited to this meeting and to be considered at all further meetings in Melbourne of representatives of these bodies' (Report of Discussion upon Proposal to Form a Confederation of Employers' Organisations, Carlton Hotel, Sydney, 19/11/51).

When the committee met 4 days later the ACMA member was not present. Instead, the ACMA wrote indicating that it was not prepared to join in discussions since it considered 'the basic idea was impossible of achievement'. Notwithstanding this, the committee set to and drafted a Constitution guided by two major considerations: the 'need for promoting unity among employers' organisations'; and the 'need to preserve the autonomy and functions of all existing employer organisations'.

The committee proposed the formation of The Australian Confederation of Employers, which, in addition to federal organisations, would include regional organisations who were 'substantially representative of a section of employers or have an interstate effect'. However, state organisations were to be represented through their federal body. The Confederation was to act as an advisory and consultative body regarding legislation, employer unity, international employer representation, government representation, the promotion of free enterprise and economic research, and the co-ordination of representation before industrial tribunals (Report of Meeting of the Committee Appointed to Draft Details of Proposed Confederation of Employers 23/11/51).

By April 1952 the ACCA and two other organisations had also indicated that they were not prepared to participate in discussions. The following month the GFCA Convention decided it would not seek to affiliate with any new body. With the withdrawal of support of the ACMA, ACCA and the GFCA, the ACEF enthusiasm waned and Confederation moves stalled.

In August Oberg reported to the ACEF Executive that the progress made in relation to the Confederation 'could not be regarded as satisfactory. Two meetings of the parties interested had been held. A subcommittee had been appointed to draft a Constitution which had not been favourably received'. He suggested that the matter 'be held in abeyance to be revived at a more opportune time'. The meeting resolved that 'the only prospect for Employer Unity lies in a Steering Committee and that the Council's representative on such a Committee keep that object in mind' (ACEF Meeting 29/8/52). The ACEF continued to press for the establishment of a Confederation for the remainder of the period but with no success.[3] It re-directed its energies towards establishing its own permanent secretariat and industrial service.

By the beginning of 1958 the ACMA was also considering establishing an industrial service. The immediate factor prompting this move was the departure of G. Gill as Secretary of the AMIA to take up a position on the Tariff Board. The ACMA, through the VCM and the SACM, had a large investment in the AMIA and had been influential in establishing it in an attempt to pre-empt the MTEA from expanding beyond New South Wales and Queensland.[4] Gill's departure, in the view of ACMA President Simpson,

> has revealed a fundamental weakness in any special purpose organisation like AMIA, devoted to the interests of one group of employers: even such an important group as the metal industries has not been able to justify an industrial organisation large enough to support a suitable executive officer and provide him with a competent understudy who can help him in his work and take his place in his absence or retirement. Other groups of employers, including non-industrial employers, have reached the same conclusion. (Memorandum 'The ACMA and Industrial Work' 27/2/58)

Simpson also considered why the ACMA (rather than the ACEF or a Confederation) ought to provide such an industrial service. 'ACMA is accepted as the leading employer organisation in such cases as the present application for increased Basic Wage and Margins. If we do not exercise this leadership, we run the risk either of a proliferation of employer bodies, all competing for the services of the few suitable men available, and none of them adequately financed and staffed, or of some other organisation being formed and doing the job, and eventually overshadowing us in this important field of service to our members'. The ACMA, Simpson considered, ought either to establish an industrial section or to arrange 'with the other members of the Policy and Consultative Committee and Working Party that they should constitute a standing body, meeting say quarterly to consider industrial matters affecting more than one State, and matters in which the interests of different members appeared to diverge' (ibid.). Shortly afterwards the ACMA determined to provide a General Industrial Service (*Journal of Industry* 26(5), 1958).

Thus, by 1958 both the ACEF and the ACMA were seeking to establish a national industrial service and were competing for recognition as the dominant employer industrial organisation. This necessarily reduced the potential for the co-operation needed to form a Confederation. The ACMA's decision, in the ACEF's view, 'was influenced by knowledge that ACEF was contemplating the taking of further steps to establish a Confederation of Employers, and also considering the establishing of a full-time secretariat' (ACEF Circular 6/6/58). Though in the short term ACMA's decision heightened competition between the ACMA and the ACEF, the long-term effect of the ACMA's industrial service was that organisation's support for the Policy and Consultative Committee and the Steering Committee being placed on a permanent basis in line with the ACEF proposals. A further outcome was the ACMA's support for the formation of the National Employers' Associations.

National employer co-ordination

The composition and operations of the Steering Committee at the beginning of 1950 have been described elsewhere. It was this Committee, under the control of the Policy Committee, that tried to implement policy formulated at a combined meeting of employers' organisations in respect to Basic Wage cases.

The ACEF had sought changes to the *ad hoc* nature of the Steering Committee during the 1940s. In July 1951 it again directed its attention to 'reforming' the Committee and, with a view to making it a Standing Committee, resolved that:

(a) ACMA and ACEF should confer with a view to jointly convening a meeting on an Executive level of all interested major organisations.
(b) The object of such a meeting would be to consider the formation of a Steering Committee and its composition.
(c) With regard to the operations of the Steering Committee and with regard to presentation of any case before the Full Arbitration Court, ACEF representatives should recommend the employment of lay advocates instead of Counsel, except in regard to questions of law.
(d) If ACMA decline to co-operate in jointly calling the meeting ACEF should itself convene the meeting. (ACEF Meeting 25/7/51)

A joint ACMA–ACEF meeting was held in October 1951. This meeting agreed 'to recommend to their organisations that for the purpose of establishing a permanent Steering Committee, ACEF and ACMA be authorised to prepare jointly recommendations for adoption by the national employers' organisations'. After discussing this recommendation in February 1952, the ACMA's Executive 'unanimously agreed that the proposal be rejected but that support be given to *ad hoc* Steering Committees created as and when necessary' (ACMA Meeting 6/2/52).

The Steering Committee was reactivated shortly afterwards in anticipation of a further Basic Wage Inquiry. This Committee continued to meet until the completion of the case in October 1953. This case, which resulted in the abandonment of automatic quarterly cost of living adjustments in favour of reviews based on seven economic indicators, was an employer victory that some organisations, including the ACEF, considered as somewhat Pyrrhic. The case had cost employers over $72 000. There was no assurance that future cases, involving the statistical evidence required by the economic indicators approach, would not involve employers in similar costs. Further, the case highlighted the lack of economic expertise on the part of employer associations in which many members did not understand simple economic concepts such as GNP (D'Alpuget, 1975:142). The ACEF responded by forming an Industrial Committee composed of federation Secretaries and other industrial advocates in September 1953. On behalf of this Committee, VEF Industrial Officer G. Polites represented the ACEF at the Margins case of the following year, thus saving the ACEF the expense of engaging Counsel.

The Steering Committee remained dormant during 1954 and until August 1955, when it became evident that the ACTU was to seek basic wage increases as well as the return of automatic quarterly adjustments. The ACMA, AMIA and ACEF held an informal discussion about the future direction of the Committee. ACEF Secretary Gibson sought the reaction of federations to the matters discussed, which he summarised as:

> — It was agreed that the composition of the Steering Committee left room for improvement.
> — That steps should be immediately taken to establish a fund for the purpose of fighting industrial cases of a general nature. The objective should be [$60 000].
> — That the same organisations and individuals should be asked to contribute annually for the purpose of sustaining such a fund.
> — That a Controlling Committee composed of ACMA, ACEF, AMIA and GFCA should be established together with the representative of any contributor of $2000. (ACEF Circular 23/8/55)

Federations responded coolly to the establishment of a permanent fund for the *ad hoc* Steering Committee. The QEF's response was typical. It objected to being 'asked to sign a blank cheque' and complained of the 'little direct control over expenditure and the insufficient use of Lay Advocates in Court proceedings'. Behind the federations' complaints lay the over-dominant role of the ACMA on the Steering Committee and an inability of other members to implement changes not supported by the ACMA. Thus, it was largely because of the ACMA's wishes that Counsel was retained for major cases, thereby adding to costs (of which the ACMA also paid a substantial proportion). Over the period the ACMA convened several meetings of employers to determine policy in relation to the conduct of national wage cases when it had already retained and briefed Counsel. Other organisations were thus forced to accept the ACMA's decision, to seek separate representation, or to opt out altogether. The latter course was likened to repudiation. The proposal to establish a permanent fund would have freed the ACMA from having to raise funds on a case-by-case approach without losing its customary control of the Policy and the Steering Committees.

Nearly 12 months later another meeting of employer organisations was convened by the VCM. This meeting considered policy in relation to the 1956 Basic Wage case, the second such case since the abandonment of ACOLA. Some 30 persons attended the meeting and 22 organisations were represented. ACMA President J. C. Hurley chaired the meeting. He noted that 'during the last 10 years we have had five major cases, including the 40-hour week case, and it seems that we are likely to be faced with enquiries of this kind at fairly frequent intervals while the country continues to expand its economy, and costs continue to rise'. The meeting voted a sum of \$30 000 to the case and resolved to reconstitute the Policy Committee to control the employers' case in the following words:

> That the Presidents of ACMA (as Chairman), ACEF, and AMIA be constituted a Policy and Consultative Committee to direct the conduct of the case (on the understanding that should any major important issue arise which they felt called for a general meeting, this would be done), and to control costs. (VCM Meeting of Employer Organisations 31/10/56)

At the ensuing case the Commission decided that Basic Wage cases would be held on an annual basis (84 *CAR* 161). This added to the ACEF's concern for the establishment of a Confederation or at least the restructuring of the Steering Committee (by now called the Basic Wage Working Party (Working Party) into a Standing Committee. A joint meeting of Presidents and Secretaries of the ACEF, ACMA, AMIA and GFCA was held in June to that end. The other organisations were not supportive of the ACEF proposals (ACEF Meeting 24–25/9/58, Report re Agenda Items).

Though these ACEF attempts were unsuccessful, by mid–1958 the ACMA was also considering the desirability of establishing the Policy Committee as a permanent body. Four factors seem to have influenced this decision. The first of these was its decision to establish a national industrial service. This gave some assurance that the ACMA would still be able to control any permanent body. The establishment of this service reduced the finance available for national test cases and by July 1958 the ACMA's contribution to the Long Service Leave case (30 per cent of costs) was no greater than the ACEF's. The second factor also revolved around finance. Though most organisations met their commitments in this respect, the ACMA was left to underwrite any shortfall. As other organisations joined the ACEF's call for a restructuring of the Policy Committee and as dissatisfaction with the ACMA's dominance grew, the likelihood of some organisations not responding to general levies increased. So too did the likelihood of national organisations seeking separate representation as happened with the GFCA in 1955 and 1958. By 1958 the ACEF was committed to the appointment of a full-time national Secretary capable of representing affiliates at national cases, and other organisations (such as the Woolbrokers) were also contemplating establishing national industrial offices. These moves increased the potential for separate representation and added costs to the ACMA. Yet other considerations were developments in the metal industry, which had the potential of robbing the VCM of its important engineering division. The loss of this division to the MTEA (which did occur in 1970) would have been a serious blow to the ACMA's finances and standing among national organisations. The fact that the Policy Committee handled the important metal margins cases after 1958 was yet another factor influencing the ACMA's desire to place that Committee on a permanent basis.

In June 1958 the ACMA's Director moved to have the Policy Committee Working Party constituted on a permanent basis. A general meeting of employer organisations convened in December 1958 to consider policy in relation to the 1959 Basic Wage case supported the establishment of both Committees 'as Standing Committees to deal with all future Basic Wage claims' (EFNSW Council Meeting 12/2/59). The Policy Committee was to comprise the Presidents of the ACMA, ACEF and AMIA and the Working Party was to comprise an industrial officer from each of these organisations and the GFCA.

Although constituted as a standing committee only in relation to Basic

Wage cases the Committee and Working Party did handle other national industrial matters because of their general application. In July 1958 the Working Party took control of the Long Service Leave case listed for hearing before the Commission later that month, and the 'White Collar and Professional Group Cases' (margins) listed for August. $8000 was set aside for the former case (BWWP Meeting 23/7/58). The EFNSW's Annual Report for 1958 (p.2) noted that 'Whilst the Policy and Consultative Committee and Working Party have no mandate in regards to national proceedings other than Basic Wage cases, they are recognised as the appropriate organisations for general liaison purposes and they have in fact been responsible for joint policy, joint submissions etc.'. In 1959 the Policy Committee handled the Metal Trades Margins case, which cost employers over $18 000.

The 1959 Basic Wage case cost employers in excess of $33 000. In contrast, the ACTU was not represented by Counsel but rather by four union officials. The substantial wage increases awarded ($1.50 or 5.7 per cent per week), caused the Working Party to reconsider its traditional approach to such cases. The need for reconsideration was accentuated shortly afterwards when the Metal Trades Margins case resulted in yet further wage increases of about 28 per cent. The ACEF was particularly disturbed by the general conduct of wage cases in which employers rejected union claims as a matter of course. In October its Executive was told:

> In the past years it has been customary for employers to adopt a policy of straight out opposition to union claims . . . This policy does not appear to be appropriate at all times, and the 1959 case recently concluded is an illustration of this . . . With the exception of the rural sector, all economic indicators showed improvements, and from the point of view of maintaining workers' purchasing power and therefore of maintaining high levels of business activity, the case for an increase of approximately $1.30 a week seemed to be unanswerable. That indeed was the view taken by members of the Commission . . . Employers have declared themselves to be in favour of the highest wage the economy can sustain . . . Employers' submissions tend to become ineffective if (to quote from the words of a member of the Commission) employers continue to adopt the traditional role of opposition to all union claims. The Working Party considers that it is possible for the attitude of employers to be determined from time to time according to stated governing policy, the general economic situation, and trading prospects. The Working Party has expressed the view that employers should discontinue traditional automatic opposition to basic wage increases on each occasion . . . Employers should not then be so vulnerable to criticism from the Bench, from trade unions, from political parties and from other sections of the community, that they have been proved wrong on each occasion that they have claimed that basic wage increases could not be afforded. The Working

> Party considers that the employers' policy should be flexible so that appropriate decisions can be made according to the circumstances existing at any time. (ACEF Meeting 15–16/10/59, Industrial Report)

The Working Party's suggestions were not without their complications. The Policy Committee and the Working Party had a mandate to carry Basic Wage proceedings through to finality without reference to other employer organisations only in cases where straight-out opposition was contemplated. The proposals therefore entailed a reversion to the previous situation in which employer organisations formulated policy on each occasion in which a major test case was presented. The ACEF was determined that this would not result in a reversion to the old *ad hoc* situation, but rather in some formalised and permanent arrangement. The ACEF raised this question with other members of the Committee and Working Party (ACEF Circular 83/1959, 1/9/59). For good measure it resolved that its newly appointed Executive Director be seconded to the Working Party for the 1960 Basic Wage case, 'that it be the objective of this Council that it be represented by its own officer in subsequent Basic Wage cases; that for that purpose, the question is to be further reviewed at the conclusion of the 1960 case, including the representation of employers collectively at further cases' (ACEF Meeting 15/10/59). Other members of the Policy Committee found these arguments persuasive, or were moved by the ACEF's new-found ability to act independently at national cases through its Executive Director. The establishment of a formal national organisation of employer organisations became a common objective of Committee members, resulting in the establishment of the National Employers' Associations in 1961.

Summary and conclusion

The decade under review was one of consolidating the developments of the wartime period. Though in the early part of the decade the ACEF experienced organisational problems, which hampered its ability to maximise the potential for growth, by the end of the decade it had abandoned public relations and political liaison functions and concentrated its resources on industrial relations functions. Its internal problems reflected an inherent weakness of its federation structure in which any dominant member could become the source of strong divisions. They also reflected difficulties about power sharing between affiliates, as well as personality clashes. The fact that the other important employer organisations of the day — the ACMA, ACCA, AMIA and GFCA — were similarly constituted, and thus potentially the subjects of similar internal organisational problems, added to the

ACEF's difficulties in trying to establish some permanent and formal national co-ordinating machinery.

The need for such machinery became more obvious during the decade. The Ministry of Labour Advisory Committee made demands on the five major organisations that they were not properly equipped to handle. The regular MLAC meetings further necessitated a high degree of co-ordination between the ACMA, ACEF, ACCA, MTEA and the GFCA at a time when no recognised machinery existed for this purpose. The frequent complaints of the Prime Minister and the Minister for Labour and National Service concerning the need for a single employer voice was another factor, the importance of which became greater with the demise of the MLAC and the loss of direct access to the Minister by employer representatives. Attempts at constitutional reform, the needs of ILO conferences, industrial legislation and the question of penal sections, Long Service leave provisions, and the perceived need to counteract ACTU activities were all quoted as factors necessitating some permanent co-ordinating machinery. By far the most important factor, however, was the abandonment of cost-of-living adjustments in 1953 in favour of periodic reviews of the basic wage. Such reviews became yearly after 1956 and incorporated a greater degree of economic evidence and sophistication than had been the case in the past. This of necessity created the need for a better research base for employer submissions. As the Policy Committee came to take over other cases such as the metal margins cases, the white collar and professional margins cases and the Long Service Leave case, the need for a permanent research base became evident. The frequency of 'general' cases also made it desirable to create some permanent apparatus for administering the considerable amounts of money involved.

These needs did result in the Policy Committee and the Working Party being placed on a permanent basis, albeit with a very limited mandate. The ACEF's continued efforts to create a Confederation of Employers, however, continued to fall on barren ground despite early prospects of success. The ACEF's own internal instability removed its ability to pursue the matter as forcibly as it might otherwise have done. By the time the ACEF had restored internal order, the need for a Confederation had become less urgent for most employers. They had scored a significant success in 1953 in having the Arbitration Court reverse its historic attitude towards automatic Basic Wage indexation, and the Labor split gave an assurance of Coalition rule in the foreseeable future. Organisations considered the *ad hoc* co-ordinating machinery that existed as adequate for most of the period. In addition to these inhibitors, there existed a number of organisational problems that loomed larger than the potential advantages of any Confederation. One of these was the historic legacy of previous co-operative venture failures. This involved not only the Canberra Secretariat, but also, as the GFCA reminded the ACEF, the Sydney-based research service, which it had continued to sponsor after the other instigators had pulled out. The GFCA expressed the view that it 'had little faith in the effective permanency of employer organisations' efforts in joint undertakings'. It also indicated a problem for federal organisations in 'being over-organised with too many affiliations'. A Confederation could have reduced the status of the organisations constituting the Policy Committee and the Working Party, and could lead, in the GFCA's view, to the duplication of activities and to the government 'brushing aside the view of substantial minorities'. Further, though by the 1950s the ACEF affiliates had largely settled on the question of federal regulation of standard employment conditions, this matter was still one that divided other organisations, including the ACMA. Organisational rivalry also intruded. The ACMA considered itself as the 'accepted leading employer organisation' in major cases, the ACEF that it was the only non-sectional organisation capable of representing all employers. Trade considerations were also paramount and the ACMA considered a Confederation 'impossible of achievement because of the diversity of interests represented and the fact that the only common ground is that we are all employers'. Even when the ACEF tried to convince organisations that the Confederation would have only industrial relations functions, problems persisted. Many organisations, such as the Coal Proprietors, the Wool and Meat Producers and the GFCA considered that their own industries had special and unique problems. The GFCA claimed good industrial relations was essentially a matter for individual industries and individual employers. In short, though there were pressing reasons for adopting better co-ordinating machinery, these were not seen as sufficiently pressing, nor sufficiently general in their ramifications, to overcome the antipathy of most organisations — particularly when they were opposed by the ACMA.

As in the past, the ACMA remained a major hurdle to the ACEF's dream of a Confederation. Why did it remain obdurate in its opposition? In other chapters the issue of tariff protection was suggested as a major cause of division between the ACMA and ACEF. Though the ACMA continued in its ultra-protectionist stance and continued to lobby against the General Agreement on Trade and Tariffs (GATT) and the Japanese Trade Treaty (Hall 1971:824), the question of protection did not appear a major stumbling block in ACMA–ACEF relations in the 1950s. Whatever the views of commercial and trading interests affiliated to employers' federations, the ACEF's official position was one of support for the McEwen policy of post-war development under the umbrella of protection. The ACMA's aloofness towards other organisations, which at times bordered on disdain, may have been the result of its successful protectionist strategy. For the Chambers of Manufactures this was a golden decade. As their resources increased, so did the ACMA's dominant position among national employer organisations. By the end of the period the ACMA had greater access to government Ministers by way of its Canberra headquarters. Its representation on the MLAC had been increased to three times that of any other employer organisation. Together with the ACEF it had nominating rights over Australian employer representatives at ILO Conferences. Its President chaired meetings of the Policy Committee, while an affiliate's Industrial Officer was Convenor of the Working Party. To the ACMA, a Confederation represented a potential dilution of its dominant position — a major reason for the ACEF's interest in such a body.

Notes

1 In this case the High Court determined that the same tribunal could not perform both judicial and arbitral functions. This resulted in the Commonwealth Court of Conciliation and Arbitration being replaced by the Commonwealth Industrial Court (subsequently renamed the 'Industrial Division of the Federal Court') and the Conciliation and Arbitration Commission (renamed the 'Australian Conciliation and Arbitration Commission').

2 Up to this day the VEF has been reluctant to provide any list of affiliated associations. Other federations publish such lists in their annual reports.

3 For greater details concerning Confederation attempts during this and other periods see D. Plowman, 'The Origins of the Confederation of Australian Industry', 1988.

4 The formation and composition of the AMIA is discussed in the next chapter.

7

THE NATIONAL EMPLOYERS' ASSOCIATIONS 1960–1972

The previous chapter reviewed developments in the 1950s. Though the ACEF had still not been able to persuade other organisations of the need for a Confederation of Employers, developments during that decade provided a firm basis for the introduction of better and more permanent machinery for co-ordinating employers' national test case submissions. By the end of the decade both the Policy and Consultative Committee and the Basic Wage Working Party had been constituted as standing bodies. By then, too, the ACEF had provided for the appointment of an Executive Director capable of overseeing its national industrial service, while the ACMA had established an industrial service.

Developments on the national wage front, and in particular the major wage gains won by unions at the Basic Wage and Metal Trades Margins cases of 1959, forced the Policy and Consultative Committee to review its traditional approach of straight-out opposition to union claims. In order to determine policy on a case-by-case basis without a return to the *ad hoc* approach that had previously prevailed, the National Employers' Associations (NEA) was formed in 1961. This loose-knit organisation met as required and provided the funds for test cases. The conduct of the cases was administered by two NEA Committees, a Policy Committee and an Industrial Committee. These Committees resembled, in most respects, the Policy and Consultative Committee and the Basic Wage Working Party.

The NEA was the vehicle of the employers' major triumph of the period — the adoption of the total wage in 1967. Its ability to bring about employer unity, however, was hampered by other wage developments and the move to 'accommodative bargaining' in the mid-1960s. Of particular significance for employer unity was the split in employer ranks in the metal industry, the dissolution of the AMIA and the formation of the Metal Trades Industry Association (MTIA). The MTIA sought a system of 'collective negotiations' for its industry. This was opposed by other employers because of the potential wage flow-ons from the bench-mark award.

These developments are reviewed in this chapter, which covers the period 1960 to 1972. The latter date is associated with the formation of the Central Industrial Secretariat by the ACMA and ACEF as a counter to the rising pressures from national industry associations. This joint venture was to result eventually in the merger of both organisations and the formation of the Confederation of Australian Industry. The date is also associated with the ending of the post-war Coalition rule.

The total wage and its aftermath

The long post-war Menzies hegemony continued until his resignation as Prime Minister in January 1966. Whereas his period of office in the 1960s was marked by economic discontinuity, the remainder of the period was marked by political and industrial discontinuities. H. Holt, who replaced Menzies, drowned, and J. Gorton took over as Prime Minister in January 1968. He was replaced as Party Leader and Prime Minister by W. McMahon in March 1971. In December of the following year voters heeded Labor's slogan 'Its Time', and brought an end to 23 years of Coalition rule.

Government fiscal and monetary policies during most of the period were designed to prevent the economy from 'overheating'. Employers were particularly critical of the 'on–off' nature of these policies and attempted to have some consultative machinery established to enable them to have an input into economic policy formulation. The Government did not accede to these attempts but did establish the Committee of Economic Review (the Vernon Committee) in 1963 to which associations were invited to make submissions. The Committee's report was presented to Parliament in September 1965. The ACEF claimed that 'many of the matters contained in the report follow closely the submissions made by this Council'. It further noted that 'the Committee approves many of the submissions made by the employers in 1964 national arbitration proceedings. These submissions, of course, are substantially based upon the propositions put by this Council to the Vernon Committee' (ACEF Meeting 29/10/65, Supplementary Background Paper). The ACEF submissions, and those of employers at the

1964 Basic Wage case, reflected the major preoccupation of employers since 1960 — the abandonment of the bifurcated wages system and its replacement by one based on the total wage.

The large increases in the basic wage in 1959, together with the 28 per cent increase in margins in the same year, had caused the Policy Committee to evaluate its traditional approach of straight-out opposition to any wage increases at national test cases. One result of this evaluation was the formation of the National Employers' Association reviewed below. Two other outcomes were the greater use of economic expertise in the form of witnesses at national cases and the total wage campaign. The first part of this strategy soon had to be abandoned. By early 1965 the ACMA was advised that 'because of the vicious cross-examination by Mr Hawke on irrelevant and embarrassing matters witnesses have refused to give evidence. For this one reason no reputable economist would agree to give evidence for any consideration whatever . . . the Commission has indicated its disapproval of his conduct but found itself very doubtful of its powers to control him' (SACM 'Circular to Chambers' 16/2/65). Of particular note was the case of Dr J. Perkins from Melbourne University who had been called by employers to give evidence on the area of his expertise, the Balance of Payments. He sought protection from the Commission not to be cross-examined outside the field covered by his paper. Hawke successfully objected and Perkins elected not to give evidence and withdrew from the case.

Though the ACTU got the better of employers in respect of expert witnesses, in the long run the Policy Committee's strategy of 'positive' submissions, which offered wage concessions in return for the adoption of the total wage, paid off. So too, did its submissions for the abandonment of the basic wage when Full Benches indicated great difficulty in turning their backs on 60 years of history. Instead, the Policy Committee sought joint hearings in which one Full Bench would consider both the basic and secondary components of wages and thus give effect to total wage determination. This strategy proved successful. By 1966, employers had effectively won their total wage campaign. The 'total wage' principle was formally adopted by the Commission at the 1967 National Wage case (118 *CAR* 75).

As noted in the previous chapter, union dissatisfaction with the penal sanctions had brought about the demise of the Ministry of Labour Advisory Council. The employers' total wage success, which resulted in the Commission ordering a work evaluation of the Metal Trades Award, provided unions with an explosive vehicle for bringing about an emasculation of penal sanctions. This, in turn, led to metal industry employers seeking industrial peace through direct negotiations, a situation objected to by other employers concerned about the wage flow-ons. The outcome was to dissipate the employer solidarity that had been generated by the total wage campaign.

The Metal Trades Work Value case was an unwanted (though not unexpected)[1] outcome of the employers' total wage drive. In order to provide the appropriate bench-mark for total wage adjustments, the 1966 Full Bench directed that the Metal Trades Award be work valued. It is apparent that the Commission took account of the Vernon Report published in 1965, which considered over-award payments (or the 'wages drift' as economists increasingly came to call these payments) as a threat to full employment and economic growth, as a source of inflation, and as a reduction in the status and authority of the Commission. Over-award payments further indicated that the Commission's awards were not set at the maximum that the economy could afford — the avowed aim since the abandonment of automatic cost-of-living adjustments in 1953. Whatever the original intention of the work value exercise, it soon degenerated into one of seeking to remove over-award payments in the industry. Thus, the fitters' award rate was increased by $7.40 per week (about 16 per cent) — the amount of over-award pay claimed for this classification in the 1966 National Wage case.[2] The majority judgement of December 1967 provided that employers could 'absorb' out of over-award payments the increases awarded. A bitter absorption struggle ensued and the Commission was forced to reopen the case. In February it ordered that 70 per cent of the increases granted in the original decision be paid as from 22 January 1968 and the '30 per cent residual' be deferred until the National Wage case of that year. By strong industrial action metal unions had broken the authority of the Commission and forced it to rescind an important decision. Equally strong action by other unions made nonsense of the Bench's ruling that, as a work value case, wage increases to metal workers were not to be automatically passed onto others.

It was in this industrial climate that Clarrie O'Shea, Secretary of the Victorian branch of the Australian Tramway and Motor Omnibus Employees' Association, was gaoled for contempt of Court. The case was both unusual and bizarre and highlighted the problems caused by the division of arbitral and judicial functions when the body concerned with the latter function took no account of the industrial implications of its actions (Sykes and Glasbeek 1972:521–6). O'Shea's gaoling brought about combined union agitation for the removal of the penal provisions of the Act. A national stoppage was averted when the union's fine was paid anonymously and the Government amended the Act to remove employers' direct access to the Industrial Court. The ACEF and other national employer associations, which, up until 1969, had paid scant regard to the ACTU pressure for changes to the penal provisions of the Act, now became actively involved in National Labour Advisory Council deliberations designed to bring about greater harmony between the Conciliation and Arbitration Commission and Industrial Court activities.[3] The Policy Committee's attempts at formulating the employers' approach to these deliberations was a further source of charged divisions between those who considered any dilution of the penal provisions was a capitulation to industrial muscle and those who considered that a pragmatic assessment of realities made such a hard line impractical. In the final outcome these changes to the Act preserved penalties but removed the automatic enforcement of awards by the Industrial Court. Before the Court could be approached for the imposition of any penalty a certificate had to be obtained from the Commission. In the first instance the Commission would seek the settlement of the dispute. Because of the Commission's vested interest in dispute prevention and settlement, the effect of these provisions was to force employers away from using the penal sanctions.

EMPLOYER UNITY AND DISUNITY

ACEF initiatives

Mr G. Polites was appointed the ACEF's Executive Director at the beginning of 1960. Under his direction its activities increased as did its influence. Within 3 years the professional staff had grown to four. Over the period its annual budget increased by $12 000 to $45 000. The latter figure was supplemented by earnings of between $10 000 and $20 000 from the ACEF's industrial services to national companies. In a period of unparalleled internal stability, the only organisational problem was the QEF's continued parlous financial position, which prevented it from contributing its apportioned share (13 per cent) of ACEF levies.

In 1962 the ACEF determined to extend its influence further by providing for associate membership of national organisations. By January 1965 the method of incorporating Associate Members had become crystallised. The ACEF would continue to function as a body of affiliated federations, which would have overall charge of policy and financial matters. In addition to the meetings of Secretaries (now called Executive Directors) and of the members of the Executive, provision would be made for the establishment of a General Council that would enable Associate Members to participate in policy debates. The proposed General Council was to consist of the ACEF's President, Immediate Past President, Vice-President, Life Members and Treasurer; the Presidents and two delegates from each member federation; and two delegates from each Associate Member. Associate Members were to have no rights in relation to the management of the ACEF; could attend Council meetings on the invitation of the Council; were to have similar aims and objectives as the ACEF; were to be national organisations; and their state branches, if any, were to be members of state federations (ACEF Meeting of Executive Officers 25/1/65).

A Special General Meeting in October 1965 voted for the rule changes providing for the General Council. Within a short time the Employers' Federation of Papua New Guinea, the Northern Territory Employers' Federation, the Australian Capital Territory Employers' Federation, the Australian Federation of Civil Engineering Contractors and the Australian Farmers' Federation had been admitted to associate membership. The two territory federations were subsequently admitted to full membership.

At much the same time, developments in the metal industry also brought the ACEF into a closer relationship with its historic rival, the ACMA. In January 1971 Polites reported on the 'various negotiations which have taken place between member Federations and other organisations regarding the establishment of closer co-operation and possible merger'. He also reported on 'discussions which had been held with ACMA in regard to this question at the National level' (ACEF Meeting 29–30/4/71, Background Paper: 10). A Joint Working Party was established to liaise on the formation of a joint industrial secretariat. This national co-operation venture stimulated similar ventures at the state level and in July 1971 the QEF reported on the outcome of talks with the Queensland Chamber of Manufactures. Agreement had been reached whereby the chamber would lease premises to the federation as a first step in bringing the organisations into a closer working relationship. The chamber proposed changing the name of its building from 'Manufacturers' House' to 'Industry House' to help with the transfer. A 'co-ordination of services was planned' (Letter, James to Polites, 6/7/71). Merger plans were also in train in Tasmania and Western Australia.

By November 1971 the Joint Working Party had produced a 'working document' for consideration by the two organisations in which it was proposed that the Central Industrial Secretariat would come into operation on 1 January 1972 and would 'act in national and international industrial affairs on behalf of the constituent members of ACMA and ACEF and would be financed jointly by the two organisations' (ACEF Meeting 11–12/11/71).

Despite the previous long history of the ACEF's collaborative attempts being aborted, both organisations saw value in merging their national industrial relations divisions. The ACEF resolved to accept the establishment of the Secretariat on the terms and arrangements set out by the Working Party. This provided for both the ACEF and ACMA to contribute $32 500 towards the operation of the Secretariat for the year 1972 (ibid.).

Polites was appointed Director of the Secretariat. By then the ACEF's pivotal role in national employer co-ordination was highlighted in its 1972 Annual Report (pp 1–2). This noted that under the direction of Polites the Secretariat took over a number of functions previously carried out independently by each organisation. The Report further noted:

> The new organisation has allowed for much closer co-operation between Employers' Federations and Chambers of Manufactures throughout Australia and has brought greater unity of purpose into industrial policy. The Council has continued to provide Secretarial and administrative services to the NEA, following the re-election of the Executive Director as Secretary of the Policy Committee and as Convenor of the National Employers' Industrial Committee. The Council also provides specialised services to a number of international industrial corporations. The Secretariat has also continued its work of co-ordinating the activities of member Federations in a number of major industry arbitration matters.

The ACMA and the metal employers' split

If the ACEF's star was in the ascendancy during the period, that of the ACMA was on the wane. During the 1950s the ACMA had virtual control of the Policy Committee and the Working Party. The ACMA's President was Chairman of the former and the VCM's Chief Industrial Officer was Convenor of the latter. With the reconstruction of these two bodies under the National Employers' Association (NEA) umbrellas the ACMA lost that degree of control. The Chairmanship of the renamed National Employers' Policy Committee rotated between the constituents and it was also intended that the position of Convenor of the National Employers' Industrial Committee (the renamed Basic Wage Working Party). The Convenor was to act as Secretary to the NEA and the Policy Committee. In fact D. Fowler (AMIA) held the position until 1967 and Polites took over for the next decade. As noted in the previous chapter, the ACMA set out to establish an industrial department in the 1960s. This Canberra-based Department proved no match for the ACEFs Industrial Service. When B. French resiged as Chief Industrial Officer in 1968 he was not replaced. The loss of its Victorian metal trades division further reduced the ACMA's dominance.

As a major component of the manufacturing industry, the metal employer bodies had developed good relations with the ACMA over the years. In 1942 the Australian Metal Industries Association (AMIA) had been formed. In this conglomerate the Metal Trades Employers' Association was given an effective monopoly of metal trades employers in New South Wales and Queensland. In the other states they were represented by way of the chambers. In Victoria the Engineering and Allied Trades Divisions catered for such employers and in South Australia the Metal Industry Association of South Australia (MIASA) was affiliated with the AMIA. Though a separately registered organisation, the MIASA was effectively a Division of that state's chamber. In Tasmania and Western Australia, metal employers were members of the respective chambers. In the latter state the WAEF undertook the industrial relations work of the chamber. Thus it can be seen that the AMIA consisted of an industry association with respect to two states and sections of umbrella or inter-industry organisations with close connections with the ACMA in other states.

In 1942 the ACMA and AMIA had established a joint Secretariat in Canberra. After the war the ACMA continued to provide liaison services and a Canberra office for the MTEA. This relationship was dissolved in 1962 when the MTEA decided to 'discontinue its formal link with ACMA'. The letter of intent indicated 'that this was not to be considered as being a break in policies between the two organisations but had been brought about by a desire to concentrate resources and efforts on one national organisation' (EATD Meeting 28/1/62). In its desire to replace the metal industry conglomerate with a single industry association the MTEA resigned from the AMIA the following year and established a Victorian office in competition with the VCM's Engineering Division.

To forestall the MTEA push the Engineering Division was reconstituted with a large measure of autonomy as the Metal Industries Association Victoria (MIAV). It was registered under that name in 1966. However, by 1970 the MTEA had persuaded this organisation to merge with it to form the Metal Trades Industry Association (MTIA). The MTIA was particularly successful in attracting all but one of the former 16 MIAV staff to its Melbourne office.[4]

The formation of the MTIA did not alleviate the philosophical problems giving rise to its formation. The bench-mark role of the Metal Trades Award had made it difficult for employers in that industry to enter into negotiated settlements with metal unions. Invariably metal margins cases became test cases, resulting in a host of intervenors and necessarily a conservative settlement to unions' claims. Unlike employers in most other industries, those in the metal industry were not in a position to negotiate freely and independently over award matters. This constraint limited the metal employers' associations' ability to buy industrial peace and added to the overaward problems in the industry. The MTIA sought to overcome these shackles by the creation of an industry association that would negotiate with unions by way of 'collective conciliation within the legal framework'. To multi-industry associations such as the federations and the VCM such a policy was an industrially naive one. Flow-ons from metal industry settlements were inevitable and so those likely to be affected had a right to be consulted and to participate in the outcome. The VCM set out to regain lost territory. Its newly appointed Director, Mr I. Macphee, announced in early 1971:

> for many years the VCM has rightly rejoiced in the fact that it is the largest employer organisation in the Southern Hemisphere. This Chamber, like the other State Chambers, has provided a diversified set of services for a very wide range of industry groups. By far the largest of these is the Metal Industries Group. Because of its size and special problems, arrangements are now being made to provide all metal members with a far more extensive service than has been provided previously . . . This service will be more comprehensive and more effective, both on a national level and state level, than has so far been provided for this beleaguered industry by any employer organisation (VCM Director's Address to Council 18/2/71).

The Metals Industry Department was established shortly afterwards with C. Mews, who had refused to move across to the MTIA with other former MIAV colleagues, as Manager. This Department, with its sizeable membership and the resources of the VCM behind it, was in a position to compete with the MTIA for policy influence in the metal industry.

For the remainder of the period, relations between the VCM (and by implication ACMA) and the MTIA (which had now taken the AMIA's place on the NEA's Policy and Industrial Committees) remained strained. By 1972 the MTIA was seeking to put into effect its policy by having National Wage cases abandoned in favour of industry-by-industry negotiations. It had unilaterally entered into negotiations with metal unions to this end. This necessarily brought it into conflict not only with the VCM but also with other members of the Policy and Industrial Committees, which, over the previous decade, had devised machinery for handling national cases. The fact that metal employers were not alone in seeking a stronger industry association — similar developments were taking place in the printing, coal mining, stevedoring, civil engineering and construction, woolbroking, banking, motor retail trade, hotel, petroleum and primary industries — helped to strengthen the ACEF–ACMA axis. As the Melbourne newspaper *The Age* recognised, industry associations could be at the expense of 'general employer groups'. This paper (1/10/71) commented:

> In the past four years the MTIA and the VCM have been involved in an all-out contest for members. Both the Chambers and the Employers Federations believe they should rightfully represent all employers and that the development of industry associations and agreements is a bad trend. They see the long-term effect on the general employer groups as a dissolution of their power in the face of increasingly powerful industry associations.

The potential for industry groups to dissolve the power of 'general associations' led to greater collaboration at the state and federal levels and, as noted above, the formation of the Central Industrial Secretariat.

The National Employers' Associations

The major national co-ordination machinery in 1960 consisted of the Policy and Consultative Committee and the Basic Wage Working Party, both of which had been constituted as standing bodies in December 1958. Three organisations — the ACEF, ACMA and AMIA — had representation on each body, and the Graziers' Federal Council of Australia was entitled to a representative on the Working Party. The first two organisations each contributed 25 per cent of the funds and the AMIA 10 per cent. The remaining funds were contributed by 38 other organisations. Of these the GFCA contributed 3 per cent of the total funds.

The wage decisions of 1959 in which the basic wage was increased by 5.7 per cent and margins by as much as 28 per cent had caused the Policy Committee to reconsider its traditional approach to union claims, an approach increasingly being criticised by the Commission. A more positive approach, however, was not without its complications. The Committee had a mandate to carry out basic wage cases without reference to other organisations only in cases where straight-out opposition was contemplated. Machinery enabling national policy to be determined on a case-by-case basis gave rise to the possibility of a return to the *ad hoc* situation that had existed prior to 1958. The Committee was therefore amenable to the ACEF's offer to propose plans for new co-ordinating machinery that would maintain the existing status of the Committee and the Working Party yet provide an avenue for other national organisations to be involved with policy formulation as cases arose.

In May 1960 the ACEF presented restructuring proposals for consideration by the Policy Committee. These envisaged the renaming of the

Committee and the Working Party as the 'National Employers' Policy Committee' (NEPC) and the 'National Employers' Industrial Committee' (NEIC) respectively. It proposed that the three major organisations constituting the Policy Committee and Working Party would continue to nominate representatives to the newly named bodies, but that the Graziers' Federal Council also be able to make an appointment to each Committee. It further proposed that the Convenor of the Industrial Committee act as Secretary of the Policy Committee. The functions of the former would be 'to supervise matters associated with the conduct of national industrial proceedings and the raising and control of funds for the purpose of financing those proceedings'. The Industrial Committee would be responsible for the 'detailed conduct of national proceedings including the engaging of advocates, witnesses and other persons' and 'general industrial, statistical and economic research in relation to pending and future national proceedings'. In addition, the ACEF proposed the establishment of machinery that would enable a loose-knit body of other national organisations 'to be consulted from time to time to decide the policy in connection with national proceedings including the question of finance'. This envisaged the calling together by the Chairman of the Policy Committee of contributing national associations. The ACEF proposed a list of 40 such associations that it considered ought to be involved in the consultative processes (ACEF 'Re-Constitution of Policy and Consultative Committee etc.' n.d. (May 1960)).

These proposals were considered at a mass meeting of associations in February 1961. This unanimously agreed to the following ACEF resolution:

> For the purpose of effectively safeguarding the interests of employers in national industrial proceedings and recognising that effective action can be achieved only on the basis of proper co-ordination between major national associations of employers, this meeting of National Employers' Associations resolves:
>
> 1. The National Employers' Associations shall meet not less than twice per annum for the purpose of considering generally policy in connection with actual or pending national industrial proceedings and over-all questions of finance relating thereto.
> 2. There shall be a National Employers' Policy Committee which shall consist of one representative (other than Officer) from each of the following National Employers' Associations:
>
> Associated Chambers of Manufactures of Australia
> Australian Council of Employers' Federations
> Australian Metal Industries Association
> Australian Woolgrowers' and Graziers' Council

The Policy Committee shall elect at a convenient time each year one of its members to act as Chairman.

The Policy Committee shall arrange the conduct of its business in such manner as it may from time to time decide. It shall be responsible to the National Employers' Associations for:

(i) General supervision of the conduct of national industrial proceedings.
(ii) The raising and the control of funds for the purpose of financing national industrial proceedings.
(iii) The calling of general meetings.

3. There shall be a National Employers' Industrial Committee. It shall consist of one officer with industrial experience nominated by each member association of the Policy Committee.

It shall from time to time nominate for the approval of the Policy Committee one of its members to act as Convenor, who shall also act as Secretary to the Policy Committee.

Subject to the direction by the Policy Committee, the functions of the Industrial Committee shall include:

(i) The detailed conduct of national industrial proceedings.
(ii) General industrial, statistical and economic research in relation to pending and future national industrial proceedings.

The meeting also voted a levy of $20 000 to finance the 1961 Basic Wage case (NEA Meeting 7/2/61).

In addition to these proposals, 'Working Rules' for the Committees were accepted. These, in summary form, provided for each member of the NEPC 'to have the right to be accompanied at any meeting by one adviser, in addition to an officer who is a member of the NEIC'; the NEPC to meet as required but in any event not less than bi-monthly; and 'the power to co-opt and engage expert assistance if and when necessary' (ACEF Meeting 23–24/2/61, Attachments A-B).

The inaugural meeting of the NEPC was held on 15 June and H. Robinson of the ACEF was elected first Chairman. In the same month the ACEF endorsed the decision of the NEPC that there should be no increase in the membership of the NEPC or NEIC. ACEF also agreed that the powers of both committees should be widened to encompass matters outside national arbitration proceedings, if such matters were referred for consideration of the Committees by the NEA (ACEF Secretaries Meeting 26/6/61). The NEA approved constitutional changes to this effect in July 1962.

In August 1962 the NEIC sought further constitutional changes enabling the NEPC to become involved in industrial proceedings not involving arbitration 'if the ACTU or any other composite body of national Trade Unions is involved in any way in any industrial matter, the NEPC shall be empowered to intervene and act if requested by a subscribing member' (NEIC Meeting 10/8/62). The major reason for this was to give the NEPC greater flexibility. It was also 'felt that, having regard to recent disputes, such as the dispute between the Clerks' Union and Ford Motor Company, and the Queerah Meat Works dispute, which was referred to the NEIC, that some flexibility should be given to the NEPC to enable it to act on behalf of employers generally in these matters, if they were truly national in character' (NEPC Circular 28/9/62). A meeting of the NEA adopted the proposed changes in December. No further changes were made until the formation of the National Employers' Consultative Committee in 1970 (see below).

In his report for 1963 NEPC Chairman H. W. Robinson noted that the NEA had developed 'into the organisation now accepted as being responsible for the formulation of wages policy on behalf of employers generally in arbitration proceedings and national affairs'. He also announced the objective of a 'positive wages policy, freed from the anomalies which followed the last Metal Trades decision and which will demand every effort and skill, with unity of thought and action' (NEA Meeting 16/8/63).

The total wage campaign that accompanied this 'positive wages policy' resulted in a degree of national employer unity and co-ordination not previously witnessed. Groups, particularly the rural interests, that experienced special problems were able to subordinate their industries' special needs to those of the NEPC's objective. Where previously the Policy and Consultative Committee had been able to get united policy only by stooping to the lowest common denominator, which resulted in total opposition to unions' claims, under the NEPC, employers were able to agree on policies that provided the Commission scope for wage increases. Changes in the NEA's constitution permitted an expansion of NEPC activities beyond those of national wage cases. National organisations, which had not previously lent support to the national bodies, came to show an interest in their operations. In addressing the Annual Convention of such an organisation, the Master Builders' Federation of Australia, NEPC Secretary D. Fowler noted that the 'emergence of the NEPC was a manifestation of the gradual unfolding of a movement within the employer organisational structure to have at the apex a body which symbolises leadership and co-ordination of employer thinking at the national level'. 'Each one of the 66 employers' organisations registered under the Act', Fowler said,

> covers a particular industry or occupation. Apart from the registered organisations, there are linked organisations not registered, the function of which is to co-ordinate the policies of an industry or an occupation on a national basis . . . Only in the last five years has emerged the NEPC which is a

> monumental recognition that the divisions of the past are buried, and employers' organisations are going forward, united and strong. The compulsive need for a closer working relationship among the major employer organisations was recognised and consummated. Unity in this sense need not necessarily be synonymous with unanimity . . . It must be apparent by now that the promulgation and pursuance of a Total Wage Plan would never have been possible prior to the emergence of the NEPC ('The NEPC: Its Work and Value to Employers', Address to MBFA Annual Convention 27/10/66, mimeograph).

Even as Fowler spoke, however, the Metal Trades Margins Inquiry had intensified divisions between the MTEA and VCM. Because of the national nature of the Inquiry, and the AMIA's membership of the NEPC and NEIC, it was but a matter of time before such divisions were elevated to a national level. Increasingly, the forces leading the MTEA to seek a national industry association, the basis of its confrontation with the VCM, also led to confrontations at the national level as metal employers sought to free metal industry negotiations from the encumbrances and scrutiny of other organisations. This led not only to policy differences within the NEPC, but also to the MTEA/MTIA seeking organisational changes that would increase the role of national industry organisations within the NEA. The MTIA was in conflict with other NEA members over the conduct of the Metal Trades Work Value case (1967), the '30 per cent residual' and 1968 National Wage cases, and the Equal Pay case (1969). Its attempts to deal with unions outside arbitration were also a source of aggravation to NEA members.

Illustrative of employer divisions over wages policy is the NEA meeting of October 1970 in which the Australian Mines and Metals Association complained of the independent action of the MTIA in the making of new awards for the metal trades and for engine driver and firemen classifications in its industry. The MTIA responded that 'many industries were now negotiating within the framework of the arbitration system and the MTIA had the same right'. The Australian Wool Growers' and Graziers' Council (AWGC) indicated the peculiar problem of unilateral action in the metal industry 'in that whatever happened in the metal trades would affect other awards . . . hence they should have had an opportunity to make some observations in relation to the issues involved'. To the MTIA claim that it 'was concerned with and would like to see the elimination of the 'test case' atmosphere which surrounds the award', the AWGC responded that 'although this may be desirable, the realities of the situation seem to make such a concept impossible'. Feelings ran sufficiently high for the MTIA to be threatened with expulsion from the NEA, a move that would have reduced even further the peer group pressures being exerted on it (NEPC Circular 14/10/71).

As a result of such divisions the ACEF informed its members that both the NEPC and NEIC 'were under strain' and added:

> One lesson which seems to emerge from these events is that the NEPC cannot expect to conduct a Metal Industry Case on behalf of that industry's association in the future. It would seem that the Policy Committee's role must be confined in present circumstances to general matters which affect all employers with equal force and which further must be of the type which precludes any argument that one group has a special position, for there does not yet appear to be sufficient willingness present in all member associations of the National Employers' group to hand over the conduct of industry affairs, no matter how specialised, to a central body. (ACEF Meeting 21-22/11/86 Background Paper)

Trying to steer clear of industry matters and limiting activities to 'general matters', which 'affected all employers with equal force', did not prove easy as long as any dominant group persisted with its 'special position' viewpoint or in setting a wage pace that created flow-ons. Thus, the NEA, which had been created in the united atmosphere of the total wage drive, found itself incapable of reaching common policy in the climate of accommodative bargaining that followed the adoption of the total wage. Disagreements about wages policy also brought calls from a number of industry associations for a restructuring of the NEPC so as to reduce the dominant role of the umbrella organisations — the ACEF, ACMA and the AWGC — or for the creation of a more formal organisation, which would be less dependent on the 'big four'. The ACEF, which for nearly 40 years had been active in seeking employer support for a national confederation, was, after 1960, the major opponent of such a development. Such opposition may have reflected its endeavours to ensure that its own dominant position was not eroded. Equally, it may well have reflected the ACEF's public position, namely that employers' interests at this time were better served by a loose-knit organisation such as the NEA.

Early in 1967 the AMIA formally requested the NEPC to consider 'the question of possible reorganisation of the NEPC'. It requested that consideration be given to the appointment of a permanent staff; 'the examination of the Constitution to ensure that it meets present day needs'; and the method of finance. Members agreed to 'consider these and cognate matters' (NEPC Meeting 1/3/67). In discussing this development ACEF reported that 'there is no doubt that other people have been pushing a similar view' and that 'one officer' of the AMIA was forcibly trying to bring about such changes. 'It is interesting to note', the paper added, 'that the pressure for change has quickened since the internecine dispute between members of AMIA has developed. Certain members of AMIA outside the two major groups of ACEF and ACMA seem to be the spearhead of the view and the movement to increase the power of the NEPC. One explanation of this attitude is that it is an attempt to create a climate for the promotion of that organisation to direct membership of the NEA'.

The report noted that 'the whole function of the NEPC and the NEIC needs to be reviewed before any real decision can be taken. There is no genuine support on the part of employers, except perhaps in some very isolated areas for the proposal that the Committees should be on a permanent basis and a permanent organisation take over from the present loose-knit group'. The costs of such an operation would militate against its acceptance by employers generally. The costs in both money and in prestige to the two major bodies of the ACEF and ACMA would probably make it unacceptable to them and thus place the whole concept in jeopardy (ACEF Meeting 20–21/4/67 Background Paper:6–8). It should be noted that the ACEF and ACMA collectively contributed 50 per cent of the running costs of the NEA and its Committees. The ACEF resolved that 'it was of the view that the interests of employers generally are best served by building and strengthening the present structure rather than by, at this time, making any permanent staff appointments or substantially altering the rules'. (ACEF Meeting 20–21/4/67). There was little support for the AMIA proposal.

The formation of the National Labour Advisory Council at this time brought new pressures from the AMIA for a more formal body, which would determine employer representation on that Council. The ACMA, ACEF and AWGC had been invited to nominate representatives to the Council. This situation contrasted with the former Council, the MLAC, in which the AMIA also had representation rights. The AMIA considered that the three organisations ought to relinquish their nomination rights to a more representative body such as the NEA. The ACEF and ACMA considered 'they could do nothing but accept the Government invitation' and refused the AMIA's request. Thus, while the major umbrella organisations were insisting that the metal industry association should allow the NEA to formulate wages policy for the metal industry, they themselves were not prepared to surrender to the NEA the determination of employer representatives to national tripartite discussions.

In October 1968 reconstruction moves were again put into motion by a letter from the Printing and Allied Trades Employers' Federation (PATEFA) seeking membership of the NEPC and NEIC. It would appear that this had been done at the instigation of the MTEA. At the NEPC meeting of that month, the ACEF sought a deferral of discussion to permit the 'constituent organisations of the NEPC to consider the matter'. The ACMA suggested that the NEIC first discuss the matter. AMIA delegate Morgan advised that his organisation had considered the matter and had approved the following resolution:

> That AMIA is of the opinion that PATEFA should be invited to join the NEPC because of the following points:
> 1. They are a national organisation.
> 2. [They] are able to provide a suitable national Industrial Officer to join and work with the NEIC.
> 3. They are of a significant size and cover a field outside the existing coverage.
> 4. They contribute not less than 5% of the total Annual Levy or Levies.

The AMIA also reported that its Executive had resolved that it was 'in the interests of National Employers that an independent Secretary be appointed by the NEPC'. The AMIA suggested that the NEA's firm of solicitors (Messrs Moule, Hamilton and Derham) be asked to provide a Secretary, on a part-time basis, and that the Rules of the NEA be altered accordingly. The AMIA further noted that it 'envisaged other organisations than the Printing Association being permitted to join the NEPC' (NEPC Meeting 8/10/68).

This new strategy in opening up the composition of the NEPC was one that could have had a degree of support from those organisations meeting the AMIA's criteria for admission to the Committees. Unlike other AMIA approaches, which had been frustrated through delaying tactics, this approach necessitated some counter-proposal. In the following month, the ACEF proposed the creation of an Advisory or Consultative Committee within the NEA that would have an input into policy formulation without diluting the position of NEPC members. The ACMA supported this ACEF plan, which was accepted by an NEA meeting in May 1970. The advisory committee was constituted in the following terms:

> (1) The proposed committee should be known as the National Employers Consultative Committee.
> (2) The Committee should consist of 9 members, being members for the time being of the NEPC and 5 members elected by members of NEA other than those who provide members of the NEPC.
> (3) Voting shall be by show of hands unless a member demands a poll when voting will be by secret ballot according to contributions — members being allocated 1 vote for each 1% contribution or part thereof to the NEA levies.
> (4) To be eligible for election to the Consultative Committee a candidate

must be a member of a Committee of Management or like body of a member Association and have the endorsement of that Committee.

(5) Members shall be elected annually at a meeting of the NEA called specifically for that purpose and shall hold office for one year.

(6) Any member of the Committee unable to attend a meeting may appoint a proxy. Such proxy shall comply with the provisions of paragraph 4.

(7) Casual vacancies on the Committee shall be filled by the remaining elected members of the Committee. The person appointed shall hold office for the balance of the term of the member replaced.

(8) The Committee shall meet, as required by circumstances, but shall hold at least two meetings in each calendar year.

(9) Minutes of the Meetings of the Consultative Committee to be made available to all NEA members, it being understood that Members of the Consultative Committee will receive NEPC and NEIC Minutes.

The Consultative Committee was formally established in June 1970 and began meeting in September of that year.[5] Though the NEPC met almost monthly in 1971 and the NEA itself met on 10 occasions in that year, the question of further restructuring of the NEA was not discussed. By then four other major considerations took greater priority. In the first place, there were significant changes contemplated to the *Conciliation and Arbitration Act* in the wake of the penal sanctions ruction. This consumed much of the NLCA activities and the NEPC attempted — with a high degree of success — to get a common employer approach to such amendments. On the political front employers sensed that internal ructions within the Liberal Party could bring about an end to the post-war Coalition rule. On the industrial front, test cases relating to the national wages, accident pay, hours of work, annual leave and the metal trades log also required a considerable degree of co-ordination. The metal trades log heightened the effects of the third over-riding consideration — organisational developments in the metal industry. By now the Metal Trades Industry Association had been brought into being and this organisation became a member of the NEA committees. The MTIA's independent activities in relation to the Metal Trades Log of Claims focused NEA activities on making the existing national co-ordination machinery work rather than seeking further changes.

In April 1971 ACEF Executive Council members were advised that it was clear from meetings of the National Employers' Consultative Committee that 'there was no general desire for substantial change to the rules of the group as it now exists'. While there would be 'some recommendations relating to the financing of the organisation and perhaps the nature of the NECC itself . . . it does not appear that any proposals for a formal reorganisation of employers will emerge'. Council members were also informed that the functioning of the NEA and its Committees would 'also need to be reviewed carefully in the light of the possible change in the relationship between this Council and ACMA. The Executive would need to give consideration to the rate at which any change in the structure of NEA is allowed to proceed if the suggestions in relation to ACMA and ACEF are likely to come to fruition' (ACEF Meeting 29-30/4/71, Background Paper:2-3). By then, as a reaction to the emergence of the MTIA, the ACEF–ACMA axis had developed to the extent that they were considering combining their industrial relations departments. The ACMA had already endorsed such a move by April 1971, when the ACEF agreed to the formation of a Working Party 'for the purpose of seeking to unify' the two organisations' industrial activities (ACEF Meeting 10/4/71).

In November 1971, by which time agreement had been reached on the creation of the Central Industrial Secretariat (CIS) in 1972, ACEF Executive Officers reported that the ACEF's best interests, and those of the ACMA, would be served by the preservation of the present loose-knit structure of the NEA and that it was undesirable to support proposals for the establishment of a more formal organisation. 'The present structure', they claimed,

> has enabled the parties to deal effectively with all the matters which have presented themselves to employers, as effectively as if there had been some formal organisation in existence, as it must be realised that no industrial organisation will totally abandon its right to make unilateral decisions if it believes that those decisions are in the best interests of its members. It is not considered that the creation of a formal organisation would alter this position and, therefore, no good purpose would be served by creating a new organisation which would substantially increase the costs of operations. (ACEF Executive Officers' Meeting 9–10/11/71)

At this time, these Officers were informed that the NEPC had 'been under some strain as, indeed, had the whole of the NEA. The strain has been caused in no small degree by the continued determination of the Metal Trades Industry group to pursue a unilateral course in industrial relations, whilst at the same time seeking to have its policies endorsed by the general body . . . This is an untenable position for the umbrella organisations and one which requires the urgent consideration of ACEF and ACMA if the CIS, which comes into operation in January 1972, is to operate meaningfully and in accordance with pre-determined policy directives' (ACEF Meeting 11-12/11/71, Background Paper: 2–3).

With no apparent difficulties, the two major organisations that had traditionally competed for industrial relations dominance were able to reach agreement on the CIS, which, with Polites as Director, began operations on 1 January 1972.

Summary and conclusion

The period under review was one of both great unity and disunity in employer ranks. The formation of the NEA brought into being the first continuing body for national employer co-ordination. The roles of the previous Policy and Consultative Committee and Basic Wage Working Party were subsumed under the NEA Committees that operated on a permanent basis and had charge of the conduct of all major cases on behalf of employers. This machinery was successful in containing wage costs through arbitration procedures and in having the Commission abandon the bifurcated wages system and adopt the total wage. Indeed, it could be argued that employers were sufficiently successful in arbitration cases to cause unions to seek wage increases outside arbitration. Though full employment and economic circumstances assisted in the unions' move outside the arbitration fold, if these conditions were sufficient in themselves for such a movement to take place, such a movement could have been expected to have taken place much earlier. By the time of the movement in the 1960s Australia had had some 30 years of relatively full employment.

The period was the era of National Employers' Associations in more than just the sense that an organisation so named helped to co-ordinate employer activities: this was an age of national employer associations also in the sense that during the period a number of national industry associations (and conversely unions) came into being. This chapter has documented the rise of one such organisation — the MTIA. As already noted, other industry associations also came into being or were restructured during the period. They operated in a wide range of industries — printing, the hotel industry, stevedoring, the maritime industry, oil refining, civil engineering, the private hospital industry, aviation, road transport, building and construction etc.). In addition, older established national associations, both umbrella federations — the ACEF and ACMA — and industry-based associations — AMIA, AWGC, PATEFA, MATFA, AMMA, ASOA, etc. — took a more federal stance in relation to their own industries and a more active role in national arbitration affairs.

In such a context, and in the context of wage *anomie* following the demise of the Commission's penal powers, the NEA and its Committees were able to prevent the return to the fragmentation that had characterised employer approaches to national cases. Relationships with the MTIA were strained and this organisation continued to be separately represented. The MTIA highlighted some of the problems confronting the emergent national industry associations in the context of a highly centralised wage determination system. It sought to free its awards of their bench-mark role and in the process sought the abandonment of National Wage cases. This necessarily brought it into conflict with national federations, which dominated the NEPC, and the possibility of expulsion from the NEA. This would have militated against its decentralist aims, which required the support of other associations.

For the national federations (as opposed to the national associations) the decentralist approach would have undermined the basis of their existence. Decentralised wage determination involving national industry associations was also a threat to the state affiliates of these national federations. For these reasons, and the compelling fact that they did not consider the MTIA capable of eradicating comparative wage justice, they opposed the MTIA's wage philosophy and its attempts to restructure the NEPC so as to reduce their influence. Other associations supported the ACEF–ACMA stance. They, of course, were not in the first line of battle as the MTIA was. It was not their members who bore the brunt of the metal workers' wage drives. Nor were they the associations pressured by governments and other employers to hold the line, while being equally pressured by their own members to find alternative wage mechanisms to the blood-letting industrial disputation accompanying the 'holding the line' approach.[6] To the MTIA, other associations wanted the best of both worlds: the ability to bargain freely with unions in their own supposedly 'special' industries, while denying this freedom to the MTIA because metal settlements would flow-on to other industries. On balance, the MTIA's independence had a limited impact on national proceedings. Governments had a vested interest in a unified employer approach to national policy matters and chose to exclude the AMIA (and subsequently the MTIA) from national forums such as the National Labour Advisory Council. The Commission followed a similar policy and prevented the MTIA from dividing employers' national wage submissions. In matters impinging more directly on industry matters, however, the MTIA's independent line was the cause of disunity. In arbitration proceedings, such as the 1969 Equal Pay case, hostilities between employers were sufficiently strong to cause ACTU advocate Hawke to comment: 'We think at the end of this table that we heard Mr. Robinson crying out a moment ago, "who needs enemies when you have friends like mine!"' (De Vyver 1972:32). It was outside of arbitration proceedings, however, that MTIA activities caused the greatest divisions. The NEA was relatively powerless to prevent these developments, though it is obvious that peer-group pressure did have a restraining effect on the MTIA. The organisational changes in the NEA to cope with this new situation — the formation of the National Employers' Consultative Committee — did not materially alter the situation.

The other major development resulting from the growth of industry organisations — the Central Industrial Secretariat — was to have a long lasting impact upon employer co-ordination. Both the ACMA and ACEF opposed moves to restructure the loose-knit NEA by the formation of a more formal national body. Ironically, the formation of the Secretariat paved the way for such a development.

Notes

[1] As early as 1963 the ACEF prepared a paper for discussion by the NEPC and NEIC entitled 'Some Observations on the "Total Wage Concept" and "Work Value"' in which it argued the inter-relationship between the two concepts (Polites 1963).

[2] More accurately the figure was that of boilermakers who had the same award rate as fitters.

[3] The National Labour Advisory Council was established in 1967. Its charter was similar to that of the Ministry of Labour Advisory Council discussed in the previous chapter.

[4] MTIA sources claim to have attracted all of the city-based metal industry members of the MIAV. The VCM denies this claim. In addition to country enterprises, the VCM claims that about half of the metal establishments, particularly the small and medium sized ones, remained members of the VCM. In an interview with the author in 1984 the industrial officer responsible for the metal division of the VCM claimed that the VCM represented half of the metal employers in Victoria.

[5] A special NEA meeting to elect members of the Consultative Committee was held on 27 July. There were seven nominations, the five successful ones being F. S. Anderson (Mines and Metals), E. A. Witts (Vehicle Manufactures Association), W. K. Jones (BHP), D. Holstock (Victorian Automobile Chamber of Commerce) and M. Farley (Printing Federation). J. S. Box (Master Builders) and E. W. Horton (Meat Trades Federation) were the unsuccessful candidates.

[6] For an account of the pressures exerted on the MTIA at this time see Collicoat 1972.

8

CONFEDERATION 1973–1988

The previous chapter reviewed developments in the period from 1960 when the National Employers' Associations (NEA) came into being, to 1972, when post-war Coalition rule ended. 1972 is also associated with the formation of the Central Industrial Secretariat by the merger of the ACMA's industrial relations division with the ACEF's national secretariat. Though the NEA maintained many of the voluntaristic elements of the previous co-ordinating machinery, it had a formal constitution. Further, its two committees, the National Employers' Policy Committee and the National Employers' Industrial Committee, had a wider mandate than their predecessors. The formation of the NEA resulted in a high degree of employer unity and the successful execution of the 'total wage' campaign. The new total wage environment, however, led to metal industry employers seeking the removal of the centralised wages system. This threatened the rationale of the NEA as well as the dominance of umbrella organisations such as the ACEF and the ACMA. It also resulted in major divisions within the NEA.

This chapter reviews national employer developments in the period from 1973 to 1980. It was during this period that a confederation, which subsumed the functions of the NEA, was finally brought into existence. Unlike the Confederation of Employers advocated by the ACEF and opposed by the ACMA in the earlier periods, however, the Confederation of Australian Industry (CAI) followed the British model and included a trade wing. Further, unlike earlier proposals that envisaged the ACEF maintaining its identity, the CAI was formed by changes to the ACMA's constitution, which provided for an ACEF merger, with the latter going out of existence. In a reversal of historic roles the ACMA came to support confederation moves and the ACEF to oppose. For a number of reasons, however, including the emergence of a new force — the 'Big 50' — the ACEF acceded to the ACMA merger. These developments are detailed in the second part of this chapter, which also reviews NEA operations to 1977 and CAI operations after that date. The first part of the chapter examines the industrial context, which was largely influenced by the Labor initiatives in the period to 1975. These wide ranging initiatives were not only an impetus to greater employer cohesion, they also cast a shadow on industrial relations developments in the years following Labor administration. The *ad hoc* approaches to wages policy by the Fraser Governments were also a cause of concern to employer associations. In the post-1983 period, the recentralisation of wage determination as part of the Labor Government's Accord placed added strains on the CAI.

The Conciliation and Arbitration Act

The use of the public sector as a pace-setter for industrial conditions, the frenetic pace at which social and industrial 'reform' was attempted, and the economic recession that accompanied Labor administration quickly brought a defensive response from employers. Within 3 days of the December 1972 election the 'duumvirate' — Prime Minister G. Whitlam and his Deputy L. Barnard — was sworn in and established a pace for change that other Ministers tried to emulate:

> The duumvirate immediately abolished conscription, freed seven imprisoned draft-resisters, dropped pending prosecutions of another 300 odd and issued pardons to 150 men absent without leave from the Army . . . Negotiations were begun for an exchange of ambassadors with the People's Republic of China. It re-opened the Arbitration Commission's hearing of the claim for equal pay for equal work for women. It announced plans for massive spending on Aboriginal welfare and suspended the granting of mining leases on Aboriginal reserves. Among other early measures were the abolition of British titles and of the sales tax on contraceptives. Spending on education, the arts and culture was to be massively increased. Most significant of all was the announcement that henceforth 'race' or skin-colour would cease to be a criterion for admission to Australia and that racially selected sports teams would be banned from Australian soil (Ward 1983:400–401)

This expansive quest for change flowed into industrial relations. Clyde Cameron was appointed Minister for Labour (the 'National Service' addendum now being superfluous) and immediately announced a program of transformation, including the seeking of expanded constitutional powers over industrial matters. A referendum to this effect in December 1973 was unsuccessful.

The *Conciliation and Arbitration Act* was a major vehicle by which

Cameron attempted to bring about radical changes to the arbitration system. The scope of change sought was indicated by his Second Reading speech when re-submitting the Conciliation and Arbitration Bill 1973. 'This Bill', Cameron claimed, 'is the first stage of a radical transformation of industrial relations in Australia. Later stages of this transformation will involve an examination of all aspects of industrial relations in Australia by a Special Committee of Inquiry to ensure that policies and procedures for handling labour relations will be suitable for our needs over the next decade or so'.[1] The examination was to be made up of two parts. The first was to deal with the quality of work. 'The second — a much larger and longer inquiry — will make an in-depth study of the institutional framework of labour relations'. Of special concern to this Inquiry would be constitutional reform, desirability of experimenting with new forms of agreements, voluntary mediation and 'ground rules for collective bargaining in Australia'. Union amalgamation and education, plant-level relationships including worker participation, the concept of workers' councils, the role of National Wage cases and other cases setting national standards were also to be considered.

The specific purposes of the 1973 Bill were to remove barriers to union amalgamations, protect industrial organisations from civil action for tort, remove the Commission's authority to ban strikes, remove all penal sanctions, establish procedures to ensure that certain types of agreements were acceptable to the rank and file affected, provide for direct voting for all positions within industrial organisations, extend to six years the period in which action could be taken for recovery of wages, and eliminate the awarding of costs in proceedings before the Courts, Registrar or Commission.

The VCM responded by preparing 'an amendment which could be moved in the Senate by the Liberal/Country Party team' (Memo, VCM Legal Officer J. L. Webb to VCM Director I. Macphee 28/2/73). The NEPC also sought the opinion of Counsel about the likely success of a High Court challenge to certain proposed amendments (NEPC Meeting 13/7/73). The Cameron Bill was rejected by the Senate and allowed to lapse. A second Bill, which was substantially modified by the Senate with 'the removal of most of the provisions to which objection had been taken by employers', was assented to in November 1973 (NEA Meeting 2/11/73).

The NEA Report for 1974 noted that during that year 'a great deal of attention has been directed towards changes in the Act'. On two occasions amendments were sought to the Act directed at 'changes to the Act which incorporated the Minister's personal philosophy concerning the procedures for the submission of proposed agreements to rank and file union members'. The first Bill lapsed with the double dissolution of that year and the second was rejected by the Senate. The Minister also presented two Bills designed to facilitate the amalgamation of unions. These Bills met a similar fate to the others (NEA Report 1974:5).

In 1975 Senator J. McClelland replaced Cameron as Minister for Labour and Immigration and announced his intention to amend the Act to remove the appeal mechanisms and require Commissioners to follow Full Bench decisions. These provisions were thought necessary because of the different approaches taken by members of the Commission to the newly introduced indexation principles and the difficulties created when Full Benches quashed the decisions of Commissioners on appeal (Plowman 1978:111). This announcement produced adverse reaction from unions and some members of government. It was referred to Caucus for consideration (NEA Report 1975:3). Events overtook Labor before Caucus had resolved the matter. In November, the Governor-General dismissed the Whitlam Government. The Coalition won the elections of the following month.

The new Government lost little time in seeking to amend the Act. In 1976 it introduced Bills to 'secure the observance of Full Bench decisions and consideration of economic factors by Full Benches'. The Bills also proposed giving the Minister 'the same right as a party to an industrial dispute to apply for a reference of the dispute to a Full Bench'. In addition the Bills altered the direct voting requirements for organisations introduced by Cameron and replaced them with a system of postal voting that allowed for either a direct or a non-tier collegiate voting system (NEPC Circulars 10/5/76 and 19/10/76).

In March 1977 another amending Bill, which sought to establish the Industrial Relations Bureau (IRB), was introduced. This 'third arm' was to take over the functions of the Arbitration Inspectorate but would also have powers to seek to invoke the sanction provisions against unions. Where employers were not prepared to take legal action against unions, the IRB would do so. The amendments loosened up the 'conscientious objector' provisions of the Act, thus attempting to make non-union membership easier (NEPC Circular 19/4/77). The NEA opposed the IRB and advised 'non-co-operation' from affiliates (e.g. NEA meeting 30/6/78 and CAI–NEIC Officers meeting 26/10/78). For its part, the IRB had a poor regard for employer associations (see IRB's *First Annual Report* June 1978). This third arm was abolished by the Hawke Government in 1983.

The thrust of Coalition legislation was to force the observance of the indexation guidelines and reduce union power. This confrontationist approach sparked further legislation such as the *Commonwealth Employees (Employment Provisions) Act* 1977, which introduced new suspension, dismissal and stand-down powers in respect of industrial action; *The Commonwealth Employees (Employment Redeployment and Retirement) Act* 1977, providing for 'management initiated retirement' of public employees; the 1980 amendments to the *Trades Practices Act*, which introduced section 45D making secondary boycotts an offence; the 1979 amendments to the *Conciliation and Arbitration Act* prohibiting the Commission from seeking to settle any dispute in which the unions involved were on strike; and amendments in the same year giving the Government its most direct involvement in the enforcement provisions of the system and enabling it to deregister unions and suspend unionists. Employers and their associations bore much of the brunt of this confrontation. For the NEA this was particularly so in the area of national tripartite conferences. Tripartism became even more pronounced with the 'consensus' style of government that accompanied the return to office by Labor in March 1983.

National tripartite consultation

Following the demise of the Ministry of Labour Advisory Council in 1958 new tripartite mechanisms, in the form of the National Labour Advisory Council were introduced in 1967. Labor inherited this Council but Cameron allowed it to fall into disuse by not convening any meetings. This was a cause of concern for employers who believed the ACTU had a ready entrée to the Minister that was denied them. In January 1974 the Minister convened a tripartite Industrial Peace Conference. This discussed several areas: mediation and conciliation committees, wage indexation, the authorisation of agreements by rank and file members, worker participation in management, immunity of unions from tort action, union amalgamation and administration, the extension of federal jurisdiction, and the establishment of an Office of Economic and Social Research. Many of these matters will be recognised as ones that the Minister had failed to get the Senate to accept in his Bill of the previous year. At the end of the Conference employers pressed for the establishment of 'appropriate machinery for continuing consultation between the parties' and alluded to the 'former NLAC . . . as an illustration of what might be possible'. The Minister agreed to establish some machinery 'the form and nature of which would be advised later' (NEA Circular 4/2/74). In fact Cameron made no effort to establish any machinery for on-going consultation.

Within days of Labor losing office the NEPC met the new Minister, seeking the re-establishment of tripartite machinery. It was agreed that a conference be convened for January 1976 to discuss this and other matters (NEPC Meeting 19/12/75). The strained political climate following the dismissal of the Whitlam Government made the three peak union councils — the ACTU, the Australian Council of Salaried and Professional Associations and the Council of Australian Government Employee Organisations — reluctant to take part in such machinery. Following the January conference the ACTU announced its decision not to participate in any tripartite machinery (CIS Council Meeting 29–30/4/76). With proposed amendments to the Act in the air, however, the ACTU later relented rather than be bypassed in deliberations. In May 1977 a Bill was introduced to establish the National Labour Consultative Council. This Council, in most respects, resembled in structure and operations those of its predecessors, the MLAC and the NLAC. Unlike the other councils, in which different employer associations had representation rights, in this case the NEPC had sole nomination rights. This was an indication of the extent to which the NEPC had become recognised as the national employer voice in industrial relations (NEPC Circular 30/5/77). The NLCC also differed from its predecessors in the wide range of topics discussed and the creation of a large number of national committees that required national employer representation and input. By 1980 a dozen such committees, the scope of which is outlined more fully in the second part of this chapter, had been brought into existence. Under the Hawke Labor Government, the CAI also became actively involved in other national tripartite machinery, notably the Economic Planning and Advisory Council and the Advisory Council on Prices and Incomes. The fact that the CAI was not given exclusive employer representation rights on these councils, or for that matter at the Economic Summit that spawned them, is indicative that the CAI has not been altogether successful in its quest for recognition as the employer mouthpiece.

The recentralisation of wage determination

The previous chapter recounted the successful employers' total wage campaign. This removed the bifurcated system composed of the basic and secondary wages. Together with the demise of the penal sanctions, however, the adoption of the total wage resulted in a 'move from arbitration' on the part of many unions and a hybrid bargaining–arbitration system. In this system National Wage cases, the chief source of wage increases to 1967, lost their relative importance and industry award cases became dominant. Australian Bureau of Statistics data suggest that between 1961 and 1967 about 85 per cent of award wage increases resulted from national reviews of the basic wage and margins. Such reviews thereafter accounted for a decreasing proportion of award increases. In 1968–69, 41.4 per cent of award rate increases came by way of National Wage cases. This figure fell to 28.2 per cent in 1971–72 and to only 19.1 per cent in 1973–74 (Plowman 1986:23). In such a situation the Commission lost control over wage determination and its continued espousal of egalitarian norms added to inflationary cost-push pressures. The wage increases negotiated by strong unions were relayed to weaker unions by way of the Commission.

In the period 1968–74 Full Benches prevaricated between wooing unions back to the national wage fold (for example the 6 per cent increase in 1970 was justified on this ground (135 *CAR* 299)) and either eliminating National Wage cases or at least discounting these to take account of 'gains in the field' (143 *CAR* 803). Employers were divided on these questions. Some associations, in particular the MTIA, strongly advocated the abandonment of National Wage cases until 1975. Thereafter they publicly supported wage indexation. On both counts these approaches were out of step with the general body of employers whose views were closer to those of the Central Industrial Secretariat. In 1974 this organisation noted that if the prevailing system continued 'it could only contribute substantially to inflationary pressures'. It noted that average weekly earnings were then rising at a rate in excess of 17 per cent per annum and if unions' claims at that year's National Wage case were granted the rate of acceleration would be in the order of 30 per cent. The Secretariat considered the decentralised system as being the major cause of wage inflation. 'Experience since the disastrous Metal Trades Work Value decision of 1967', it claimed, 'should by now have converted even the most doubting of the fact that the operation of the principles of comparative wage justice will not permit any one group of wage earners to secure a permanent advantage over any others. The doctrine of maintenance of relativities is so ingrained in the tribunals, in employers and in trade unions that arguments for the restoration of a loss of relativity arising from an increase in wage rates are almost irresistible'. The Secretariat noted that since 1969 employers had 'reverted to the negative role of reacting to union demands. It would seem that if some order is to be brought back there will be a necessity for employers to take a positive approach towards the problem. Undoubtedly there will be difficulties in achieving agreement in the approach to be adopted' (CIS Council Meeting 15–16/5/74). Though at this stage the Secretariat did not advocate any specific approach to wage determination, its thrust was clearly centralist.

Two months later, at a meeting of the NEA to determine policy in relation to the 1974 Wage Principles Conference, the Central Industrial Secretariat affiliates (ACEF and ACMA) presented the case for a centralised system. By then metal unions had secured wage increases of the order of $15 per week by way of negotiations. Not only was there evidence of this amount flowing onto other awards, but also of relativity leap-frogging. This was a situation in which other awards were increased by a greater amount thus distorting existing relativities. Subsequently, by way of arbitration, the metal unions received a further $9 per week, which brought them up to the Transport Workers' standard. Thereafter, though the Metal Award remained the Standard bench-mark award, it no longer set the pace for federal awards.[2] The ACEF–ACMA paper commented on the three-tiered wages system that had developed (National Wage cases, industry awards and agreements, and over-award bargaining) and claimed:

> Having regard to the rigidity of the Australian wage fixing system it seems impossible in present circumstances to avoid some form of general enquiry into wage levels being conducted regularly by the Commission, whatever that enquiry might be called and, therefore, it is suggested that it is more appropriate to propose ways and means of containing the extent of general increases rather than the abandonment of National Wage Cases. It is suggested that the employers submit, inter alia, that 'the decentralised wage fixing system in operation in Australia would seem to require the adoption of some co-ordinated approach to wage fixing which recognises the principles of comparative wage justice and the institutional role of the Commission, unions, and employers' organisations. Restraint needs to be exercised in respect of non-wage incomes, such as profits, and in this connection it might be appropriate to relate the arbitration of the Prices Justification Tribunal to the arbitration of the Commission and then set limits for increases in prices arising from wage increases based on the 1969 principles'.[3] (ACEF–ACMA 'Conference on Wage Fixation: Proposals for Discussion', NEA Meeting 15/7/74)

General agreement on the need for a centralised system was one thing. Formulating the details of that system, and getting Commission support and union acquiescence were more problematic. In 1973 the government, conscious of the electoral impact of stagnation, also sought the centralisation of wages by way of indexation. The following year, in concert with the ACTU, it again pressed for the adoption of indexation but also promised 'supporting mechanisms' to ensure that indexation would not merely provide a tier from which unions would then press for other gains.[4] Employers were unsuccessful in opposing the return to a system of national wage adjustments in which wages were adjusted in accordance with price movements. Indeed, under the quarterly indexation system introduced in March 1975, employers' success in the Total Wage case became something of a millstone around their necks. The plateau form of indexation accompanying basic wage cost-of-living adjustments was no longer industrially acceptable to unions. Further, in anticipation of indexation, some unions had successfully negotiated paid rates awards. This resulted in the over-award component being 'absorbed' into the awards, and thus being indexed.

Not surprisingly, the NEA opposed the indexation system, which reversed its earlier victories. Despite this opposition, however, indexation continued to dominate wage determination and condition NEA and, subsequently, CAI policy. These organisations adopted a reactive and negative position to the system of wage indexation that was to condition industrial relations until its abandonment in 1981, a system that was to consume much human and financial resources, and that was to force a tenfold increase in association contributions.

In its meeting of 24 July 1981, the National Employers Industrial Council of the CAI resolved to press for the abandonment of indexation on the ground that the strike action accompanying unions' claims for increased wages and a shorter working week were totally incompatible with the indexation guidelines. On 31 July, the Commission abandoned indexation in favour of the case-by-case approach to wage claims. ACTU strategy, however, negated this approach. In effect, a 'metal trades round', involving a sizeable wage increase and a reduction in working hours, became the order of the day.

In December 1982 the Government prevented a second wage round by imposing a 12 month wages freeze on its own employees and by asking the Commission to impose a similar freeze on private sector employers. The Commission imposed a 'wages pause', which was to be reviewed in June 1983. By then Labor had gained office and persuaded the Commission to reintroduce indexation as part of its Accord incomes policy approach to economic management. Full indexation was the order of the day until June 1987 when Balance of Payments difficulties caused a review of this approach. In March 1987 the indexation guidelines were scrapped in favour of a two-tiered wages system. The CAI had made submissions for such a system, which, it hoped, would provide for greater wage flexibility.

TOWARDS CONFEDERATION

NEA operations 1973–1977

The previous chapter described the origins and operations of the NEA. This consisted of nearly 40 associations and companies that contributed to national arbitration cases. NEA policy was formulated at general meetings and the NEPC had charge of implementing such policy. In practice the NEPC (which consisted of the nominees of the ACEF, ACMA, MTIA and AWGC) was also instrumental in formulating policy for endorsement by the NEA membership. In order to allow for a greater input from other associations a Consultative Committee (NECC) was formed in 1970. This consisted of the four NEPC members and five others chosen by a general meeting of the NEA. The NECC acted as an advisory body to the NEPC. A third Committee, the Industrial Committee (NEIC), had charge of the conduct of NEA arbitration cases under the direction of the NEPC. The NEIC was also composed of nominees of the four major organisations. ACEF Executive Director, Mr G. Polites, was Convenor of the NEIC as well as being Secretary of the NEPC and NECC. His pivotal role was further increased when appointed Director of the Central Industrial Secretariat, which co-ordinated the industrial relations activities of the ACEF and ACMA.

The NEA Constitution provided that meetings be held 'not less than twice per annum for the purpose of considering general policy in connection with actual or pending national industrial proceedings and over-all questions of finance relating thereto'. It had become customary for the industrial officers of NEA members to meet more frequently as the need arose. With the advent of the Labor Government such meetings became monthly affairs and tended to rotate between Melbourne and Sydney. A consequence of the frequency of such meetings, according to the NEA Report for 1973–74, was the reduced attendance rate. Indeed, including NEPC members, few officers' meetings had more than 10 per cent or so in attendance. During 1973 and 1974 many of these meetings discussed only one issue — government and union applications for wage indexation.

The human resource pressures placed on associations by the need for frequent NEA meetings were matched by equally strong pressures for financial resources. The new centralised regime that accompanied indexation was an expensive one for the NEA and finances became a perennial problem. The 'Moore Conference' and related National Wage case leading to the introduction of wage indexation cost the NEPC nearly $45 000, a sum that outstripped that year's levies of $36 000 (NEPC Statement of Receipts and Payments 30/6/75 and Accounts for Payment 22/8/75). The NEPC budget for 1975 was fixed at $100 000 and by 1980 it had mushroomed to $554 500.[5] Despite these massive increases, however, the demands of the centralised wages system ensured that expenditure continued to outstrip income.

The centralised indexation system placed resource demands on the NEPC in many ways. The first was the frequency of National Wage cases — quarterly until June 1978 and half-yearly until July 1986. In all, there were some 22 cases for the period. The frequency of such cases further necessitated the full-time engagement of research staff to prepare cases, a difficult matter for the NEPC since it had no secretariat. This facility was effectively provided by the Central Industrial Secretariat with assistance from two Melbourne University economic consultants. Over the period the guidelines were amended after exhaustive Wage Fixing Principles Conferences, which replicated the 'Moore Conference'. The NEPC and its successor took part in six such conferences to 1980. The indexation regime also involved the NEPC in a large number of industry cases, an area traditionally left to affiliates. At the behest of the NEA, in the first 5 months of indexation the NEPC intervened in cases involving the metal, building, oil, wool selling, maritime, banking, municipal, vehicle building, coal, printing and insurance industries. In all cases it submitted that the matters in dispute were precluded by the indexation guidelines (NEA Meeting 18/7/75).

The indexation system not only created logistic and resource problems for the NEA, but also confronted it with policy problems. In essence, the indexation system marked a return to the system that had operated until the abandonment of cost-of-living adjustments in 1953. Rubbing salt into employers' wounds was the fact that their other major post-war triumph — the acceptance of the total wage — now militated against the plateau system of indexation that had operated between 1922 and 1953. The total wage, in some instances on a paid rates basis, would now be indexed. The previous system of basic wage indexation that employers had helped to scuttle looked benign in comparison with the new proposals. Thus it was not surprising that most associations strongly opposed the introduction of wage indexation. The NEPC's inability to provide an industrially acceptable alternative at a time when union acquiescence was essential, however, necessarily placed the NEA in a defensive and negative role. In this context some associations came to consider indexation a régime preferable to the wage wilderness that preceded it. The NEA was forced into a position of accepting indexation, but always on a conditional and short-term basis.

By April 1976 the NEA had adopted a reactive policy that characterised the national employers' approach for the rest of the period, namely to 'support with reservation, the indexation package' but to seek changes to the guidelines. The changes sought over the period varied and, at times, seemed anything but a support for indexation. They included the tightening up of wage gains outside indexation, greater recourse to the discretionary powers granted under Principle 1, 6-monthly (and subsequently 12-monthly) hearings, discounting for 'policy induced' price increases, discounting because of the lack of substantial compliance, the tightening of the work value principle, and the move 'to annual hearings in which the prime consideration would be the movement in national productivity' (CAI–NEIC Meeting 27/7/79). This approach assumed the ability of the Commission to regulate wages and enforce its decisions, that economic logic would prevail over industrial strength, that employers able to do so would not seek to buy industrial peace notwithstanding the guidelines, and that government policies would tame unions into submission. As the indexation system came under greater pressure, so too did the NEPC.

From Secretariat to Confederation

The Central Industrial Secretariat was brought into being on 1 January 1972 and combined the industrial relations functions of the ACMA with the ongoing functions of the ACEF. It was effectively staffed by the ACEF, the ACMA having provided only one person to the Secretariat. Thus, for the ACEF, the Secretariat provided a major boon and boost. It had a leading hand in formulating the ACMA's industrial relations policies without in any way having to sacrifice its own autonomy. Since the ACEF had a dominant influence in formulating secretariat policy, the Secretariat a dominant influence over the NEPC and NEIC, and the two committees a controlling interest in the NEA, the ACEF became the dominant national policy-initiating organisation. Most NEA policies of the period can be traced by way of a Polites–ACEF–CIS–NEIC–NEPC–NEA linkage.

The previous chapter recounted the problems posed for the NEA by the domination of that body by the 'Big Four'. In an attempt to overcome this the National Employers' Consultative Council had been created in 1969 with a view to increasing the role of other organisations in NEPC policy formulation. Though this development dissipated tensions, the NECC's effectiveness was minimal. By February 1973 secretariat members were being warned that 'the constitution of the National Employers' Group is again under consideration in many quarters. Various proposals for restructuring the group into a formal organisation are being canvassed' (CIS Officers Meeting 9/2/73).

Active in the development of such initiatives were the MTIA and AWGC. In addition to organisational power brokerage, the MTIA's major concern was the state orientation of the ACEF and ACMA even though the Secretariat had strengthened national control over policy vis-a-vis state affiliates.[6] The AWGC's major misgivings related to the potential trade and commerce implications of a strong ACEF–ACMA alliance. The rural groups' interests in these areas conflicted with those of the ACMA. The AWGC feared the breakdown of the industrial relations co-ordination that had been achieved through the NEIC–NEPC–NEA troika should the ACEF become partisan in the commercial field. This consideration coloured its approach to any ACMA–ACEF relationship.

Another factor spurring the reorganisation thrust was the emergence at this time of a new force — the 'Big 50'. In February 1973 a group of 54 large companies met 'to consider the establishment of a new employer organisation aimed at combating the influence of the ACTU and its president'. It proposed the establishment of a confederation, albeit one that included only companies employing not less than 1000 employees, a figure subsequently changed to 5000 (Letter, Sir Henry Somerset to ACMA President Nichols 9/4/73 and ACMA Board Meeting 13/2/73).

The formation of such an organisation on a company, rather than association, basis posed a problem for all NEA members and not just those keen to reduce Central Industrial Secretariat influence. In Victoria, associations formed the Congress of Victorian Employers whose inaugural address by VEF Secretary Spicer — 'Strengthening the Future Role of Associations' — is indicative of associations' defensive thinking. In New South Wales associations began meetings of 'Joint Organisations'.

In the 1960s ACEF had responded to threats to its industrial relations dominance by broadening its basis by way of associate membership. It now proposed that the Secretariat membership be broadened 'as a way of promoting employer unity', a move that the Secretariat approved (CIS Council Meeting 5-6/4/73). In addition the presidents of both organisations met, with a view to seeking total amalgamation. They had little difficulty reaching agreement on 19 'basic principles for a merger' (Appendix 3). This provided for Foundation Members (chambers and federations) and Inaugural Members (other NEA members). The organisation would be administered by an executive committee composed of Foundation Members. A General Council, representative of all members, would determine policy. This council would also elect the president. Where voting was required, voting rights would be according to contribution. Foundation Members would meet the costs of the organisation, less subscriptions of Inaugural Members. A Chief Executive Officer would be responsible to the Chairman of the Executive Committee for administration and to the President of the Council for policy. There would be two operating wings, a Trade and Commerce Division and an Industrial Relations Division, the directors of which would be responsible to the Chief Executive Officer. Each division would have a Consultative Committee to advise on areas of that division's activities. The organisation would be staffed by existing personnel of the ACMA, the ACEF and the Secretariat.

The Heads of Agreement reached by the President was endorsed by the ACEF in November 1973 with a view to a merger being achieved by the beginning of July 1974 (ACEF Council Meeting 22/11/73). By the latter date, however, other considerations and developments intruded, which made it reconsider merger plans. It became apparent that the proposed voting rights and management structure would have enabled ACMA affiliates to determine policy. The VEF considered that this could have led to a situation in which industrial relations considerations were subordinated to trade matters. It gained the support of other federations in seeking the establishment of a confederation that, in the first instance at least, would limit itself to industrial relations. In essence, this would have meant converting the Central Industrial Secretariat (or the NEA) into the proposed confederation. The ACMA and ACEF entered into protracted discussions over the next 3 years with the ACMA pushing for a merger and the ACEF being the reluctant party. The discussions came to include the federal government, which was pushing for a merger, and the 'Companies Group', which had delayed forming a confederation so as to facilitate the ACMA–ACEF merger. This group was now threatening to act independently.

Discussions also came to include the 'NEA Group'. This group consisted of the associations representing the metal trades, the printing trades, mines and metals, farmers and pastoralists, the meat industry, the retail trade, wool-selling brokers, and the banking industry. This group considered that 'the unity of employers already established on industrial relations would be endangered by seeking to establish a Confederation to deal with wider issues including trade and tariffs on which there is no uniformity of interest and on which markedly different views are held' (Letter MTIA President Kirby and AWGC President Burston to NEPC Chairman Dillon 3/6/77). Thus the NEA group supported the ACEF's position, namely the creation of a Confederation of Employers, rather than the creation of a Confederation of Industry. The NEA group further proposed that a confederation should be created by formalising the structure of the NEA and NEPC rather than by an ACEF–ACMA merger. The MTIA and AWGC threatened that they would not join a Confederation of Industry. The Companies Group, however, insisted that any confederation would have to incorporate all of the 'Big Four' members of the NEPC.

The ACMA was not interested in a national body that did not encompass trade matters and considered ACEF procrastination as a breach of its agreement. The imperatives that had driven it to form the Central Industrial Secretariat and rationalise its industrial relations functions equally affected its trade activities. The development of major industry associations such as the MTIA and PATEFA had the potential to reduce the ACMA's long standing influence as the manufacturers' voice. The formation of such bodies as the Conference of National Manufacturing Industry Associations and the Australian Industries Development Association were challenges to ACMA's historically dominant role as the employer mouthpiece for manufacturers. Its stand for a composite Confederation of Industry was supported by the Companies Group.

Thus, by mid-1976 a complicated set of organisational considerations and strategies had evolved, which shaped merger developments over the next 13 months. All associations were confronted with the possibility that the 'Big 50' might form their own organisation. This was not to their advantage and could be forestalled by the formation of the Confederation. The companies' insistence that the MTIA and AWGC be members of the new Confederation gave those organisations bargaining leverage likely to steer the Confederation into a replication of the NEA. The 'Big 50's' insistence on a 'composite' confederation, however, strengthened the ACMA's hand in ensuring that the Confederation had a trade division. Further, the ACMA had the ability to frustrate the formation of a confederation of employers (rather than of industry) by refusing to join and by disbanding the Secretariat. Constituents of the ACMA and ACEF feared the diminution of the state organisations and sought a privileged position for Foundation Members. National associations sought to diminish the state orientation by refusing to join if Foundation Members had over-riding control. This consideration had to be tempered by the fact that the Government was likely to recognise the new Confederation irrespective of whether or not NEA members joined. Thus NEA members could not overplay their hand since such recognition could deprive them of representation on the NLAC and other tripartite bodies. In the three states where federations and chambers had merged (Queensland, Tasmania and Western Australia) the new bodies did not want to contribute to two national organisations and actively supported a national merger. On the other hand, the failure of amalgamations in two states (New South Wales and South Australia), and the refusal of the VEF to seek a merger with the VCM, had a chilling effect on the national merger proposals.[7]

Though the ACMA refused to give way on the formation of a composite confederation, it did compromise on the proposed Memorandum of Articles so as to alleviate the federations' fears about control and the diminution of industrial relations interests. The Articles were amended to provide for a confederation in which the trade and industrial relations wings would be separate and autonomous in their own areas of responsibility, and for each wing to have charge of its own financial affairs. Instead of there being two divisions whose directors were responsible to the Chief Executive Officer, there were to be two independent councils — the National Employers' Trade and Industry Council and the National Employers' Industrial Council. The latter would be concerned with industrial relations issues, the former with trade matters. The restructuring arrangements also removed the position of Chief Executive Officer. Instead there was to be a secretariat, which would act as a linking mechanism between the two autonomous councils. The ACMA also made concessions on voting rights. Proposals for embodying these changes were accepted by the ACMA on 28 October 1977. At that time it resolved to change its name to the Confederation of Australian Industry and to adopt a new Memorandum of Association and Articles as from 1 December 1977. A special meeting of the ACEF held earlier that day had resolved to merge with the ACMA to form the Confederation as from 1 December. The Central Industrial Secretariat also resolved to merge with members of the ACEF and ACMA under the name of the Confederation of Australian Industry and to transfer to the Confederation all assets and liabilities at the date of merger (CIS Council Meeting 27–28/10/77).

In the same month the VEF, the federation least disposed to the merger, formally indicated its preparedness to join the CAI as a Foundation Member. A Special General Meeting of the ACEF was held to consider 'resolutions designed to facilitate the merger'. Changes were needed to ACEF's constitution to enable it to merge with another body. These were approved together with a resolution that the merger take place on December 1 1977. Due obsequies were then observed as federations paid tribute to the work performed by the ACEF since its inception (ACEF Special General Meeting 28/10/77).

The merging of the ACEF and ACMA was only the first step in the formation of the CAI. The second involved enticing other national associations to join one or both of its two Councils. A special NEA meeting had been convened in October 1977 with a view to those wishing to become Inaugural Members being able to join at the time of the ACEF–ACMA merger. This did not prove possible for a number of reasons and the NEA continued in existence for 7 months after the merger.

As expected, Mr G. Polites was appointed Director of the National Employers' Industrial Council (NEIC), the body that effectively subsumed the NEA. The Council determined to continue with those methods of operation that had evolved since the foundation of its predecessor. There were to be regular meetings at officer level 'so as to ensure that there is as great a degree of consistency and uniformity in approach as possible'. As with the NEA, the Council was to meet at half-yearly intervals 'to determine general policy on a wide range of issues'. Meetings of officers of all members were to be held monthly. These would alternate between Sydney and Melbourne and follow a format already established by NEA officers. The NEIC Committee, which in many respects resembled the former National Employers' Consultative Committee, 'was to meet as required but at least every 2 months to oversee the activities of the Secretariat'. These meetings were to be similar in form to those of the former NEPC. General statements of policy were to be issued by the Chairman of the Committee with the Director having authority 'to make day-to-day comments on immediate issues'. Subject to the general policy guidelines laid down at council meetings, policies for arbitration cases were to be determined by the Committee. The Secretariat was to have responsibility for the detailed drafting of submissions and reports, which were to be presented to regular meetings of officers. The Secretariat was also to prepare submissions for Inquiries and for representation before governments on the authority, and with the approval, of the Committee (NEIC Circular 19/12/77).

Thus, apart from differences in the constitution of the various bodies, the major administrative difference between the NEA and NEIC was that the latter had its own secretariat (the former Secretariat staff) whereas the NEA relied on the good graces of other organisations to perform these functions. Another major difference was that the NEIC was a formalised secretariat-driven body as opposed to the loose-knit organisation it replaced. Further, though autonomous, it was nonetheless a part of a two-winged body with a joint board of directors. The physical separation of both wings increased their sense of autonomy. The NTIC and CAI administration took over the ACMA's Industry House in Canberra and the NEIC operated from the Central Industrial Secretariat offices in the VEF Hawthorn building until taking up offices in Exhibition Street, Melbourne, in January 1979.[8]

The first general meeting of the NEIC was held in May 1978. It had the task of electing the committee, which, in turn, had to elect its chairman and one additional member to the Board of Directors. The meeting also considered a number of important industrial relations matters that were formerly the province of the NEA. These included the formulation of policy in relation to wages, hours of work, termination of employment and general arbitration proceedings. The latter included redundancy and severance pay for the construction industry, qualification by continuous service for annual leave eligibility, delayed payments of workers' compensation, maternity leave, interstate and country wage differentials in the building industry, metal industry award wage claims, additional public holidays, and leave for trade union training. In addition to these policy areas the NEIC reviewed developments in a number of areas in which submissions or publications were being considered. They included multinational enterprises (publication of CAI guidelines for operation in Australia), worker participation in management (publication of CAI documents), education and training (including the National Training Council and Trade Union Training and position paper), population and immigration (submissions to the Green Paper), employment and unemployment (CES changes and the Secretariat's discussion paper on youth unemployment), Commonwealth legislation (*Conciliation and Arbitration Act*, Prices Justification Tribunal and *Trade Practices Act*), National Labour Consultative Council, and international affairs (NEIC Council Meeting 2/5/78). Following the format established in the ACEF and then the Secretariat, the council meeting was preceded by that of the officers of member organisations. This meeting made recommendations for consideration at the council meeting.

The first CAI General Meeting was held the next day and elected Mr Max Dillon (formerly ACMA) President and Mr K. W. Mason (formerly ACEF) and Sir Samuel Burston (AWGC) Vice-Presidents.[9] The Board of Directors was duly elected with each Foundation Member having a nominee, Mr R. L. Duprey (Australian Chemical Industry Council) being elected by members other than Foundation Members, Messrs H. G. Aston (Textile Council of Australia) and K. D. Williams (Chamber of Commerce and Industry of South Australia) being appointed by the NTIC and Messrs R. G. Kirby (MTIA) and W. B. Burgess (Iron and Steel Industry Association) being appointed by the NEIC. Mr J. Walker (CAI) was elected Treasurer.

The meeting of the Board of Directors on the following day noted that Inaugural Membership had been finalised at a total of 26, namely

The Association of Employers of Waterside Labour
The Australian Associated Brewers
Australian Bankers' Association
Australian Chemical Industry Council
Australian Electrical and Electronic Manufacturers' Association
Australian Farmers' Federation
Australian Federation of Construction Contractors
Australian Maritime Employers' Association

Australian Mines and Metals Association (Inc.)
Australian Retailers' Association
Australian Sugar Refiners' Industry Association
Australian Woolgrowers and Graziers' Council
Commonwealth Steamship Owners' Association
Federal Industrial Council of the Retail Motor Industry
Federation of Australian Radio Broadcasters
Growers Conciliation and Labour League
Insurance Council of Australia
Insurance Employers' Industrial Association
Iron and Steel Industry Association
Life Offices Association of Australia
Master Builders' Federation of Australia
Meat and Allied Trades Federation of Australia
Metal Trades Industry Association
The Oil Industry Industrial Committee
Printing and Allied Trades Employers' Federation of Australia
The Textile Council of Australia.

Only five of these associations did not have membership of the NEIC. Four organisations (including the AWGC, which had previously protested against any involvement with the trade division) had membership of both councils. Thus, taking into account Foundation Members, the NEIC had been successful in enticing most NEA members. By the time of the CAI's official launching by the Prime Minister on 19 June, two other NEA members, the Australian Hotels Association and the Australian Wool Selling Brokers Employers' Federation, had joined the Confederation.

A fortnight later the NEA was wound up at a large combined CAI-NEA meeting, which recorded its appreciation of the 19 years of work carried out by the NEA and NEPC. The only organisation present at this meeting that had not joined the CAI was the Australian International Airlines Operations Group (i.e. Qantas). Notwithstanding this, Qantas was represented at subsequent meetings of NEIC Officers. It finally joined the CAI in 1979, by which time all former NEA affiliates had joined the NEIC. The addition of the Pharmacy Guild of Australia and the Cinematograph Exhibitors Association in that year increased NEIC membership to 36. In the same year the AWGC and Australian Farmers' Federation merged in the formation of the National Farmers' Federation, which replaced these organisations on the NEIC. Membership was maintained at 36, however, by the admission of the Australian Council of Local Government, 'the first major involvement by a non-private sector association in national employers' affairs' (CAI Board of Directors Meeting 22/11/79).[10] By the end of 1980 membership of the NEIC stood at 34 as a result of a merging of the Chamber of Manufactures and Employers' Federation in Western Australia and the disaffiliation of the Australian Broadcasters' Federation. Membership of the National Trade and Industry Council had increased to 25 by this time.

A notable difference between NEA and NEIC membership was that the former included companies while the latter catered only for national associations. In practice this difference was more apparent than real. Three companies had been active in the NEA — BHP, CSR and Qantas. Oil industry companies had also been represented but in a less consistent way. The companies adopted the simple strategy of forming national associations in which they had a controlling influence. Qantas formed the Australian International Airlines Operations Group, CSR the Australian Sugar Refiners Industry Association (ASRIA) and BHP effectively increased its representation through control of the Iron and Steel Industry Association and the Australian Maritime Employers' Association (AMEA). The ASRIA and AMEA illustrate the structure of these new associations. The latter was formed in March 1976 with a membership of three large companies (BHP, CSR and the Australian National Line) and three small companies (Fenwick & Co., Hetherington Kingsbury Pty Ltd and the Western Australian Shipping Commission). Fenwick and Co. was one of the three major operators of tugs in Australian ports. These six members accounted for 63 per cent of 'the total Australian manned fleet'. As with the Iron and Steel Association, the Australian Maritime Employers' Association has operated out of BHP's Sydney offices since its inception. In May 1977 it successfully sought membership of the NEA. The ASRIA was formed in June 1977 and had two members — CSR and Millaquin Sugar Co. Pty Ltd — and has operated from the offices of the larger company.

CAI operations 1978–1980

The NEIC inherited not only the basic membership and methods of operation from the NEA but also that organisation's financial and wage policy formulation problems. The CAI was formed on the understanding that Foundation Members, who had a controlling influence over CAI affairs, would underwrite the bulk of its costs. At the time of merging the ACEF, ACMA and Central Industrial Secretariat injected nearly $1.5 million into the CAI's coffers. Despite this, it was anticipated that operational and establishment costs would result in a shortfall of 'not less than $40 000 by June 30 1978' (CAI Board of Directors Meeting 3/5/78). Shortfalls of a similar magnitude accompanied each financial year. Initially the CAI sought to redress this problem by way of Foundation Members, subsequently by way of Other Members. Despite the latter being given greater representation rights, no acceptable subscription formula could be found.

In May 1978 a sub-committee was formed to 'develop a formula for determining the proportion of subscriptions payable to the CAI by Foundation Members, which formula might be based on subscription paid by companies and firms to Foundation Members' (CAI Board of Directors' Meeting 3/5/78). The sub-committee was not able to find an acceptable formula. The VCM and CMNSW, whose insurance companies were experiencing difficulties, indicated that they were not prepared to contribute to 'CAI by way of subscription in 1978–79 an amount greater than their existing contribution, i.e. $208 182, being the total of their subscription to the ACMA ($194 820) and their proportion of the levy payable to NEA ($13 362)'. A provisional budget was drawn up for 1978–79 in which subscriptions of Foundation Members were to be equal to their respective contributions to the ACMA, ACEF and NEA as at 1 December 1977, plus a surcharge, which did not apply to the VCM and CMNSW. The net result was to increase the subscriptions of Foundation Members by $66 179 to $718 914. As Table 8.1 shows, the chambers' contribution outweighed that of federations.

The surcharge on most Foundation Members was merely a temporary expedient. In August 1978 the Board again attempted to find a more permanent formula but without success. A special meeting of Presidents of Foundation Members was convened in the following month but again was unsuccessful. This meeting concluded that it was not desirable to adopt a fixed formula for apportioning subscriptions of Foundation Members, that CAI should look at the possibility of funding special CAI projects through contributions from individual companies, that contributions by Foundation Members calculated on a state basis (with the chamber and federation in each state apportioning the state quota between them) be examined, and 'that account be taken of possible levels of contributions to funding from non-Foundation Members' (Meeting of Presidents of CAI Foundation Members 26/9/78). In the final outcome the VCM and CMNSW refused to pay any more than $200 000 and $180 000 (a reduction of $8 000 and $28 000 respectively) and the contributions of other members were increased by 10 per cent.

In May 1979 the CAI Board met again to consider finances and prepare

Table 8.1 *CAI Foundation Members' subscriptions 1978–79*

Member	Subscription
CMNSW	$208 182
EFNSW	$59 340
VCM	$208 182
VEF	$45 850
CCISA	$65 770
SAEF	$11 520
CWAI	$17 560
WACM	$23 730
TCI	$18 580
QCI	$54 950
ACTEF	$3 550
CI (NT)	$1 700
TOTAL	$718 914

Source: CAI Board of Directors' Meeting 20/6/78, Agenda Background Paper.

Note: The estimate for the total subscriptions of Inaugural/Ordinary Members was $171 500. Services, secretarial fees, interest and the surplus of rent income over expenditure of Industry House were expected to realise $265 600 giving a total income of $1 146 760.

the 1979–80 budget. The prognostications were that the shortfall for 1978–79 would be in the order of $38 000. The VCM advised that it would not in future be prepared to pay a greater contribution than the CMNSW. Only the NT Confederation indicated a willingness to increase its contribution by the 10 per cent contemplated. The South Australian Chamber advised that it was unable to increase its contribution beyond 5 per cent and the VEF and EFNSW indicated an inability to increase contributions at all. The Board was unable to get Foundation Members to accept any subscription formula and in the end had to settle for an increase in the following year's deficit to $47 750 (CAI Board of Directors Meeting 23/5/79).

It was not until mid-1980 that the Board was successful in having

Foundation Members adopt a subscription formula. The 'Wheeler Formula' provided 'for determining the proportion of subscription income payable based upon the industrial intensity factor for each State expressed as a percentage of the Australian total using statistical data relative to civilian employment by relevant industry groupings'. At the same time it determined that the 'proportions of total subscription income received from Foundation Members and other members (76.5 : 23.5 in 1979–80) should be reduced to 60:40 over a period of five years 1980–81 to 1984–85'. As from 1 July 1980 the proportions were to be set at 73.4 : 26.6. Total subscriptions were increased to $924 404 (out of an expected total income of $1.28m). As the result of the subscription redistribution Foundation Members' contributions were increased by 6 per cent and those of Other Members by 14 per cent. Despite these increases, and the probable alienation of some members, the Board anticipated a shortfall of $35 000 for the 1980–81 financial year (Letter, CAI Treasurer Wheeler to EFNSW Director Darling 12/6/80).

Despite some attempts to have the Wheeler Formula abandoned it continued to provide a stable basis for Foundation Member subscriptions. The Board next tackled the accompanying problem of having Other Members agree to increase their proportionate subscriptions. The Board quickly came to the conclusion that increased representation of Inaugural/Ordinary Members on the Board would have to accompany such a movement. Prior to calling meetings of these Members, the Board put into train amendments to the Articles of Association, increasing the number of association representatives elected to the Board from one to five (CAI Board of Directors Meeting 10/9/80). These amendments still gave Foundation Members a majority on the Board but reduced the potential gap between the different levels of membership on the Board.[11]

At a meeting of Inaugural/Ordinary members in October 1980 Treasurer R. N. Wheeler outlined financial problems and developments. In the case of these members, subscription levels had originally been fixed, within broad parameters determined by the CAI Board, following negotiations with each individual member. Subsequent increases had been applied under an *ad hoc* arrangement, which, in the view of the CAI Board, was inappropriate and in need of rectification. The Board had been able to develop a formula for fixing subscription levels for each Foundation member and now sought a formula for Other Members. As in the case of Foundation Members this proved no easy task. The meeting agreed

> to seek a review of the decision to allocate subscriptions in the 60:40 proportions, a further discussion paper which explores available options, that

> no decision on a subscription formula should be taken by the CAI Board until Other Members had been fully consulted; Other Member representation on the Board should be increased; the CAI Board should examine the possibility of seeking more members so as to spread costs on a wider base; subscriptions paid by members should be available and not kept confidential by the Board; and that $2 500 was a reasonable minimum subscription for Other Members. (Meeting of CAI Inaugural/Ordinary Members 30/10/80)

By the end of 1980 no formula had been achieved in relation to Other Members. By then the budget for 1980–81 had been set for just over $1.3m of which $554 500 was marked for NEIC operations. About half of this amount was set aside for salaries and $140 000 for 'National Arbitration Costs' (CAI 'Budget for Year Ended 30 June 1981', 28/5/80).

The NEIC inherited a range of industrial activities from the NEA. In addition governments were quick to seize on this employer mouthpiece for representation on a large number of tripartite bodies. At the end of 1978 the NEIC reported being engaged in 'activities embracing a wide range of industrial matters on behalf of members and employers generally'. These activities included representation of employers at the Inquiry into Wage Fixation Principles in which they were successful in having the Commission adopt half-yearly indexation. The NEIC made submissions to three separate National Wage hearings and the Maternity Leave case. It was involved in a large number of 'anomalies' conferences and intervened in a number of arbitration proceedings on behalf of employers generally. Such proceedings included the claims for the insertion of supplementary payments in the metal industry award, appeal proceedings against the decision of the Commission to grant severance payments in the construction industry, claims for reduced standard hours of work in the electricity generating industry, and claims for the inclusion of rostered overtime in the payments made to employees on annual leave. On the tripartite plane the NEIC not only represented employers on the revamped National Labour Consultative Council, but was also represented on the National Training Council, the National Employee Participation Steering Committee, the Australian Population and Immigration Council and the Trade Union Training Authority. Other NEIC activities included the making of a submission to the Curriculum Development Working Party and the publication of four booklets — one on youth employment, the others on education and training in Australia, employee participation and national wage determination (Report of NEIC for year ending 31 October 1978).

The NEIC was involved in a similar flurry of activity in subsequent years. In 1979 it represented employers at the two national wage cases and at the

Wage Principles Conference. It took part in 18 anomaly conferences and intervened in 27 industry cases involving the application of the indexation principle. It was further involved in 10 'general principles' cases, including Maternity Leave and Trade Union Training Leave (Report of NEIC for 12 months ending 31 October 1979).

Tripartite obligations continued apace. Not only was the NEIC involved with the quarterly meetings of the NLCC, it also became involved in a growing number of sub-committees of that Council. These included the Committee on Labour Market Questions, the Committee on Women's Employment, the Committee on Manpower Policy Matters, the Committee on Financial Reporting of Organisations, the Committee on Rationalisation of Industrial Tribunals, the Committee on International Affairs, the Committee on Amalgamation of Organisations, the Committee on Employment Discrimination, the Committee on the *Administrative Decisions (Judicial Review) Act* and the Working Party on the *Conciliation and Arbitration Act.* The NEIC continued to represent employers on the other non-NLCC bodies identified earlier and also became a member of the Commonwealth Employment Service Advisory Committee. During 1979 the NEIC made submissions to five major inquiries, namely the Inquiry into Technological Change in Australia, the Senate Standing Committee on Education and the Arts, the Inquiry into the Effectiveness of Australian Schools in Preparing Young People for the Workforce, the Senate Standing Committee on Foreign Affairs Inquiry into Australian Relations with ASEAN, the Inquiry into the Training of TAFE Teachers in Australia, and to the Minister for Immigration and Ethnic Affairs on the Operations of the Proposed Institute of Multicultural Affairs. 'The wide range of these activities', the NEIC Report for that year noted, 'indicates the change which has occurred in the traditional concept of industrial relations. The subject is no longer confined to simple but fundamental questions such as wages and conditions of employment. It now embraces a wide range of diverse social issues which have an impact upon the relationship between employers and their employees' (Report of NEIC for 12 months ending 31 October 1979).

This message was reiterated in the 1980 Report (Address, NEIC Chairman R. Kirby to CAI Special General Meeting 28/11/80).

One method of trying to assist the Secretariat in dealing with such a range of activities was the creation of working parties. The first of these became operational in July 1979 and helped formulate wages policies. Two other working parties, one to review the *Act* and industrial relations systems, the other reduced working hours, came into being during the period. The first of these bodies indicated the increasing divisions within employers over the continuance of a centralised or decentralised wages system. By November 1979 it reported 'a strong but not unanimous view that Industry cases, rather than National Wage cases, should have the predominant role in Wage Fixation'. It further reported, however, that 'in the meantime there was no alternative but to support the existing Council policy' (CAI–NEIC Officers Meeting 2/11/79). This policy was for a centralised system based on productivity rather than price movements — a policy that led to a negative sniping at the existing indexation guidelines; the seeking of annual rather than more frequent reviews; the quarantining of work value and industry cases; the greater discounting of price movements for government 'policy induced price rises'; a policy that proffered ever longer litanies of strike indicators to demonstrate the absence of the substantial compliance required by the indexation guidelines. As the wages Working Party admitted, the NEIC had not been able to formulate either a positive or a long-term wages policy. That seemed a feature common to other major actors in the system. Thus the indexation system, which by mid-1979 the Commission had declared to be on the brink of abandonment, limped on for another 2 years. By the time indexation was abandoned in July 1981, the NEIC still had not formulated a wages policy. Divisions on this score, and the vexed question of finances, led to many associations going their own way. Associations serving the building, retailing, insurance, meat slaughtering, entertainment, woolbroking and broadcasting industries disaffiliated, as did the National Farmers' Federation. The loss of membership occurred at a time when the union movement was consolidating its resources by way of ACTU mergers with the ACSCPA (1979) and the CAGEO (1981) and at a time when the CAI was confronted with 'the growth in single-company awards which meant that a large number of members were drifting away from employer association structures' (CAI-NEIC Officers Meeting 6/9/79). Perhaps reflecting this company drift, the 'Big 50', which had threatened to form their own organisation in the 1970s, did so in the early 1980s — initially Round Table and subsequently the Business Council of Australia (BCA). The BCA made separate wage submissions (through the NEIC) in 1983 and fragmented the CAI's representative role at the 1983 Economic Summit and the 1985 Tax Summit.[12]

Post-1980 strains

The divisions and ructions that characterised the first 3 years of CAI operations became more pronounced after 1980. This was the case notwithstanding the very competent input by the NEIC at national test cases, and the greater need for employer unity under a Labor administration that placed great demands on employers' lobbying and representative skills. The CAI experienced increased organisational and financial difficulties. It also became the victim of economic and political circumstances.

The previous section recounted the financial difficulties that confronted the newly formed Confederation and its industrial relations wing, the NEIC. Those difficulties became more pronounced in the early 1980s as the employer association insurance companies, the mainstay of Confederation finances, made losses. The Manufacturers Mutual Insurance Limited (a subsidiary of the CMNSW) made a loss of $18.5m in 1980–81. The VEF's subsidiary, Federation Insurance, made a similar loss, which was partially offset by the sale of $10m in shares and $4.5m from other investments. This left it with a net loss of $3.8m. The VCM's subsidiary, Chamber of Manufactures Insurance Limited, reported a $1.5m loss for the 1980–81 financial year. 'Altogether', one commentator noted, 'these three organisations, the source of 70 per cent of the operating income of the Confederation of Australian Industry, sustained losses amounting to $24m, with the annual reports indicating little likely improvement during the current year' (Dobson 1982). With the loss of revenue from its staple sources, the CAI was forced to substantially increase levies on other members. For example, the membership fee of the Australian Retailers Association for 1980–81 was $11 800. This was scheduled to increase to $56 600 over the 6-year period to 1986–87. The Association chose to disaffiliate rather than pay such an increase. Other associations also came to question the need for such enormous increases. In particular, 'the amount of time and money both divisions were allocating to frequent overseas participation in International Labour Organisation and Business Co-operation Committees, the benefit from which was not apparent, was becoming a topic of more frequent discussion' (ibid.).

The massive affiliation increases, in some cases in the order of 400 per cent, provided a ready-made excuse for disaffiliation by some organisations who had other reasons for doing so. For example, the Australian Woolselling Brokers' Federation became critical of the NEIC's support for a centralised wages system. Developments on the industrial relations and wages front since the Total Wage campaign of 1967 had caused this federation to press, not only for the abandonment of national wage cases, but also for the removal of the arbitration system. In the process, relationships between Polites and his former supporter, B. Purvis (Executive Director of the Federation), became embittered. The Federation's disaffiliation, on the grounds that the CAI had not honoured its financial commitment to inaugural members at the time of its formation, enabled both organisations to side-step the more difficult underlying philosophical rift (Interview, B. Purvis 29/1/86).

The raising of affiliation fees did not have the desired effect. Some organisations disaffiliated, thus reducing contributions. Others merely argued that the fee increase was in breach of the Foundation Members' undertaking at the time the NEA was persuaded to join the Confederation. In the view of many, CAI finances were the primary responsibility of the Foundation Members who were cynically referred to as 'the founding fathers in perpetuity'. Many affiliates simply refused to accept the fee increases. In some cases these associations adopted a 'take it or leave it' attitude but did agree to index the fees set at the time of joining the Confederation (Interview, B. Evans 17/12/85). As well as leading to tensions within the CAI membership, the fee increase may have dissuaded some potential new members from joining the Confederation.

Economic recession compounded the CAI's financial difficulties since it increased the perception on the part of many groups of the need for special interest representation. Thus, the National Farmers' Federation (NFF) maintained that a centralised wages system, with its uniform wage increases, militated against the depressed rural sector. In the NFF's view, the rural sector did not have the capacity to pay wage increases similar to those of other sectors of the economy. It disaffiliated from the CAI, supposedly because the Confederation's support for centralism was a cause of hardship to rural employers. Scrutiny of Confederation national wage case submissions would indicate that the Confederation's centralist policies, which were based on productivity rather than price increases, could not be construed as being against the interests of this sector. Further, the Confederation was successful in getting the national wage guidelines altered in such a way as to take account of those sectors claiming an incapacity to pay general wage increases. Despite these efforts, the Confederation proved a useful 'coconut shy'. The NFF itself was unable to make effective use of the 'economic incapacity' guidelines accompanying indexation after 1981.

The NFF experience suggested other inherent problems for the Confederation: the restructuring of competing umbrella organisations and the turnover in officials whose long association with national wage cases had led them to see merit in effective co-ordination mechanisms. Just as the restructuring of the manufacturing sector led to the ACMA courting the ACEF, so too the decreasing political influence of the Country Party (now the National Party) and the lower rates of return to rural interests led to the formation of the National Farmers' Federation. As part of this restructuring, the AWGC, the mainstay of the NFF, underwent a metamorphosis similar to that of the ACMA in its CAI transformation. In 1979, it merged with the Australian Farmers' Federation to provide the nucleus for the NFF. Though the AWGC had evolved primarily into an industrial organisation (its only full-time paid officer for much of its post-1890 history was the industrial officer), the NFF was formed primarily as a lobbying organisation. Thus, the merger diluted the former AWGC's concentration on industrial relations. Further, shortly after the formation of the NFF, Mr E. Cole who had been AWGC's industrial officer for over two decades, and had been a member of the NEA Industrial Committee, and was a strong supporter of Polites, resigned. He took with him the conviction the need of effective employer co-ordination mechanisms. The retirement of other NEA activists (including that of Polites himself in 1983) meant that Cole's experience was not an isolated case.

While the NFF may have considered that the Confederation's approach was too 'soft', other groups objected to the Confederation's scrutiny, intended to reduce any leakages outside the national wage guidelines. This impaired the ability of associations in productive industries to buy industrial peace through generous wage increases or other concessions. In the view of some, the disaffiliation of the building and construction industry associations was an attempt to remove Confederation scrutiny and peer group pressure on these associations.

Thus, relations between the CAI and its inaugural and ordinary members were not smooth. Excluding the Foundation Members, by the end of 1979 the CAI had been successful in attracting 31 members. Over the next 8 years it suffered 16 disaffiliations.[13] It partially compensated for this loss by gaining five new members.[14]

Other problems encountered by the CAI included the emergence of new employer organisations whose New Right philosophies were at odds with those of the Confederation. The most notable of these was the Australian Federation of Employers (AFE). Spurred by the perceived lack of action by established employer groups against the anti free enterprise activities of Labor, this organisation sought to counter its inability to attract mainstream employer groups by public criticism of the CAI. Its industrial relations philosophy, as articulated by Chairman Andrew Hay, sought the removal of the Conciliation and Arbitration Commission, and the 'development of a system of negotiated labour contracts which, in the breach, would entitle either party liable for the monetary damages incurred' (Plowman 1987). The AFE made appearances at national wage cases, where its submissions were out of tune with those of the CAI. This nuisance value was compounded by its frequent criticism of the CAI, which heightened the perception of employer disunity.

Yet other organisational problems impacted on the CAI . To the larger organisations which, through the 'Big 50', who had been a factor in the formation of the Confederation, the CAI interests were seen to be primarily aligned to the small and medium-sized firms, which form the bulk of the federations' and chambers' membership. The large companies formed their own organisation, the Business Council of Australia (BCA). Though this Council presented its national wage submissions through the CAI, on trade and commerce matters it was afforded partner status with the CAI by the Hawke Governments. This reduced the status of the CAI.

If larger companies reacted to the perceived small business orientation of the CAI, small businesses reacted to the formation of the BCA by forming, or revitalising, their own national organisations — the Australian Small Business Association and the Council of Small Business Organisations. This development added to the number of organisations seeking to speak on behalf of employers.

Problems also developed within the Foundation Members' ranks. In the view of many manufacturers, the ACMA-ACEF merger seriously diluted manufacturers' lobbying capacity. This led to lower tariffs, increased foreign competition and a substantial erosion of Australia's manufacturing base. In part, this perception led to the disaffiliation of the Metal Trades Industry Association in 1987. It has also led to the creation of the Australian Chambers of Manufactures (ACM), which, by 1988, had two divisions — the Victorian division (formerly the VCM) and the CMNSW. In effect, the ACM took up the protectionist mantle of the former ACMA. This served to consolidate the free trade coalitions. The former Associated Chambers of Commerce of Australia was reconstituted as the Australian Chambers of Commerce.

Organisational problems were not limited to the trade area. The ACEF agreed to the ACMA merger on the clear understanding that the trade and industrial wings would each be autonomous. The geographic separation of the wings, the former being located in Canberra and the latter in Melbourne, reinforced this commitment to autonomy. In time, newer brooms sought to 'rationalise' the CAI's schizophrenic existence. In December 1981 a move to appoint a board of management under a super director (a move that would have reduced the NTIC and NEIC to CAI sub-committees) was defeated. At that time the NTIC was renamed the 'CAI Trade Council' and the NEIC renamed the 'CAI Industrial Council'. Also at that time, an

Executive Officer was appointed to head up the whole organisation, a move explicitly rejected in 1977. There was a perception by many associations that over time the Executive Officer operated in such a way as to encroach on the autonomy of the industrial wing. In August 1987 there was yet another move to integrate both Councils still further. This was thwarted, in part, because of the realisation that many affiliates of the Industrial Council (including perhaps some federations) would have disaffiliated in protest.

Summary and conclusion

The beginning and end of the period under review coincided with the only two Labor Governments of the post-war period. Employer unity at the beginning of the period was not strong. The National Employers' Associations suffered major dissensions as the result of the sectional activities of particular groups, in particular the Metal Trades Industry Association. By the end of the period the new, and more formalised, co-ordination machinery could hardly claim any greater record of unity. In part, this was the product of the difficult economic and political circumstances and of the pervasive structural changes taking place within the Australian economy. In part, it was because the Confederation itself had been formed as a negative response to those changes. It was argued earlier in this chapter that a major factor impelling the ACMA to merge with the ACEF was its attempts to maintain its own influence in a changing world, and in particular one in which national industry associations had come to usurp the previously privileged position of the ACMA and ACEF. If this is a true assessment, then the merger may have merely bought these umbrella organisations time; it did not alter the fundamental shifts leading to an erosion of the influence and importance of the chambers and federations or their national organisations. The CAI's more formal structure, which sought to maintain the pivotal role of the federations and chambers, was less flexible than that of previous co-ordination machinery. Though the previous loose-knit arrangements had provided a malleable forum capable of absorbing many of the ructions between employer groups, the more formalised structure of the Confederation was less amenable to such conflicts. Inevitably this led to disaffiliations, which militated against the co-ordination role assumed by the CAI. This became particularly so as the Foundation Members, who occupied a more privileged position within the CAI, had greater difficulties in sustaining the economic viability of the Confederation.

On many fronts the Confederation experienced instability. By 1988 nearly half of the inaugural and ordinary members who had joined the CAI had disaffiliated. This included the two associations that, together with the

ACMA and ACEF, had formed the 'Big Four' who controlled the co-ordinating committees since the end of the Second World War. By that time, too, there was the potential for Foundation Members, both the chambers and federations, to withdraw from the Confederation. The formation of the Australian Chambers of Manufactures created the potential for the two largest chambers to act independently, and perhaps against the policies, of the Confederation. There was also the potential that these chambers could disaffiliate leaving the CAI, in essence, a renamed ACEF. Moves to reduce the autonomy of the CAI Industrial Council triggered the potential disaffiliation of some federations.

The disaffiliation of any Foundation Member would prove catastrophic for the continued existence of the CAI. Already, the erosion of membership has reached a point where it is questionable whether the Confederation can effectively co-ordinate national test cases on behalf of employers in general. Its existing capacity to do so depends, in no small measure, on the co-operation of important non-affiliates not to present contrary claims or, in the case of the BCA, to process their claims through the CAI. Should this co-operation not continue, the Confederation's Industrial Council may have to re-evaluate its rationale for existence. Other associations will have to consider the age-old question of maximising their collective goals while maintaining sectional autonomy and freedom of action.

Should associations be forced to seek new co-ordinating machinery, that machinery will undoubtedly reflect the evolution that has taken place on the economic, political and organisational fronts. In any such search, associations will have a rich history to draw on. The establishment of the Business Council of Australia would suggest that the 'Companies' model would attract greater attention today than when first proposed in 1974. The failure to bring into being a confederation that has not successfully combined, nor yet kept apart, industrial relations and trade activities could impel searches for a Confederation of Employers, rather than a Confederation of Industry. The establishment of such a Confederation was a long-time goal of the ACEF. It was also the model proposed by the 'NEA Seven' in 1977. The existence of the CAI Industrial Council's research and professional staff with their enormous expertise in national test cases, would complement either of these courses. It would also complement a return to a less formal method of organisation embodying many of the attributes of the National Employers' Associations. Such a loose-knit organisation may be the only approach capable of accommodating the industrial relations co-ordination needs of national employer associations with their conflicting sectional claims.

Notes

1 Interest in a committee of inquiry into the arbitration system persisted over the next decade notwithstanding changes in governments. Such an inquiry was finally instituted by the Hawke Government in July 1983. It reported in April 1985. The Committee, headed by Professor K. J. Hancock, Vice-Chancellor of the Flinders University of South Australia, included Mr G. Polites. The third member of the Committee was Mr C. H. Fitzgibbon, a former Secretary of the Waterside Workers' Federation and Vice-President of the ACTU.

2 Post-1974 developments have confirmed the Transport Workers' Awards as the major pace-setters. As well as initiating the $25 standard for 1974 they also initiated the 'work value' round under indexation. It was in response to disputes in this industry that indexation was finally abandoned in July 1981 and the settlement then reached with employers provided the basis for the 'metal industry standard', which dominated the post-indexation period.

3 These principles provided for national wage cases as the major source of increases, with work value cases for consideration of 'non-economic factors'.

4 These supporting mechanisms included refraining from using the public sector as a pace-setter, seeking greater co-ordination between federal and state tribunals, supportive fiscal and monetary policies, government intervention in cases where the parties sought to breach the guidelines, the use of the Prices Justification Tribunal to dampen price rises and, after December 1975, tax indexation.

5 This figure was the sum voted to the industrial relations wing of the Confederation of Australian Industry. The total budget for the CAI that year was $1.3m.

6 In the Central Industrial Secretariat structure national and international policy was technically determined by the Central Council, consisting of three delegates from each constituent organisation and two delegates from each of the ACMA and ACEF. Assuming constituents were able to combine forces (which was rare) this gave them a total of 14 votes as against ACMA/ACEF's four votes. This Council met only twice yearly and it was the Secretariat that was responsible for the preparation of material for policy formulation. The Central Council was advised in policy matters by a national Industrial Affairs Committee comprising the Council Chairman and three representatives each from the ACMA and ACEF. By 1976 the VCM was expressing concern at the intrusion of the Central Industrial Secretariat into areas traditionally handled by ACMA constituents (ACMA Board Meeting 2/4/76).

7 For greater details of the power play and intrigue accompanying confederation discussions at this time see D. Plowman *A Long Haul: The Origins of the Confederation of Australian Industry*, Industrial Relations Research Centre, University New South Wales, 1988.

8 The NEIC offices were subsequently moved to Nauru House, Collins Street, the building in which the Australian Conciliation and Arbitration Commission has its headquarters.

9 The Australian Woolgrowers' and Graziers' Council had insisted during negotiations leading up to the formation of the CAI that the NEIC have full autonomy and that none of its contributions be used other than by the industrial relations wing. Curiously the AWGC elected to join both the NEIC and the Trade Council following the formation of the CAI.

10 This statement was not correct. The Victorian Municipal Government Association had taken part in the deliberations of the Committee of Control re Basic Wage in the early 1920s.

11 Until the amendments to the Articles of Association the Board consisted of a President (elected by all members of the CAI), two Vice-Presidents (one from Foundation and the other from Other Members), twelve elected from Foundation Members, one elected by Other Members, two elected by the Trade Council, who could be Foundation or Other Members, and two, elected by the NIEC who could also be either Foundation or Other Members. In the unlikely event of Other Members being elected to all positions to which Foundation Members did not have a right, Other Members would have held seven positions

as against the Foundation Members' 13 positions. In 1979, to facilitate the merger between the Confederation of Western Australian Industry and the Chamber of Manufactures of Western Australia, the Constitution was amended to provide that where Foundation Members amalgamated in any state that state would still be entitled to two Board positions. In consideration of the Queensland and Tasmanian positions where such mergers had already taken place the Articles were amended to provide for an additional Board position for each of these states' Confederations. Thus at the end of 1979 Foundation Members held a minimum of 15 Board positions and Other Members a maximum of seven. The 1980 amendments bridged this gap and provided for the possibility of 15 Foundation Members and 12 Other Members constituting the Board.

12 In addition to the Confederation of Australian Industry the following employer groups were represented at the Tax Summit: the Business Council of Australia, the National Farmers' Federation, the Australian Retailers' Association, the Council of Small Business Organisations, the Australian Chamber of Commerce, the Federal Council of the Automotive Industries, the Australian Mining Industry Council, the Metal Trades Employers Association, the Life Insurance Federation of Australia, the Australian Bankers' Association, the Australian Associated Brewers, the Master Builders Federation of Australia, the Housing Industry Association, the Australian Federation of Construction Contractors, the Travel Industry Association, the Real Estate Institute, Australian Small Business Association, the Association of Permanent Building Societies, the Australian Merchant Bankers' Association and the Australian Chamber of Manufactures.

13 The following associations have disaffiliated from the CAI: the Australian Electrical and Electronic Manufacturers' Association; the Federation of Australian Radio Broadcasters; the Insurance Council of Australia; the Life Officers' Association of Australia; the Master Builders' Federation of Australia; the Metal Trades Industry Association; the Australian Federation of Construction Contractors; the Federal Council of the Retail Motor Industry; the National Farmers' Federation (which includes two former CAI affiliates, the Australian Farmers' Federation and the Australian Woolgrowers' and Graziers' Council); the Australian Hotels Association; the Australian Wool Selling Brokers' Federation; the Cinematograph Exhibitors Association; the Australian Council of Local Government; and the Meat and Allied Trades Employers' Federation of Australia.

14 These new members are: the Banks' Industrial Association; the Carpet Manufacturers' Federation of Australia; the Pharmacy Guild of Australia; the Tractor and Machinery Association; and the Vehicle Manufacturers' Association of Australia.

9

MODELS OF NATIONAL EMPLOYER CO-ORDINATION

This study has sought to examine the factors leading employers to form national co-ordinating machinery as well as to explain the reasons for the different forms of co-ordination adopted at different points of time. Several co-ordinating models, some containing variants, were developed by employers over the period under review. These models may be described as:

- the mutual defence model
- the federation model
- the alliance model
- the secretariat model
- the confederation model.

Successive sections of this chapter examine each of these models of co-ordination and the factors behind their development.

The mutual defence model

This was the earliest form of proposed national (and state/colonial) organisation identified in the study. Its rationale was not so much the co-ordination of employer policies or the negotiation with unions at the national or state levels as a method of stiffening employer resistance to union militancy. Under this scheme individual employers, and associations of employers, could insure themselves against the whip-sawing actions of unions. It was hoped that compensating employers for strike losses would enable them to resist union demands and thus prevent the percolation of new industrial standards. This method of mutual defence was the counterpart of the unions' method of mutual insurance and of strike funds, which attempted to make strike action less of a financial burden for members.

The logistic problems associated with the implementation of such a scheme on an Australia-wide basis, and the very different negotiatory styles adopted by employers and their associations, made such a concept difficult to bring into being. Interest in this form of mutual support was, in great measure, the outcome of national strike panic accompanying the disputes of the 1890s. It dissipated with employers' victories and the decline in union power at that time.

At the state level it is uncertain whether the New South Wales Mutual Defence Fund ever became operational. Its Victorian counterpart soon succumbed to employer disinterest. At this level, employer victories reduced the need for such funds. The evidence also suggests associations had difficulty in bringing into being effective mechanisms for administering the funds. The heterogeneity of industrial undertakings and of trade associations, and the lack of a recognised peak employer body, made it difficult to administer funds other than on an *ad hoc* basis. This made such funds transitory. The emerging divisions between the protectionist manufacturers and free-trade primary and commercial interests ensured that no peak body came into being in these states.

It was only in Western Australia and South Australia that the Mutual Defence Model experienced any longevity. The Federated Employers' Assurance of Western Australia (FEAWA) was formed in 1912 and brought into being the WAEF the following year. The federation's activities were underwritten by the FEAWA. The WAEF, in turn, provided the machinery for assisting at the operational level different employers and associations, and for helping FEAWA directors determine appropriate 'test cases' for financial subsidy. Further, by trying to bring about settlements to disputes, the federation helped minimise the FEAWA's financial liabilities to strike-bound employers. In South Australia the SAEF operated the Employers' Mutual Fund. As in Western Australia, the major role of this fund was not so much compensating employers for strike losses, but rather for the costs involved in fighting test cases before the industrial tribunals.

The successful operation of the funds in these two states may be explained by three major factors. In the first place these federations quickly emerged as the dominant state employer organisations. In Western Australia, for example, the WAEF was able to entice most of the existing trade associations into membership because of its assurance and industrial services. Further, it actively set about organising associations for those sections of industry that had not been organised. In South Australia the federation had a monopoly over industrial matters until the late 1940s. In both cases the dominant role of the federations was enhanced by the support of key associations such as the Chamber of Mines in Western Australia and the Iron Trades Association in South Australia, by the small scale of manufacturing in each state, and the lack of major clashes over the question of protection. An important factor enabling these federations to dominate employers' industrial relations services and operate defence funds was that the federations in these states quickly adapted to the new tribunal situation, rather than undertaking futile efforts of trying to eradicate the tribunals. In Victoria and New South Wales on the other hand, the federations continued to thwart, rather than operate within, the tribunal system. As outlined in the case of Victoria, the latter approach necessarily led to other employer bodies having to play a representative role before tribunals, which undercut the VEF's industrial influence. The SAEF and WAEF quickly developed the expertise to operate within the local tribunal system thus reducing the need for individual associations to develop their own industrial departments. This situation broke down in South Australia in the late 1940s for reasons outlined in Chapter 5. With the breakdown of the SAEF's dominant role, the establishment of an industrial division within the Chamber of Manufactures and the advent of the Metal Industry Association of South Australia, the Employers' Mutual Defence Fund ceased to operate. In Western Australia, the Federated Employers' Assurance became a public company (the Associated Employers of Western Australia) in 1957. This company amalgamated with the WAEF and became the latter's Finance Board in 1961.

The federation model

The federation model consisted of trade associations joining to form an employers' federation in each state. The federations, in turn, confederated at the national level to form the Central Council of Employers of Australia (Fig. 9.1). The coming into being of such a national Council, and the rationale of this mode, were outlined in Chapter 1, which explored the inauguration of the EFNSW and the formation of the CCEA. The impetus for the formation of these organisations was not, in essence, very different from that which earlier had called for the establishment of indemnity funds, namely an overt challenge to the employer situation. In this case, however, it was not the challenge of industrial unionism that called for an organisational response, but rather that of industrial legislation, which attempted to alter bargaining relationships and which struck at the heart of employers' newly won freedom of contract. The establishment of industrial tribunals, and especially of compulsory arbitration tribunals, required of employers machinery for dealing with unions that was less transitory than previously. The federation model was attractive on a number of scores. It enabled trade associations to devote themselves to those things they knew best — the economic and commercial interests of their members. Such interests often conflicted with those of other trade associations. The creation of a separate industrial body enabled trade associations to continue in their sectional interests in the knowledge that the federation would defend the industrial interests common to all employers. The federation would also develop the necessary expertise to represent employers before the new tribunal system and act as a clearing house for industrial information. The federation model offered employers the potential for establishing their organisation equivalent to the Trades and Labor Councils. The federation model was also attractive in that it had the potential of providing a better lobbying organisation than could be provided by a number of disparate trade associations.

Figure 9.1 The Federation Model (1904)

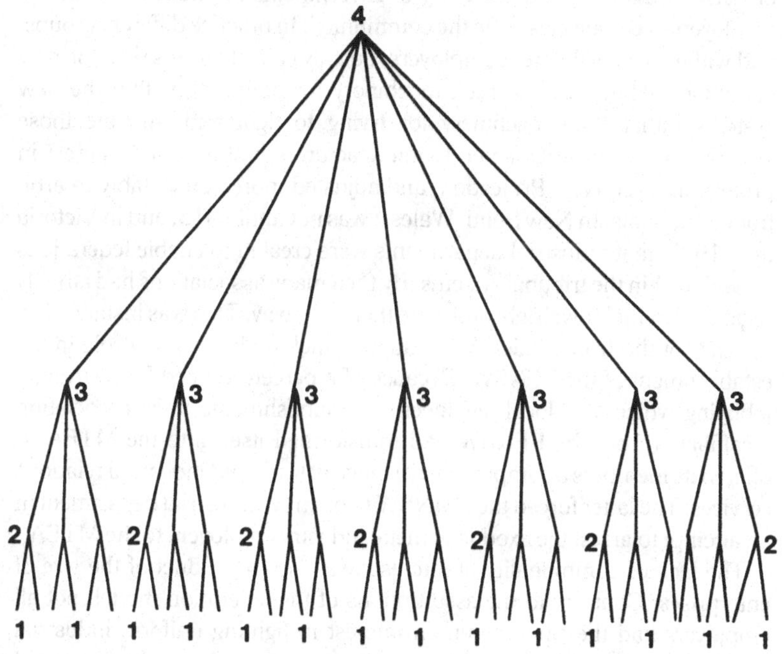

Individual employers (1) are grouped into Trade Associations (2). The Trade Associations are affiliated with the State Employers' Federations (3). The Federations confederate to form the Central Council of Employers of Australia (4).

Apart from Western Australia and, until the 1940s South Australia, the federation model soon proved inadequate for a number of reasons. In particular it presupposed a greater unity of interest and commonality of purpose on the part of employers than turned out to be the case; it assumed that industrial relations and trade considerations could be isolated from each other; it overstated the complexities of operating within the new tribunal systems; and its twin role of an industrial and political agency necessarily led to divisions about the appropriate balance between these functions. At the national level other problems also existed. Interstate rivalries, financial and voting rights and obligations, and the question of autonomy from state affiliates all reduced the potential effectiveness of the federation model.

The federation model presupposed a common objective against which all employer interests could combine. The industrial legislation, and the new lease of life given unions by this legislation, were seen to provide such an objective. So too was the tendency of governments to 'make the State the employers of certain classes in the community'. In practice different groups, and within groups different employers, quickly came to terms with the new conditions. They came to seek machinery for operating within the new systems rather than machinery for trying to fight and frustrate those systems. As noted in Chapter 1, manufacturers had a vested interest in protection, even New Protection, and adjusted more comfortably to arbitration tribunals. In New South Wales it was not until 1915, and in Victoria until 1927, that industrial departments were created to enable federations to work within the tribunal systems. By then many associations had already registered in their own right and gone their own way. This was instanced by the case of the Iron Trades Association, which took a leading role in the establishment of the EFNSW. Because of a perceived need for a stronger lobbying voice for local engineering establishments this association disaffiliated from the EFNSW and transformed itself into the MTEA. It offered its members a comprehensive range of trade and industrial relations services. The latter forced the CMNSW to open an industrial department in an attempt to arrest the exodus of metal industry employers to the MTEA.

The lack of commonality of interests was also a product of the size of enterprises. Contrary to the assumptions of the federation model, not all employers had the same common interest in fighting uniform industrial standards and trade unions. In many instances, employers had a vested interest in 'taking competition out of the market', since such a situation prevented competitors from stealing a march on them by undercutting wages and costs. This was instanced by the move by employers in the brush-making industry to bring into being a wages board that would prevent sweating by competitors. In some cases large employers made 'sweet-heart' agreements with unions with a view to putting 'certain classes of competitors out of business'. In other cases tribunal standards could be used to dilute certain advantages of competitors such as proximity to public transport by requiring all shops to be closed at peak travelling times. Such considerations made it impossible for federations to provide a co-ordinating role since there were conflicting employer interests. The ability of large employers to register under the arbitration systems as employer unions in their own right added to such co-ordination problems. That the arbitration Acts provided for the registration of craft-based and industry-based associations, and of single companies as employer unions in their own right, presented the federations with yet another organisational problem: the umbrella form of organisation adopted by federations was not consistent with the form of organisation conceived by the Acts. The latter assumed direct registration and representation by parties to disputes, in most cases the trade associations, rather than a more distant umbrella inter-industry organisation. The ability of different groups to register separately (and in the case of federations to register only with respect to certain classes of members) provided a direct avenue for associations to by-pass federations when they chose to do so.

That employers could not compartmentalise industrial relations and trade considerations is evidenced by the major cleavage between manufacturers and the primary and commercial groups. It is also evidenced by the different responses of these groups to the New Protection. Manufacturers soon developed their own organisations, which, in most states and at the national level, came to rival the federations. The manufacturers own method of organisation, however, replicated the federation model and sought to provide an umbrella coverage for all employers and trade associations in the manufacturing and allied industries.

Trade divisions naturally influenced trade association membership of, or aversion towards, the federations. On top of this associations also found that, even if possessing a common trade outlook, industrial relations policies between themselves, and between themselves and the federations, could differ. As the co-ordinator and watch-dog organisation of trade associations representing disparate areas of economic activity, federations soon found that the major way of formulating policy was to sink to the lowest common denominator of consensus. This necessarily meant a negative and reactive approach to industrial problems, legislation and award-making. Sectional groups, however, could take a more pragmatic and practical approach to problems affecting their own industries. The simplest way of implementing such an approach was to take on their own industrial work, particularly when they found that industrial tribunal work was not as demanding nor as complex as initially thought. In this situation federations increasingly came to service the needs of individual employers who, for one reason or another, did not want to belong to the sectional association; of those small employers seeking some protection against the designs of larger employers and unions; and of those trade associations with insufficient funds or with a sufficiently low level of industrial activity not to warrant their diversifying into employer associations. Though many of the larger associations continued to remain affiliates of the federations, this was largely to help in state wage cases, which, as noted in Chapter 2, began as early as 1914 in New South Wales. Federation support continued to be desirable, since the federations continued to provide a useful forum for debating proposed new legislation that cut across all employers. Membership of the federations also relieved associations of the tedious task of compiling statistical and award information.

The increased association fragmentation and the inability of the federations to bring into operation the federation model also affected the similarly composed Chambers of Manufactures, notwithstanding their more homogeneous composition. Even within the manufacturing sector, policy divisions and organisational competition soon appeared. The emergence of the MTEA has already been cited. Other separate manufacturing associations developed in New South Wales, which reduced the CMNSW's ability to speak for manufacturers. Separate associations catered for such areas as the textile, footwear, clothing, hosiery, brick, paint, plaster, bread, furniture, timber, and printing (which included pulp and paper manufacturing) sectors.

The development of separate employer associations acting independently of the federations and Chambers of Manufactures restricted the scope of the federation model. A latent problem for national employer co-ordination was the potential for the industry associations to federate and form national associations that would reduce the voice of the CCEA and ACMA. It was this eventuality that caused the search for other models for national co-ordination.

The alliance model

The inadequacy of the federation model as a method of employer co-ordination was demonstrated in 1917 when the CCEA called for the creation of an Employers' Industrial Disputes Council (EIDC). The objective of this Council was 'the securing of a powerful Central Council of Employers representing important industries to deal with any serious industrial disturbances arising at any time'. The proposal to form a Central Council of Employers was a recognition by the CCEA that it had not been able to perform that co-ordinating role itself, the purpose for which it had been conceived. The CCEA proposed that the EIDC be comprised not only of the national umbrella organisations (i.e. the CCEA, ACMA and ACCA) but also of 'such large employing interests as Shipping, Colliery Proprietors, Pastoralists, and other large groups of industries'. Though the EIDC did not come into being, the form of organisation proposed served as the model for employer co-ordination in the period 1924–58. During that period the Committee of Control re the Basic Wage (1924), the Committee of Control re the Basic Wage and Standard Hours (1926), the Interstate Conference of Employers (1930), the Basic Wage Steering Committee (1947) and the Basic Wage Working Party (1956) performed the co-ordinating role envisaged for the EIDC. All these organisations had a number of similar characteristics:

- They were loose-knit informal alliances.
- They were voluntary alliances.
- They were *ad hoc* alliances, which were brought into being as the need arose.
- They were representative alliances, which brought together national umbrella organisations, national and state employer associations and national companies.
- They were confined to a restricted role involving test cases before the CCCA. They determined the policy of 'employers in general' for such cases and raised the finances necessary to prosecute cases. Policy determined as the 'general' policy was not binding. Any organisation could be separately represented in cases in which submissions on behalf of employers generally were made.
- They were all influenced, controlled by and dependent on a small number of key organisations.
- None of the alliances employed their own staff; they were reliant on the goodwill of member organisations for the necessary manpower.

This alliance model (Fig. 9.2.) represented a compromise between the desire for autonomy by employer associations and their need to work in concert in the era of test cases after 1921. Such cases were designed to provide general norms for federal awards. It was noted in Chapter 2 that Higgins J had sought to use test cases as early as the Harvester case of 1907. In this he had not been successful.

Figure 9.2 The Alliance Model (1924–58)

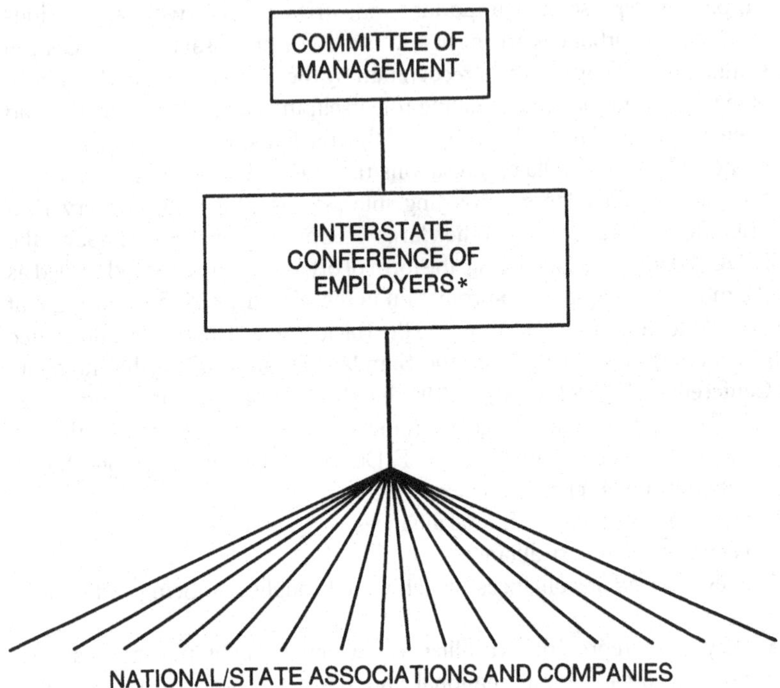

* As at 1930. As noted in the text the name of the co-ordinating body varied.

In addition to High Court challenges by employers that restricted the federal jurisdiction until 1914, the inability of the CCCA to vary awards during their currency restricted the scope of test cases. The most Higgins could do was to bring together awards expiring about the same time and determine common standards for them. The new wage standards to 1921 were not initiated by the CCCA but rather derived from the New South Wales system, which began holding test cases for state award employees as early as 1914, and which began holding six-monthly reviews of the Living Wage in 1918.

Chapter 3 reviewed the 1921 amendments to the *Conciliation and Arbitration Act* providing that awards could be varied during their currency. These amendments enabled unions to make joint applications for basic wage variations, and Powers J directed the many unions seeking the adjustment of the basic wage to reflect the findings of the Piddington

Commission to present a joint application. The 1921 amendments also provided for Full Benches to determine certain matters (which in 1926 came to include the basic wage), thus giving greater test-case value to these matters. In 1921–22 the CCCA had instituted the system of basic wage automatic quarterly cost-of-living adjustments. By then, too, unions had formed the Commonwealth Council of Federated Unions to take control of general applications. In 1927 this Council was absorbed into the newly constituted ACTU.

The employers' initial response to the new order was to ignore test cases in the hope that by doing so their scope would be reduced. By 1924, however, employers were forced to accept the new situation and legislation in New South Wales providing for a 44-hour week made it inevitable that test cases in this area would continue to be mounted in the federal jurisdiction. The CCEA sought to address the situation by proposing the establishment of a Confederation of Employers. Divisions between the Chambers of Manufactures and federations in the major states as their industrial divisions competed with each other, and the perennial pre-occupation of ACMA with tariff protection, reduced the prospects of any formalised co-ordinating mechanisms.

Despite these barriers to unity, the new test-case era necessitated some co-ordination machinery among employers both to reduce costs and to ensure that their submissions were not at cross-purposes with each other. This *ad hoc* machinery evolved gradually. The 1921 basic wage review of the gas employees' award was converted into a general review by the CCCA. The CCEA took the initiative in bringing about a united approach to the case by the four principal organisations involved.

The 1922 case to determine 'The Fairest Method of Securing the Harvester Standard to the Workers' evoked a greater response from employer associations because its outcome was seen to impact more generally than the previous case. Nine major associations took part. The VCM, MTEA, Municipal Association of Victoria and Master Carriers Association joined the Australian Mines and Metals Association and the CCEA in making a joint submission. A second joint submission was made by shipping, building and timber interests.

Between 1924 and 1928 unions threatened to apply for a general review of the basic wage formula. This threat and the Main Hours case of 1926 led to a more formalised method of co-ordination and revenue raising, namely the establishment of the Committee of Control re Basic Wage. The CCEA initiated the formation of this organisation in August 1924 and was supported by associations representing graziers, shipowners, metalliferous miners and timber merchants. The Gas Companies and C.S.R. also joined in that year. In 1926 the name was expanded to that of 'Committee of Control re Basic Wage and Working Hours'. Membership grew to 35 organisations (including state federations) by 1927. Though the ACMA was not a member of the Committee, the VCM, which undertook its industrial work, was. Members of this Committee met to determine broad general policy. An Executive or Management Committee of seven organisations, chaired by the CCEA's proxy T. Maughan, had charge of the day-to-day conduct of cases, the implementation of agreed policy and the raising of funds and allocation of costs. The Committee re Control became dormant in 1927 as recession reduced union applications for basic wage reviews.

The Committee was resurrected in February 1930 to review legislative changes by the Scullin Government and to consider means of reducing the basic wage. From then until 1940 it operated under the name 'Interstate Conference of Employers' (ICE), perhaps a reflection of the wider range of issues this body initially undertook. As noted in Chapter 4, however, the ICE was soon forced to restrict itself to test case issues and so minimise the potential for conflict among members. An Executive of seven members determined the basis of apportioning costs of any test cases and had charge of implementing policy determined by members at joint meetings. Though the ICE was very active in 1930 and 1931, when it met on 11 occasions, increasing tensions between organisations over the issue of federal uniform standards reduced its appeal to many organisations. After 1933 it met on only five occasions, the last in 1940 to seek the abandonment of the prosperity loading to the basic wage that had been granted in 1937. The 1940 meeting was the first to give the Executive Committee controlling affairs a more descriptive title — the 'Co-ordinating and Consultative Committee'. This Committee became dormant when the CCCA stood over the Basic Wage case in 1940. It was subsequently reconstituted under the name 'Basic Wage Steering Committee' in the period 1947 to 1955, and as the 'Basic Wage Working Party' from 1956 on.

Though these various co-ordinating committees were similarly composed, they did evolve to reflect the shifts in the balance of power between and within member organisations. As noted, the prototype committee of 1921 involved only three organisations — the CCEA, the Mines and Metals Association and the Gas Companies. These organisations, together with the next four affiliating subscribers in 1924 (Shipowners, Graziers, C.S.R. and Timber Merchants) constituted the first controlling executive, a necessity in view of the number of organisations represented. None of these organisations was able to maintain its membership of the Executive Committee. The Graziers' Council oscillated between supporting the employers' general case and presenting a separate case on behalf of rural interests. It was not represented on the 1927 Executive, was a member of the 1931 Executive, dropped out of subsequent Committees but was a member of the 1949 Steering Committee. It continued to prevaricate during the 1950s. The Timber Merchants and C.S.R. did not maintain membership of the Executive after 1927. Neither, strange to say, did the convening organisation, the CCEA. By 1931 internal divisions between members had led to it not being able to agree on policy, a situation replicated in the ACMA, which, to this time, had not been a member of the alliance. In addition to the Shipowners, Miners and Graziers, the 1931 Executive included two federations (VEF and EFNSW) and three members of the VCM. The AMMA and the MTEA continued to be members of the Executive until 1940. By that date the other members were the Chambers of Manufactures and federations of Victoria, South Australia and New South Wales. The interest exhibited by the Mines and Metals Association was no doubt the result of the activities of its Secretary, T. Maughan. He played a key role in CCEA affairs and in employer co-ordination. The MTEA dropped out of the Executive following the formation of the AMIA in 1942. The latter became a member of the Steering Committee in 1949, which continued to include chambers and federations.

Not only did state affiliates replace their national organisations within the controlling committees during the 1930s and 1940s, in the case of the VCM, it came to replace the CCEA as the convenor and controlling body. A number of factors gave rise to this situation. For much of the period the CCEA/ACEF President lived in Sydney rather than Melbourne, where the test cases were conducted. His Victorian heir-apparent — T. R. Ashworth — was not acceptable as a Convenor, and in any case the VCM had greater standing than the VEF, which was then experiencing internal organisational problems. Internal splits within the CCEA further reduced its ability to co-ordinate the activities of other organisations.

During the 1930s the Committees of Control undertook their own industrial work rather than engage counsel. C. H. Grant (VCM) and L. Mann (VEF) undertook the preparation and the advocacy of cases. Perhaps because of this, the Executives came to include industrial officers of organisations to the exclusion of office bearers. The establishment of a Policy and Consultative Committee in 1950 sought to give back control of policy and finances to the office bearers of major organisations, leaving the Steering Committee to look after the conduct of cases. The Policy and

Consultative Committee was composed of the Presidents of the ACEF, ACMA and AMIA. The Steering Committee was composed of industrial officers of these organisations and, on occasion, the GFCA's industrial officer.

A feature of most of the Executive Committees was their attempts to have some form of machinery constituted on a permanent basis. As noted in Chapter 3, the attempts of the Executive Committees of 1927 were brought to an end because recession removed union applications for basic wage adjustments. A decade later, attempts of the Interstate Conference of Employers' (ICE) Executive Committee to form a permanent sub-committee to take 'a long-range view of industrial matters and make preliminary arrangements for the handling of future cases' was also rejected. The CCEA rejected this proposition on the grounds that the other principal employers' organisations would not be willing to provide the financial assistance required. The VCM's approach, in which it claimed it was not agreeable to the 'setting up of a permanent organisation which would practically mean the dictation of policy by another organisation', vindicated the CCEA's view. However, actions by CCEA affiliates had gone a long way towards bringing the ICE into disrepute. As outlined in Chapter 4, the 1930s were difficult ones for the CCEA as federations split on the question of federal uniformity. The bitterness was such that the EFNSW and VEF disaffiliated in 1935 and did not rejoin until 1937. A problem that emerged was that the supporters of federal uniformity (EFNSW, VEF and NSWCM) tried to win support for this policy through the ICE after having failed to have their own federal organisations support such a policy. Within the CCEA smaller federations had pressed for a withdrawal from the ICE. It was little wonder that organisations feared a permanent organisation might attempt to 'dictate policy'. Tensions within the ICE had resulted in that organisation being bypassed in favour of independent action. Thus, although the ICE made representation on behalf of 'employers generally' in the 1930 cases, as noted in Chapter 4, between 22 and 37 employer advocates appeared at the five Basic Wage cases held in that period; and by the time the ICE was convened to formulate policy with respect to the 1940 case five organisations had already briefed counsel. Seventeen employer advocates took part in that case. The number of advocates used in these cases indicated that the ructions within the CCEA and ACMA had now intruded into employers' basic wage submissions. A number of federations and chambers appeared separately so as to counter each other's submissions. This internal instability adversely affected attempts at inter-organisational co-ordination.

War conditioned employers to accept a centrally determined basic wage. The fragmented employer approach to Basic Wage cases was not evident after 1945 when most organisations were prepared to be represented by counsel briefed by the Steering Committee. In this more stable context the establishment of an Employers' Consultative Committee was considered by the ACEF and ACMA (Chapter 5). The latter, however, refused to support such a notion. This organisation's difficulties in co-operating with any permanent co-ordinating machinery are outlined more fully in the section of this chapter reviewing the confederation model.

The alliance model proved a useful first step in bringing about some degree of co-ordination between employer organisations covering a range of industries. The fact that over 30 national associations and companies were involved indicated the need to create co-ordination machinery that extended beyond the federation model strategy. Two developments within the model occurred. As the number of organisations in the alliance grew, a smaller management committee (executive) became necessary for the day-to-day implementation of policy and overseeing of the industrial work. The second was the creation of separate committees, one to oversee finances and policy formulation and the other to oversee the industrial work. Until 1958 organisations were not prepared to take the next step — that of giving permanency to the co-ordinating committees. Several factors may be adduced for this: inter-organisational rivalries, the internal instability of the ACMA and ACEF, the lack of a national industrial service by the two umbrella organisations, the annual rotation of presidency of the ACMA, the ACMA's dominant and independent activities and general aloofness from the ACEF, and the general lack of economic and statistical expertise required at test cases to that time. However, the most compelling factor reducing any concerted effort for permanent organisation was that until 1956 there was not the sustained need for co-ordinating machinery. Following the adoption of automatic basic wage indexation in 1922, reviews of the basic wage were held in 1931, 1932, 1933, 1934, 1937, 1940, 1946, 1949–50 and 1953. It can be seen that, apart from the depression years, when unions sought a restoration of the 10 per cent cut (and when the ICE met bi-monthly), cases were infrequent. Standard Hours cases were also infrequent — 1922, 1926 and 1946–47. Further, despite the *ad hoc* nature of their co-ordinating mechanisms, employers could claim success in many of these cases — the Basic Wage cases of 1931, 1932, 1933 and 1940 with partial success in 1946; and the Hours cases of 1922 and 1926. This degree of success may have reduced the perceived need for more permanent co-ordinating machinery.

The secretariat model

The alliance model formed the first basis for co-ordinating umbrella organisations, industry associations and companies. Three key features of this method of organisation were its *ad hoc* nature, its loose-knit and voluntary nature, and the lack of permanency for its industrial and/or management committees.

As already noted, there had been a number of attempts to place some form of secretariat or management committee on a more permanent basis. By the mid-1950s pressures for greater permanency increased. Employers determined policy and co-ordinating machinery for the 1956 Basic Wage case along lines that had become standard practice, namely 'That the Presidents of ACMA (as Chairman), ACEF, and AMIA be constituted a Policy and Consultative Committee to direct the conduct of the case (on the understanding that should any major important issue arise which they felt called for a general meeting, this would be done), and to control costs'. The Steering Committee consisted of industrial officers of these organisations with power to co-opt the GFCA industrial officer. By that date, however, there was a more widely held concern about the deficiencies of the *ad hoc* nature of the machinery. Typical of the concern was the TEF's observation: 'We begin our cases at least one lap behind the opposition because we create a new loose-knit body each time an economic matter comes before the Full Court. As to funds we never know what is going to be available and there is bickering and bargaining as to apportionment of contributions'. Further, as the Policy Committee Chairman noted, the rate at which test cases were being mounted had increased. 'In the last ten years', he observed, 'we have had five major cases, including the 40 Hours case, and it seems that we are likely to be faced with enquiries of this kind at fairly frequent intervals'.

This statement was proved correct. The 1956 Basic Wage Full Bench determined that thereafter the basic wage would be reviewed annually. This decision necessitated a reappraisal on the part of both employers and unions of their methods of preparing for such cases. This need was compounded by the earlier basic wage judgement of 1953, which abolished automatic quarterly cost-of-living adjustments in favour of 'economic reviews', and the treatment of Metal Trades Margins cases from 1952 on as 'economic inquiries in miniature'. These developments were recounted in Chapter 6. Both basic wage and margins reviews required a greater degree of economic expertise than was previously the case. The 1953 case had been a costly one for employers — $72 000. There was no assurance that future (annual) cases involving the statistical evidence required by the economic indicators approach would not involve employers in similar costs.

It was these developments that convinced employers of the need to move away from the totally loose-knit *ad hoc* alliance model to one that incorporated some degree of permanency — the secretariat model. The latter was a refinement of, and shared many things in common with, its predecessor. It remained essentially a loose-knit alliance of voluntary organisations that were brought together as the need arose. These organisations shared the costs of test cases. The alliance's charter continued to be a restricted one and it continued to rely on contributing organisations for human resources. The secretariat model differed from its predecessor, however, in having its management and industrial committees constituted on a permanent basis. It also differed in that the organisations controlling these committees became set. A further distinguishing feature, from 1961 on, was provision for regular meetings of members of the alliance.

The Secretariat Model operated from 1959 until 1977 when the Confederation of Australian Industry absorbed the National Employers' Associations. The NEA was the significant metamorphosis of the period and sought to ensure a compatibility of outlook between the permanent and largely independent Policy and Industrial Committees and the general body of employer organisations.

Though there were industrial relations imperatives for the establishment of more permanent co-ordinating mechanisms, the ACMA's organisational needs were to the fore in determining the form of organisation, the scope of its operations and the timing of changes. In 1957 the ACEF had sought to have the Policy Committee and Working Party placed on a permanent basis with the Policy Committee having a wide mandate — 'dealing with such national industrial matters as the conduct of Basic Wage and other national proceedings; matters for discussion at the Ministry of Labour Advisory Council meetings, ILO Conferences, Immigration Advisory Council meetings and the like; and such other national problems as Constitutional Reform' (Chapter 6). The ACMA did not accept the need for any permanent arrangements at that time.

A year later, however, the ACMA itself was leading the movement for more permanent machinery. By then the ACEF had begun placing its national secretariat on a full-time basis and was proposing to offer a national industrial service to associations and national companies. By then, too, the ACEF had developed a degree of internal stability that eluded the ACMA as its South Australian affiliate sought to have the Commission prescribe a lower basic wage for South Australian industry. The ACMA was conscious that if it continued to obstruct initiatives to form some permanent co-ordinating machinery it might be by-passed. Its Memorandum of February 1958 noted that 'ACMA is accepted as the leading employer organisation in such cases as the present application for increased Basic Wage and Margins. If we do not exercise this leadership, we run the risk either of a proliferation of employer bodies . . . or of some other organisation being formed and doing the job, and eventually over-shadowing us in this important field of service to our members'.

It was the ACMA's proposal for the establishment of Standing Committees that was accepted by a meeting of employers in December 1958. Unlike the ACEF's wider charter, the ACMA's proposal limited the role of the Committees to basic wage claims. The Policy Committee was to be comprised of the Presidents of the ACMA, ACEF and AMIA, and the Working Party of an industrial officer of each of these organisations together with an industrial officer from the GFCA. These Committees gave the ACMA a high degree of control. It continued to provide the Chairman of the Policy Committee and Convenor of the Working Party. Further, Chambers of Manufactures constituted the bulk of the AMIA's membership. The ACMA's potential for controlling the industrial committee was further enhanced by its decision, in 1958, to create a national industrial relations division.

In addition to the question of controlling the co-ordinating mechanisms, three other reasons were adduced in Chapter 6 for ACMA's new-found interest in more permanent co-ordinating mechanisms. The first of these was financial. During the 1940s ACMA contributed up to 50 per cent of the costs of national test cases. As the costs of national test cases increased, as the number of national cases multiplied (see Table 6.1), and as affiliates such as the South Australian Chamber chose to mount their own cases at the expense of the general case, the ACMA was no longer prepared to contribute to the extent that it had in previous years. Its contribution to the 1958 Long Service Leave case, for example, was 30 per cent of the costs — the same proportion as that paid by the ACEF. As the controlling body, however, the ACMA was in the potential position of having to underwrite any shortfall in contributions. As other organisations joined the ACEF in calling for the restructuring of the Policy Committee, and as dissatisfaction with the ACMA's dominance grew, the likelihood of some organisations not responding to general levies increased. So too did the likelihood of national organisations seeking separate representation. This happened in the case of the GFCA in 1955-56 and 1958. The ACEF's 1959 decision to appoint a full-time Secretary led to the potential of that organisation seeking separate representation since it continued to oppose the ACMA's policy of representation by paid legal counsel. Other organisations, such as the Woolbrokers' Federation were also contemplating establishing their own national industrial divisions at this time.

A second, and not unrelated, reason for the ACMA's support for permanent machinery at that time was the developments from the late 1950s that threatened to rob the VCM of its important engineering division. The loss of this division to the MTEA (which occurred in 1971) would have been a serious blow to ACMA finances and standing among national organisations.

A final factor was the fact that by 1958 authority had been given to the Policy Committee to take charge of major margins cases because of their increased general application. This had the potential to increase demands for greater control of the Committees by industry associations whose awards were under review. As noted in Chapter 7, this became a major problem after 1967 but was initially headed off by the 1958 restructuring.

In its 1958 form the secretariat alliance model quickly proved inadequate for the changed industrial environment. This was clearly illustrated in 1959 when on both the basic wage and margins fronts unions made spectacular gains. In that year the basic wage was increased by 5.7 per cent and metal trades margins by 28 per cent. Employers were forced to reconsider their traditional approach to such cases, particularly the customary policy of straight-out opposition to all union claims. Employers were told by the Working Party that 'submissions become ineffective if (to quote from the words of a member of the Commission) employers continue to adopt the traditional role of opposition to all union claims'. The need to develop a 'positive' wages policy resulted in the further formalisation of the secretariat model. Under the 1958 framework the Standing Committees had a mandate to carry basic wage proceedings through to finality without reference to other employer organisations only in cases where straight-out opposition was contemplated. The positive wages policy approach necessitated greater co-ordination between the Committees and the general membership.

The bringing into being of the National Employers' Associations in June 1961 was designed to serve this purpose (Fig. 9.3). It was the first form of national co-ordination that had a set Constitution. Organisationally it differed in five significant ways from its predecessor. Firstly, the management committee, now called the National Employers' Policy Committee, included the AWGC (the successor of the GFCA). This organisation continued to be a member of the newly named National Employers'

Industrial Committee which took over the activities of the Basic Wage Working Party. Secondly, provision was made for regular — no less than half-yearly — meetings of contributing members. This contrasted with the previous situation in which members were convened when the Policy Committee thought it appropriate. Thirdly, in July 1962 the charter of the Committees was extended beyond national arbitration proceedings if such matters were referred to the Committees by the NEA. In August 1962 the charter was further increased to include industrial proceedings not involving arbitration 'if the ACTU or any other composite body of national Trade Unions is involved in any industrial matter' and if requested by a subscribing member. The fourth change was the loss by the ACMA and the VCM of their traditional leadership role in the permanent committees. The rules of the NEA provided for a rotation of the Chairmanship of the Policy Committee between the four members, and for members of the Industrial Committee to elect that Committee's Convenor. The fifth change was to formalise the secretarial arrangements, which also had the effect of integrating the two Committees. The Convenor of the Industrial Committee became Secretary of both the Policy Committee and the NEA. As noted in Chapter 7, this latter change established a firm basis for Mr George Polites to exercise a great degree of control over employer policy and co-ordination. Despite these changes, the operations of the NEA continued to depend on the goodwill of a small number of key organisations for the provision of both financial and human resources.

Two other NEA structural changes may be mentioned. The first was the establishment of the National Employers' Consultative Council in 1970, which attempted to provide a bridge between NEA members and the NEPC. It does not seem to have exerted much influence or to have operated for any long period. The second was the development of meetings of industrial officers of NEA members. By 1972 these meetings were taking place monthly and tended to alternate between Sydney and Melbourne.

In 1963 the NEPC Chairman was able to announce that the NEA had developed 'into the organisation now accepted as being responsible for the formulation of wages policy on behalf of employers generally in arbitration proceedings and national affairs'. He was also able to announce 'a positive wages policy freed from the anomalies which followed the 1959 metal trades' case. This positive wages policy consisted of trading off wage increases in return for the adoption of the total wage.

The operations of the NEA to 1967, when employers were successful in the achievement of the total wage, represented a high-water mark in employer solidarity. However, as NEIC Convenor D. Fowler (AMIA)

Figure 9.3 The NEA Model (1961–78)

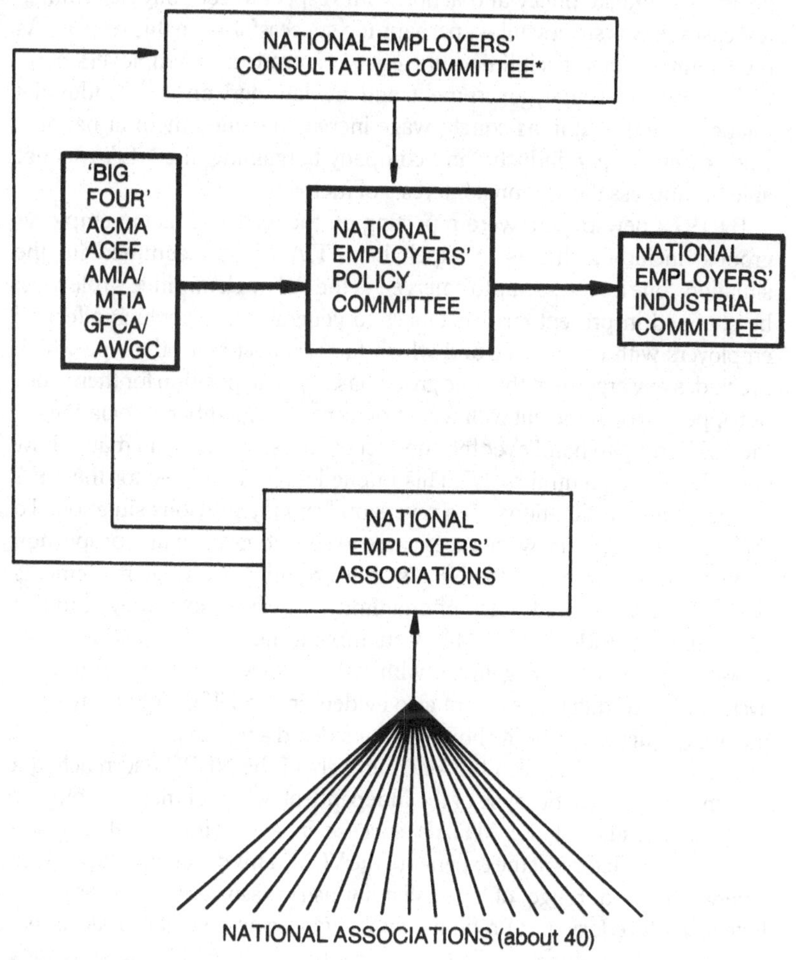

* From 1970 on.

noted, unity was not synonymous with unanimity. This became more apparent in the accommodative bargaining period following the Metal Trades Work Value case of 1967. As detailed in Chapter 7, the NEA increasingly found it difficult to marry the aspirations of the MTIA to free its members from the constraints imposed by the bench-mark role of the Metal Trades Award, with the aims of other affiliates who feared the effects of flow-ons from metal industry agreements. The NEA had been brought into being to formulate policy and action with respect to centrally determined test cases. It was successful — perhaps too successful — in this respect. As the Commission's disciplining powers were eroded, as employers complained of 'ineffectual government and no law and order in industrial relations', and as unions sought wage increases denied them at national wage cases through industry and company bargaining, the NEA was not able to suppress the sectional interests of members.

By 1972 newspapers were reporting on the 'collapse facing employer groups' including threats to expel the MTIA. Polites summed up the situation: 'one lesson seems to emerge . . . the Policy Committee's role must be confined in present circumstances to general matters which affect all employers with equal force and which further must be of the type which precludes any argument that one group has a special position for there does not appear to be sufficient willingness present in all member associations of the NEA group to hand over the conduct of industry affairs, no matter how specialised, to a central body'. This implied a restricted role for the NEA outside test case situations — a reversion from the previous situation. To the extent that national wage cases came to contribute a smaller proportion of award wage increases, the NEA's ability to influence wage movements was necessarily limited. Lack of unanimity, however, spread even to test cases, as was evidenced by MTIA attempts to have national wage cases replaced by industry bargaining 'within the framework of the arbitration system'. Major differences were also evident in the 1969 Equal Pay case, including whether or not it should be considered a test case.

These relations between the key members of the NEPC had reached a low ebb, not merely because of the independent action of metal employers but also because of the MTIA's success in absorbing metal industry employers in Victoria at the expense of the VCM. This development, and the emergence of a range of specialist industry associations in printing, hotelling, stevedoring, oil refining, civil engineering, aviation, road transport, and building and construction, spurred closer ACEF–ACMA relations leading to the formation of the Industrial Secretariat in 1972.

The NEA had been created in the united atmosphere of the total wage drive. It found itself incapable of harmonising a common employer policy in the climate of accommodative bargaining that followed the adoption of the total wage. Just as the increase in the number and regularity of centrally determined industrial standards had made for the development of an organisation such as the NEA, so too the move to a decentralised system reduced the imperative for, and moral suasion of, such a body.

The confederation model

As noted under the federation model, the emergence of parallel organisations of federations and chambers at the national and state levels necessitated some superstructure that would bring the industrial relations operations of these umbrella organisations into harmony with each other, in short some form of confederation. As also indicated, by about 1914 such a confederation would have to incorporate not only the major umbrella organisations, but also the increasing number of industry or craft associations that were adding industrial relations activities to their trade activities. This incorporation was particularly necessary at the national level, since no provision existed for national industry associations to belong to either umbrella organisation. At the state level industry associations could belong to the federations.

The CCEA first mooted the establishment of some form of confederation as early as 1917. From 1924 until the late 1950s it actively sought the formation of such a body. During the 1960s a number of NEA members pressed for the formation of a Confederation and finally during the 1970s the ACMA became active in trying to bring a confederation into being. Though many of the confederation attempts were not sufficiently long lived for any blue-print to come into being, over the period three major variants can be identified: a unitarist model, a federalist model and an integrated model. Potentially each of these models could have attempted to promote a Confederation of Employers, that is a confederation whose role was restricted to industrial relations, or a Confederation of Industry, one that combined both industrial relations and trade activities. Each of the models had the potential to incorporate both associations and companies or to restrict membership to the former.

At its 1920 Conference the CCEA deliberated on the need for, and the possible forms of, an employers' confederation. The need was seen for providing at the state level 'a connecting link between . . . independent employers' bodies, an organisation which can speak and act for employers as a whole in the same way that the Trades Hall Council can for employees'. It was at this Conference that unitary and federal systems for a Commonwealth Council of Employers in which industrial, commercial and manufacturing interests would be compartmentalised into separate departments, were first proposed. These models were articulated in the papers presented by T. R. Ashworth and S. Perry reviewed in Chapter 3. The Unitary Model (Fig. 3.1) was one in which all 'employers shall become members of a general State Association which shall be governed by an elected Central Council'. Members would be organised into trade sections that would be grouped into 'Chambers of Manufactures, Commerce, Agriculture, Mines, Building and such other bodies as may be determined'. Provision would be made for 'linking up the sections, Chambers and State Associations with similar bodies in other States in each case in which it is deemed expedient'. In essence, this method of organisation was an attempt to reassert the federation model while taking account of the greater need to compartmentalise different commercial and trade interests. The State Association, which was the lynchpin of this unitary mode of co-ordination, was to be a revamped employers' federation. The problem with this proposal, as Perry himself realised, was that it did not give sufficient autonomy to the different factions. Experience would also suggest that the combination of Chambers of Manufactures and Commerce (even if compartmentalised) into the one State Association was an impractical idea. This is discussed more fully below.

Perry recommended against his unitary model in favour of some form of 'federal scheme'. He proposed three possible forms this could take. These variants proposed employers combining into state Trade Associations which, in turn, would be grouped into Chambers of Mines, Commerce, Manufactures, Building, Agriculture and so on. In these schemas the purpose of each chamber was to be the 'promotion of the common interests of its members within the State'. Within each state there would be a State Central Council of Employers composed of either representatives of the Trade Associations (Fig. 3.2) or of the chambers (Fig. 3.3). The role of this Council would be 'the protection of the interests of Employers within the State'. An indemnity company would be formed in each state with the object of compensating employers for any losses sustained through industrial disputes. A Federal Council would be established for each of the Chambers to 'deal with Interstate questions affecting its members'. In addition there would be a Federal Council of Employers composed of representatives of State Central Councils. This body was to 'deal with questions of common interest to employers throughout Australia'. The third federalist model, one that Perry entitled the 'Practical Scheme on Federal Lines' took account of the fact that though the first two federal models presented neat and tidy methods of organisation, they did not take sufficient account of organisational competition and antagonisms. To expect that all organised employers would have to belong to a Trade Association, the associations to chambers, and the chambers to a State Council was to require too great a degree of regimentation. The 'Practical Scheme' allowed for a less tidy situation, in which individual employers could elect to by-pass Trade Associations and join the State Council (in this case the employers' federation) direct. Similarly, though some Trade Associations would choose to belong to chambers and have indirect affiliation to the federation through these chambers, other associations would choose to join the federations directly (Fig. 3.4). This was Perry's preferred option and, in great measure, replicated the situation then existing in South Australia and Western Australia.

In keeping with employer sentiments of the time, Perry's models were essentially state-based and gave only secondary consideration to national co-ordination. This was seen as little more than bringing together at the national level federations of state entities at the Trade Association, Chamber and State Council levels. The linchpins of each of Perry's federalist models were the variously entitled employers' federations. This presupposed that the federations were capable of exercising a leadership role at the state level. Perry's preferred option did approximate the situation in his own state (South Australia) until the 1940s and the situation in Western Australia. The federations, however, had greater difficulty in exercising leadership roles in other states. In Tasmania, the absence of any federation between 1918 and 1952 prevented the application of the 'practical scheme' in that state. In Queensland, employer federations had been established along regional lines. This reduced the authority and resources of the metropolitan federation (the QEF) and resulted in that state's Chamber of Manufactures becoming the more dominant organisation. In New South Wales, the Chamber of Manufactures never became a member of the EFNSW and established its own industrial department in the 1920s. In addition, some Trade Associations, notably the MTEA, established their own industrial departments, which acted independently of either umbrella organisation. In Victoria, the critical state, since this was the heartland of the federal tribunal's operations, the situation was one of intense competition and rivalry between the VEF and VCM. Further, as Ashworth noted in 1920, inter-organisational relationships in that state were extremely complex. There the VEF, VCM, Melbourne Chamber of Commerce and Chambers of Mines and Agriculture independently organised a large number of affiliated bodies and individual employers. In addition, however, there existed a further 31 'other independent sections of employers'. There was no 'connecting link between the 36 independent employers' bodies'. As noted in Chapter 4, despite his concern for greater employer unity, Ashworth himself did much to reduce the co-ordinating role of his own federation, to reduce its membership significantly, and to divide the CCEA. As also noted in Chapter 1, the VEF's preoccupation with political considerations resulted in the lack of effective employer industrial services. The VCM created its own industrial department to alleviate this situation for its own members. When the VEF decided to create its own industrial department in 1927, it was presumptuous to expect that the VCM would acquiesce and hand over industrial work to the federation. The VCM's greater financial resources, internal stability and status projected it, rather than the VEF, as the natural organisation to co-ordinate employers' national industrial activities in the pre-1960 period when such activities were facilitated through Melbourne-based state bodies.

Perry's federalist models thus had little chance of being implemented during the 1920s. Such implementation was even more difficult during the 1930s when both the CCEA and ACMA suffered major divisions over the question of federal uniform standards. Indeed, for much of the 1930s the very existence of the CCEA was in the balance. The disaffiliation of the EFNSW and VEF between 1935 and 1937, and attempts by rival factions to 'reform' the CCEA to their own liking, reduced any potential this organisation may have had as a national co-ordinating body.

By the mid-1940s, under the impetus of Labor Governments perceived as hostile, the CCEA (by now called ACEF) initiated new attempts to bring into being a confederation. During 1943 a series of meetings of 'Central Employers' Organisations' (i.e. the three national umbrella organisations the ACEF, ACCA and ACMA) considered the formation of a confederation. It was decided that the Victorian affiliates pilot such a scheme at the state level so as to determine the feasibility of any national scheme. It was in Victoria that relations between the federation and Chamber of Manufactures were most strained and nothing came of the move. This development reiterated the dependency of the national bodies on their state affiliates, a dependency further highlighted when developments at this time were yet again held in abeyance 'until the three Commonwealth-wide Employers' organisations were domiciled in Sydney'. The 'seven principles as the basis for closer collaboration between the principal employers' organisations' enunciated by ACEF President Oberg in 1944 were directly aimed at industrial relations and, as noted in Chapter 5, were essentially a restatement of the 1904 objectives of the newly founded CCEA. At a time when the requirements of war had reduced national test cases, the formation of such a confederation was not considered a matter of urgency by other organisations. Further, 'the problems of socialism', which spurred the confederation impetus, proved to be one that national employer bodies were able to handle through action other than reorganisation. In any case, the special relationship developed between the ACMA and the Labor administrations, a relationship founded on a shared objective of economic advancement predicated upon high levels of protection, militated against the ACMA wanting this relationship diluted by way of a confederation. The ACMA provided the leadership for employer representatives on the Industrial Relations Council, it had exclusive representation at the tripartite conference on manpower of 1942, its representation at the proposed Peace in Industry Conference of 1945 outweighed that of all other employer bodies, and it was the only organisation to represent employers when this Conference was finally convened in 1947. By mid-1944 ACMA indicated that it was 'not disposed to commit itself to a Confederation'. Though the ACEF contemplated a Confederation that did not include the ACMA, it was considered that the formation of such an organisation would not achieve any positive results. The developments during this and subsequent periods would indicate that the formation of a confederated organisation presupposed a degree of heterogeneity in terms of resources and political influence among the major potential sponsors of such an organisation.

The next round of confederation attempts, those of the 1950s, took place in an environment in which wartime regulation had conditioned most employer organisations to accept the determination of basic wage and standard hours of work by the federal tribunal. By July 1951, the ACEF was again spearheading a campaign for the formation of a Confederation of Employers and in August 1951 had the Memorandum and the Articles of Association of such a Confederation registered under the Companies Ordinance 1931. The registration was interpreted by the ACEF as an indication of the general support for a Confederation at that time. Another explanation, however, was that proposed amendments to this Ordinance would have made any subsequent registration more difficult.[1] Subsequent amendments to these Articles have made it difficult to determine the precise model developed in 1951. The role of the ACEF within the Confederation as that of helping to form 'a National Council of Employers for the purpose of co-ordinating the representatives of all employers and employers' organisations in relation to industrial matters' would indicate that the proposal contemplated trade as well as industrial relations activities. The fact that these proposals followed soon after the 1951 Anti-Inflation Conference in which the ACEF was critical of the lack of employer cohesion on economic matters would also suggest that a Confederation of Industry was proposed. The proposal, as outlined in the ACEF's letter to organisations, was the establishment of a 'National Confederation of Employers' Organisations'. Membership was to be limited to employer organisations of a 'federal character'. No organisation would lose its autonomy and policy would only be arrived at as the 'result of unanimous decisions'. It was proposed that the

Confederation function in one of two ways: either 'the form of a convention' in which meetings would be held at regular intervals to determine common policy, or 'the form of a permanent organisation under the control of a Council consisting of the Presidents of member organisations' and with the appropriate staff. The Confederation's functions were to determine policy matters 'of general interest', to co-ordinate opinion, to facilitate representation of employers in the international sphere, to co-ordinate amendments to industrial legislation, and to represent employers' views at test cases. In the economic field it could 'permit a concerted examination by all sections of employers of the economic problems facing the Commonwealth' and it was proposed that the organisation eventually include an economic research unit. Though there was no mention of any trade activities, an economic research unit necessarily implied that some consideration would be given to matters that would affect the vested interests of member organisations.

It will be seen that the ACEF's proposals attempted to build upon structures that already operated to a large extent. The first model of organisation, one that would only require employers to meet periodically, was not a departure from the Interstate Conference of Employers that had been operating in the 1930s and whose functions were subsumed by the Basic Wage Steering Committee. It was also the model subsequently adopted for the NEA in 1961. Though it guaranteed the maximum autonomy to members, it lacked the ability to provide any day-to-day oversight of industrial matters in the absence of the continuing operation of the Basic Wage Steering Committee. The latter, presumably, would constitute the full-time staff of the 'appropriate organisation' under the control of the Presidents of member organisations. In modified form, such a development did take place in 1958 when the Policy Committee and the Working Party were placed on a permanent footing. The proposal to establish a Council consisting of all Presidents of affiliates implied an equality of voting rights and/or of subscriptions. This situation never eventuated. When formed in 1961, the NEA's structure enabled the 'big four' to control the Policy Committee. A major difference between the NEA and ACEF's Confederation proposals of 1951 was that the former did not include any economic research unit.

The draft constitutional committee of the Australian Confederation of Employers established in 1951 to develop the ACEF's confederation proposals essentially limited the proposed Confederation's role to industrial relations matters. Despite an initial high degree of interest from a number of organisations and the work of the draft committee, these Confederation developments stalled. The ACEF's reasons explaining previous failures were equally true of this attempt: the fear of loss of autonomy on the part of potential affiliates, fear that the organisation would 'assume the character of an incubus', and suspicion that certain organisations may be ambitious to expand 'their power at the expense of other organisations'. Related to this third factor were 'the ambitions and fears of salaried executive officers'. Gibson, the ACEF Secretary, noted the 'influences within ACMA that will work against any collaboration notably Mr Hall (Director of the NSW Chamber) and Mr Curphy (Director of VCM)'. Indeed the ACMA quickly distanced itself from any confederation developments, claiming that 'the basic idea is impossible of achievement because of the diversity of interests represented and the fact that the only common ground is that we are all employers'. This view reflected the paramount concern of the ACMA with trade matters. International trade developments such as the operation of the General Agreement on Tariffs and Trade and the Japanese Trade Treaty, which liberalised Japanese imports, put it on the defensive. The general economic growth under the McEwen policy of industry development under a protectionist umbrella, however, also reinforced the ACMA's organisational strength. In many ways the 1950s was a golden age for the chambers as membership and resources expanded. This added to the ACMA's aloofness and independent disposition. It torpedoed attempts to form a joint research office in the mid-1950s by creating such a position within its own secretariat. Its President automatically assumed the position of Chairman of the Policy and Consultative Committee and its major affiliate, the VCM, appointed the Convenor of the Basic Wage Steering Committee and Working Party. A Confederation could have weakened this dominant position.

The Graziers' Federal Council of Australia also decided against joining any Confederation at this time. Its reasons for doing so indicate some of the other organisational complexities involved. It claimed its own organisation to be 'over-organised with too many affiliations all of which entail a considerable amount of work for Executive and administrative officers'. This was a problem common to the other umbrella organisations. It feared that the new body would duplicate work already being done by affiliated organisations. This presupposed an inability to differentiate between 'common' and industry-based issues and cases, or a reluctance by the organisation to surrender its role in the former where it had traditionally argued the special position of the primary sector of the economy. The Graziers' Federal Council was also fearful that the existence of a single employer mouthpiece would 'merely provide a convenient means by which governments can brush aside the views of substantial minorities'. While a confederation purported to have an economic arm, this presented a problem for most associations, which saw themselves as representing a select group of employers. A further reason given by the GFCA was its lack of faith in the 'effective permanency of employer organisations' efforts in joint undertakings'. This was no doubt inspired by the fact that the GFCA's New South Wales affiliate had been a party to the establishment of the Industrial and Economic Service in the 1940s. Within a short time the other four organisations financing this service had withdrawn their support and the Graziers' Association of New South Wales was left to shoulder the financial burden.

By 1952 the confederation drive had waned. When the ACEF made yet another attempt 2 years later it was as the result of changes in the system of basic wage determination, government support for a single employer mouthpiece, and the support of 'certain industrialists'. The latter suggested a new force in national labour relations — interstate companies. As noted these were subsequently to cause pressure for the formation of the CAI and to form their own organisation, the Business Council of Australia. By 1954, associations had not come around to see the need for a Confederation. When basic wage pressures did become apparent, the establishment of the NEA (which, as noted, approximated one ACEF confederation variant) reduced pressures for any more formalised organisation. Further, instability within the ACEF itself, with the near demise of the SAEF and independent action of the VEF, again meant that the ACEF was not able to continue with its confederation thrust. The ACEF's internal problems reflected an inherent weakness in its federation structure in which any dominant member could become the source of strong divisions. As noted in Chapter 6, they also reflected difficulties about power sharing between affiliates, as well as those resulting from personality clashes. The fact that the major national organisations — the ACMA, the ACCA, the AMIA and the GFCA — were similarly constituted and therefore potentially the subjects of similar internal divisions, added to the ACEF's problems in seeking to establish a Confederation.

By 1958 the ACEF had concluded that an alternative to the formation of a Confederation was 'to build up ACEF to the state where it would discharge the functions of the proposed Confederation'. The emergence of an era of unparalleled internal stability, the appointment of a full-time Director (G. Polites) as well as industrial and research officers, the addition of Associate Members, the establishment of the ACEF–ACMA Central Industrial Secretariat under the Directorship of Polites, and the latter's influence over the NEA Committees, all promoted the ACEF as the most dominant national employer industrial body. After 1960 the ACEF no longer provided the impetus for the establishment of a national Confederation. Initially this role fell to some national industry affiliates of the NEA and after 1972 to the ACMA.

During the 1960s the national employer co-ordination was achieved by way of the NEA. This loose-knit organisation resulted in no loss of autonomy on the part of affiliates. Over time, however, the National Employers' Policy Committee came to be recognised as the employer mouthpiece on industrial relations matters by the Conciliation and Arbitration Commission as well as by governments. Though this Committee was part of the structure of the NEA, in practice NEA members had no control over membership of the Committee. Such membership belonged to the 'Big Four' — the ACMA, ACEF, AWGC and (after 1971) the MTIA. Confederation moves, described in terms of bringing into being 'a more formal organisation', were largely directed by some industry-based NEA members at counteracting the dominant role of the 'Big Four'. Following the formation of the MTIA in 1971, this organisation, through a member of the Committee, also sought a restructuring of the NEA in an attempt to reduce the influence of state-controlled organisations such as the ACEF and ACMA. The ACMA also sought a confederation in the early 1960s apparently in an attempt to counter the ACEF's rising influence. In the 1970s it again sought the formation of a Confederation, but this time by merging with the ACEF.

In 1962 the ACEF resolved not to support the establishment of a Confederation of Employers and claimed that the NEA's Policy and Industrial Committees provided 'the best means of bringing about some unification in the action of employers'. The ACEF noted at this time that the confederation move had 'been prompted by ACMA as a counter to the rising influence of ACEF'. The ACEF claimed that the best interests of employers were served by way of a loose-knit, rather than a formal, organisation. This was its declared public position until the mid-1970s.

By 1965 the ACEF noted 'pressures from other sources for some formalisation of the NEA' seemingly directed at reducing the dominant role of the 'Big Four'. In 1967 the ACEF further noted that 'the pressure for change has quickened since the internecine dispute between members of AMIA has developed'. In 1968 two industry organisations — the PATEFA and MTEA (an organisation that had indirect membership of the NEPC through the AMIA) were pressing for a reconstruction of the NEA. The ACEF, with ACMA's support as well as that of a number of other organisations, headed off this move by industry-based associations by having the

National Employers' Consultative Council brought into being. The Council, which supposedly provided a liaison function between the NEPC and other NEA members, does not seem to have been active or have had any significant impact.

The formation of the MTIA in 1971 brought about a major realignment between the ACEF and ACMA. The emergence of national industry associations presented a threat to both organisations, which were based on the federation of state organisations. In 1972 they formed the Central Industrial Secretariat with Mr G. Polites as Director. This was the first stage towards total merger. The form of confederation that emerged from this merger differed from most previous models in two major respects. In the first place it was a Confederation of Industry rather than of employers. Though some 1920 models had considered such an option, subsequent blue-prints restricted the role of the Confederation to industrial relations. Some 1950 variants included a limited economic research function as well. Secondly, confederation was achieved not by the formation of a new formalised body to which the ACEF and ACMA affiliated, but rather by both these organisations merging and losing their identity — an integrated model of organisation.

Several factors help to explain the ACMA's turn-about and the ACEF's acceptance of a Confederation that extended beyond its traditional area of operation. The emergence of national industry associations and of the 'Big 50' threatened the long-term dominance of both organisations. The 'Big 50' sought the formation of the Central Employers' Organisation in which employer association input would be matched by that of the large companies (Fig. 9.4). The companies' proposal envisaged that they would meet half the costs of mounting major cases and that the Companies' Executive Committee would constitute half of the CEO's Policy Committee, the other half coming from the 'Big Four'. This proposal, which threatened to reduce the influence of all associations, was not acceptable to the employer organisations.

Among national associations, the 'NEA Group' sought a reconstruction of the NEA into a more formalised body that would restrict itself to industrial relations and that would give a greater degree of control to 'ordinary' members. The latter implied diminished control by the inter-umbrella organisation — the Central Industrial Secretariat.

By forming a confederation to their own blue-print in 1977, the ACMA and ACEF sought to 'create a situation in which NEA members could not in logic be able to refuse to join the Confederation', that is, a situation in which not to join the Confederation caused NEA members to run the risk of being

Figure 9.4 Confederation Models (1974–77)

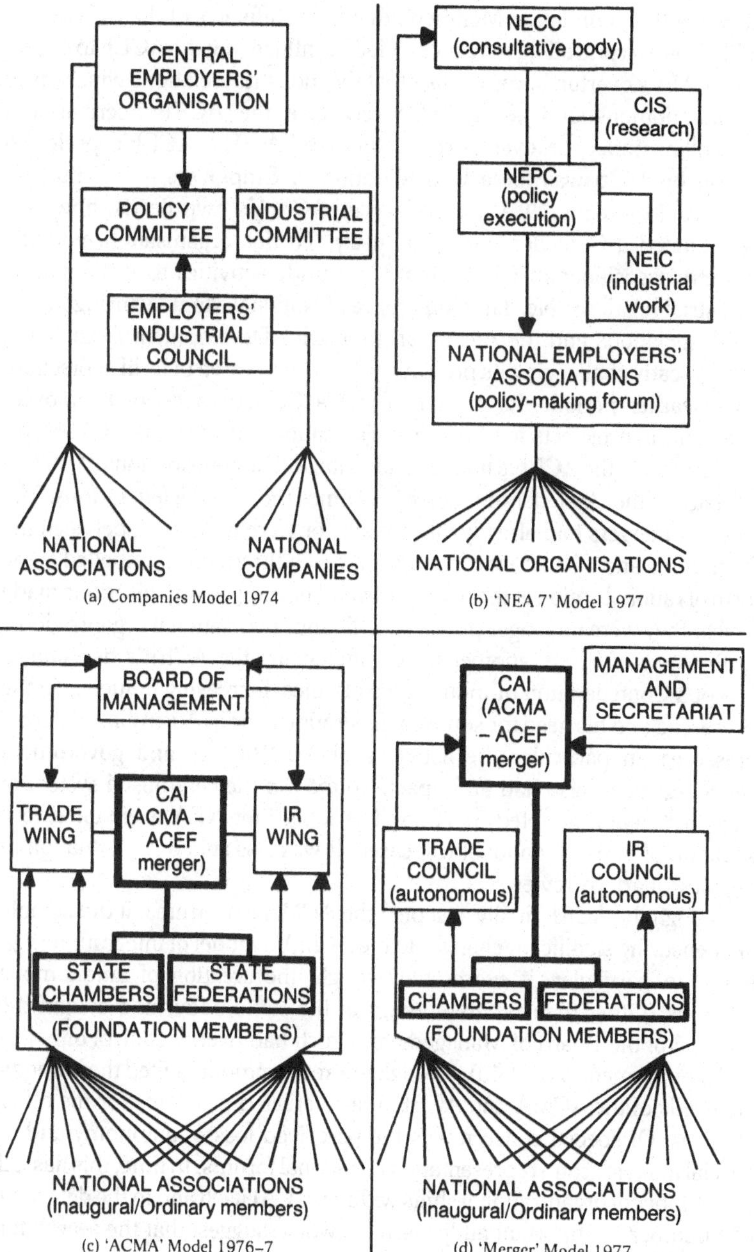

(a) Companies Model 1974

(b) 'NEA 7' Model 1977

(c) 'ACMA' Model 1976–7

(d) 'Merger' Model 1977

bypassed by governments and the Commission. The 1977 model was one in which the Foundation Members, that is the affiliates of the ACMA and ACEF, had a controlling influence. A factor influencing the ACEF to accept the ACMA's overtures was the fact that the industrial relations wing was to be autonomous and would effectively give the ACEF Secretariat a controlling influence over a restructured NEA. The ACEF's preferred option by 1976 was for a Confederation of Employers — a situation supported by many NEA members. The ACMA's own needs, however, necessitated a Confederation of Industry. To this organisation, national industry associations were a threat to its trade activities as well as to its industrial relations role. The Conference of National Manufacturing Industry Associations and the Australian Industries Development Association were already challenging its pre-eminent role in the area of tariff protection. As in earlier periods, its refusal to join a Confederation of Employers reduced the prospects for such an organisation. Further, the ACMA proposals were to the ACEF's financial advantage. The contributions of ACMA affiliates to the Confederation were four times those of the federations. The fact that mergers had already taken place, or were imminent, between the federations and Chambers of Manufactures in three states, impelled some form of rationalisation at the national level. The merged organisations made it clear they were no longer prepared to finance two national organisations. In the view of some, another factor influencing the ACEF's decision to accept a Confederation of Industry was Polites' increasing influence in the ILO arena and his need for some confederation base in Australia.[2] External pressures, in particular the activities of the 'Big 50' and government encouragement, also had an impact. So too did the centralised system of wage indexation adopted in 1975. The loose-knit NEA was suited to a situation of periodic national test cases. It was less suited to a situation of ongoing quarterly reviews.

Though the ACEF finally accepted the ACMA's overtures, it did so only after ensuring significant changes to the ACMA's model of integration (Fig. 9.4c). In particular, it successfully sought the creation of autonomous Councils (rather than separate wings of the same body) and sought the removal of the Board of Management, which had overall control of policy and management (Fig. 9.4d). Though this merger model suited the immediate needs of the ACMA and ACEF, it also created problems for the other affiliates. Of special concern was the perceived loss of autonomy and of special interest group representation at national forums. In time, this has led to a number of organisational shifts within the CAI itself and to the defection of a number of important affiliates. This would suggest that the search for effective co-ordinating mechanisms is an ongoing one. In time, the merger model itself may give way to a different variant of co-ordination.

Summary and conclusion

Many factors helped to shape the particular form of national co-ordination mechanisms that operated at any particular point in time. In general, these factors can be divided into two groups: organisational and exogenous factors. Exogenous factors included the activities of federal governments and the degree to which these pressed for a single employer mouthpiece. It included developments on the union front. Most importantly, it included the 'test case' environment operating at any particular point in time. This study has reviewed the evolution of a highly centralised system to the mid-1960s, the breaking down of such a system, and its re-institution in 1974. The gradual evolution of co-ordination machinery from the alliance model to the period 1958, the secretariat model the effectiveness of which climaxed in 1967, and the confederation model, which was finally pushed through to fruition in the mid-1970s, fits in broadly with the evolution of the centralised test case environment.

On the organisational front the study has highlighted associations' desire for self-autonomy. Any surrender of that autonomy has generally been necessitated by compelling externalities. It has also suggested that the federal structure of umbrella organisations, organisations that dominated national employer co-ordination for the period surveyed, was an inherently unstable one. Internal instability within organisations seeking to bring about co-ordination mechanisms only made their task less likely of success. Indeed, as illustrated by the example of the Interstate Conference of Employers, such co-ordination could be used by competing state organisations to win support for policies unacceptable to other affiliates of their own organisation.

The study has highlighted the fact that central to the formation of any co-ordinating bodies has been one dominant driving influence — usually the ACEF, though in the latter stages the ACMA. The needs of this driving organisation impelled it, for one reason or another, to seek inter-organisational links. This factor serves yet again to highlight the importance of internal stability — a situation not achieved in the ACEF until 1958 and in the ACMA until after the metal employers dispute — as well as the importance of leadership. An important part of the leadership function was the personality of those at the helm of organisations. Some dominant personalities such as T. R. Ashworth and G. H. Boykett were irritants and sources of organisational friction. Others such as O. D. A. Oberg and G.

Polites were major catalysts for unity. None of the participants interviewed in the course of this study failed to see the last named as a critical link in confederation developments.

The importance of national key figures such as Polites suggests that a major feature of the formation of formal co-ordinating machinery was the ability of national organisations to act with some degree of autonomy. The study of the ACEF indicated that this was not the situation until 1960. Prior to that date state affiliates controlled not only ACEF policy, but also its day-to-day secretarial affairs. In such a context petty state rivalries intruded into national organisational relations.

At the organisational level the study would suggest that agreement by dominant organisations to form co-ordinating mechanisms presupposes some homogeneity of resources or influence. The *ad hoc* nature of much of the co-ordinating machinery can be explained in terms of the ACMA's refusal to be a part of any permanent machinery. By the mid-1950s, however, the ACEF, AMIA and GFCA challenged the ACMA's dominance and were able to entice it into a standing committee, which they dominated to the exclusion of other organisations. The two-tiered structure of the NEA reflected the dominance of the 'Big Four' *vis-a-vis* other members.

The emergence of the ACEF in the 1960s as the most influential industrial relations organisation, as the research agency for the NEA, and as the 'think-tank' of NEPC policy, led to it being courted by the ACMA. The CIS was the initial result, the CAI the final product. That the ACMA could distance itself in disdain from ACEF activities to bring about a confederation for over 30 years, but could subsequently take the lead in wooing it into a confederation merger, would also indicate that for industrial organisations 'he who pays the piper calls the tune'.

Post-confederation tensions and developments would further suggest that in a world of change few things remain constant — including co-ordination mechanisms.

Notes

1 Interview, Mr A. Howard, former Research/Industrial Officer, CAI, 15/7/80.

2 Interview, Mr B. Purvis, Executive Director, Australian Wool Selling Brokers Employers' Federation, 29/1/86.

APPENDICES

Appendix 1

Employer organisations registered under CAA 1905–1987*

1905	Commonwealth Steamship Owners' Association
1912	The Renmark Growers' Association#
1912	The Federated Picture Showmen's Association of Australia
1914	The United Licensed Victuallers' Association of the Commonwealth of Australia
1917	The Theatrical Proprietors' and Managers' Association of Australia
1922–49	Sydney Bonded and Free Stores Employers' Federation
1922	The Timber Merchants' and Sawmillers' Association of Australia
1923–49	The Master Brick Carriers' Association
1923–49	Country Rabbit Packers' and Freezers' Association of NSW
1923–60	The Entrepreneurs' Association of Australia
1925–72	H. V. McKay Proprietary Ltd
1925–75	The Broken Hill Proprietary Company Ltd
1926	The Printing and Allied Trades Employers' Federation of Australia
1926	Metal Trades Employers' Association
1926	The Fire Protection Engineers' Association of Australia
1926	The Graziers' Association of New South Wales
1926	The Pastoralists' Association of West Darling
1926	The Pastoralists Union of Southern Riverina
1926–75	Nestlé and Anglo-Swiss Condensed Milk Company (Australasia) Limited
1927	The Pastoralists' Association of Western Australia (Incorporated)
1927	The Showmen's Guild of Australia
1927	The Commonwealth Jam Preserving and Condiment Manufacturers' Association
1927	The Shearing Contractors' Association of New South Wales
1927–74	The Colonial Sugar Refining Company Limited
1927	The Federated Pharmaceutical Service Guild of Australia
1928–70	The Furniture Manufacturers' Association of Australia
1928	Master Butchers' Meat and Allied Trades Federation of Australia
1929-50	The Glue and Gelatine Manufacturers of Australia

1930–70 The Metropolitan Transport Trust
1933 The United Graziers' Association of Queensland (Union of Employers)
1935 Motor Traders' Association of NSW
1936 The Hosiery and Knit Goods Manufacturers' Association of NSW
1937 The Master Builders' Association of NSW
1940 The Federation of Master Process Engravers of Australia
1940 Victorian Automobile Chamber of Commerce
1940–70 The Master Builders' and Contractors' Association of the Northern Territory
1940 Timber Trade Industrial Association
1941 The Cinematograph Exhibitors' Association
1941 The Victorian Chamber of Manufactures
1942–76 N.S.W. Combined Colliery Proprietors' Association
1942–70 Northern Collieries Committee
1943–70 Associated Furniture Manufacturers of N.S.W.
1944–82 Shirt Manufacturers' Association of N.S.W.
1944–52 Milk Zone Dairymen's Council
1944–65 The Independent Steamship Owners' Association
1945 The Victorian Showmen's Guild
1945 Tasmanian Timber Association
1946 Wearing Apparel Sections of the Chamber of Manufactures of N.S.W.
1947–74 The Retail Timber Merchant's Organisation
1948–85 The Amusement Proprietors' Association of Australia
1948–55 South Australian Chamber of Manufactures Incorporated
1948 Employers' Association of Wool Selling Brokers
1948 The Vehicle Manufacturers' Association of Australia
1949 Clothing Industries Division of the Queensland Chamber of Manufactures
1950 The Federated Sheepskin Export Packers and Allied Trades Industrial Association of Australia
1950 The Tasmanian Farmers' Stockmans' and Orchardists' Association
1951–77 The Queensland Footwear Manufacturers' Association
1951 The Graziers Association of Victoria
1953–75 The Commissioner of Government Transport of N.S.W.
1954–75 The Australian Dairy Farmers' Industrial Federation
1954–66 The Association of Consulting Engineers
1955 The Metal Industries Association of South Australia
1956–61 The Country Traders' Association
1957–78 Farmers' and Settlers' Industrial Association
1957 Victorian Sawmillers' Association
1957 The Hop Producers' Association of Tasmania
1958 The Electrical Contractors' Federation Victoria
1960 S.A. Automobile Chamber of Commerce Incorporated
1960 The Licensed Clubs Association of Australia
1960 The Victorian Authorised Newsagent Association Limited
1961 The Victorian Employers' Federation
1962–76 The Clothing Manufacturers' Association of N.S.W.

1963	The Drycleaners' Associations of Queensland
1963	The Association of Employers of Waterside Labour
1965	Proprietary Limited Hotel Companies Association
1965	Master Builders' Association of the Australian Capital Territory
1966–76	Metal Industry Association Victoria
1966	Master Builders' Association of Victoria
1966	Metal Industry Association Tasmania
1967–85	The Ceramic Wall and Floor Tile Merchants' Association of the Australian Capital Territory
1967	The Stockowners' Association of S.A.
1967	The Australian Capital Territory Employers' Federation
1968	Australian Trainers' Association
1968	The Master Builders' Association of Tasmania
1969	Metal Industries Employers' Association of Western Australia
1969	New South Wales Soft Drink Association (Country Division)
1969	Dry Cleaners' and Dryers' Association of New South Wales
1970–85	Private Hospitals and Nursing Homes Association of Australia
1970	Professional Photographers' Association of Australia
1970	Timber Merchants' Association of South Australia
1971	The Motor Inn and Motel Association of Australia
1971	Master Builders' Association of the Northern Territory
1972	The Film Production Association of Australia
1973	The Licensed Club Association of Victoria
1973–79	Victorian Farmers' Union Employers' Association
1973	Electrical Contractors' Association of South Australia Incorporated
1973	Mechanical Harvesters' Association of Australia
1974	The Retail Traders' Association of Victoria
1975	The General Aviation Association (Australia)
1975	The Master Plumbers' and Mechanical Services Association of Victoria
1976	Tasmanian Farmers' Federation Employers Association
1976	Australian Federation of Construction Contractors
1976	Australian Earthmovers' and Road Contractors' Federation
1977	The Master Builders' Association Incorporated
1977	Farmers' Union of W.A. Industrial Association
1977	The Licensed Restaurateurs' Association of Australia
1978	Master Painters', Decorators' and Signwriters' Association of NSW
1978	Tasmanian Automobile Chamber of Commerce
1980	The Retail Traders' Association of New South Wales
1980	Decorators' and Signwriters' Association of Tasmania
1981	The Bread Manufacturers' Association of Australia
1982	Australian Petroleum Agents' and Distributors' Association
1984	Australian Road Transport Industrial Organisation
1985	Australian Universities' Industrial Association
1985	The Trustee Companies Association of Australia
1987	Australian Advanced Education Industrial Association

Total number of registrations: 117
Total number of deregistrations: 32

Total still registered: 85
* Original registered name. Several name changes have occurred.
# Registered by Proclamation under section 158 A(3) of the Act.
Source: Compiled from Principal Industrial Registry records.

Appendix 2
Employers' Declaration of Policy 1945

1 We believe that the economic and social security of employers, employees and the community as a whole depends upon maximum employment and that this can best be achieved by encouraging the initiative of the individual.

The term individual initiative implies freedom for employers in the investment of funds, management's inherent right to run its business, and the placing and disposal of resources, and for employees in choosing their careers and living their own way of life.

2 We believe that efficiency and service must represent as important an objective to employers as the gaining of profitable results, and that open competitive methods are far more likely to help in the consummation of this ideal than a system of State ownership.

3 In the achieving of maximum employment to provide efficiency and service, we recognise the part that employees will play when providing their personal services and skill, and in turn we acknowledge the responsibility for providing reasonable and adequate remuneration and the best possible working conditions.

4 We believe that employees will be better able to work towards the objectives of service and efficiency if they are offered, and accept, standards aimed at achieving mutual trust and better understanding.

To this end we urge all employers to consider the following suggestions and to apply them where practicable:

(a) The acceptance of voluntary Trades Unionism and the recognition of the right of the individual to join his Union. Both employers and employees are already in organised groups and the encouragement of co-operation in industry will do much towards ensuring harmonious industrial relationships.

(b) The appointment of Staff Relations Officers and Committees to encourage such matters as discussion groups, merit-reward systems for suggestions and skill and general facilities for the improvement of employer–employee relations, including sports clubs and recreation areas.

(c) The translation of friendly encouragement towards technical and educational training for apprentices and others into terms involving financial help and special leave facilities.

(d) The initiation of plans to provide for the economic well-being of all concerned. Such plans to incorporate subsidised schemes for superannuation, sickness and accident benefits and the establishment of welfare funds for general purposes.

(e) The encouragement of a sense of social and moral independence among workers.

(f) Equal opportunity for all engaged in industry for the promotion to higher responsibility positions commensurate with their ability and qualifications.

5 We endorse the principle of preference to ex-service personnel.

6 We believe that the principles of Industrial Conciliation and Arbitration is [sic] the only satisfactory method for determining the just rights of employers and employees, and we deprecate all acts of lawlessness in the shape of strikes or lock-outs.

7 We believe that the community in general should be educated to assess and resist any false ideology which encroaches on the economic and social life of Australia and endangers the Nation's prosperity.

8 We believe that a determined effort must be made to create conditions where all can enjoy freedom from unemployment, poverty and fear. It is realised that this can only result from intelligent work, the willingness to face realities which, in turn, bring about maximum employment, and the necessary high standard of efficiency.

9 We endorse the principle of contributory National Social Security plans.

10 As a necessary prerequisite to social security we urge the immediate acceleration by the Commonwealth Government of all matters affecting the rehabilitation of ex-servicemen and women, particularly plans for psychological tests, vocational guidance, technical and educational training methods and adequate repatriation benefits. A special responsibility devolves upon the Commonwealth Government in the rehabilitation of those who enlisted either straight from school or before they had become established in industry.

We urge all employers to accept their full obligations and responsibilities in respect of the rehabilitation of their employees enlisted in the services. Advance plans should be prepared by the employers now in order to accomplish the complete rehabilitation within their own organisations, even to the extent of assisting these employees to engage upon both technical and handicraft courses within the employer's time.

Source: The Employers' Review, 31/5/45, p.145

Appendix 3
Heads of Agreement ACEF and ACMA Basic Principles for Merger 1973

1 That ACMA and ACEF seek to merge into a single organization, the name of which shall be matter for further discussion.

2 The new organization to have as foundation members the existing Chambers of Manufactures and Employers' Federations at the time of its establishment.

3 That the new organization may have as inaugural members any association being a member of the National Employers' Association willing to subscribe to its aims and objects.

4 That the new organization be administered by an Executive Committee consisting of representatives of its foundation members and the President of the General Council (see Point 7).

5 That policy making for the new organization be determined by General Council, consisting of representatives of all members.

6 That the Chairman of the Executive Committee be elected from representatives of foundation members.

7 That the President of the General Council be the President of the organization and be elected by that Council.

8 That a voting procedure be established which would permit all questions being determined in the first instance on the voices.

9 In the event of any member demanding a poll, the matter be determined by vote, each member having a vote strength according to contributions.

10 That inaugural members and members pay subscriptions according to a fixed scale.

11 That the cost of the organization be met by the foundation members, account, of course, being taken of the subscription paid by members.

12 That the administration of the organization be in the hands of a Chief Executive Officer, who would be responsible to the Chairman of the Executive Committee for administration and to the President of the General Council for Policy.

13 That the organization consist of two operating divisions, namely: a Trade and Commerce Division, and an Industrial Relations Division.

14 That Directors be appointed to each of these divisions, both to be responsible to the Chief Executive Officer.

15 That Consultative Committees be established to advise the Chief Executive Officer and the Directors of the Divisions on Policy matters relating to the areas of activity covered by the organization.

16 That members of such Consultative Committees be appointed on the nomination of members of the General Council.

17 That the present staff of ACMA and ACEF and CIS be integrated into the new organization in positions appropriate to their qualifications.

18 That a Constitution and Rules be drawn up taking account of present aims and objects of both organizations and the above policy proposal.

19 That the document referred to in paragraph 18 be referred to the constituent organizations of ACMA and ACEF for consideration.

Source: CIS Council Meeting 22/11/73, Background paper.

BIBLIOGRAPHY

Anderson, G. (1929) *Fixation of Wages in Australia*, Macmillan, Melbourne.

Black, G. (1929) *Arbitration's Chequered Career From 1901 – 1927*, Sydney (privately published).

Carboch, D. (1958) *The Fall of the Bruce–Page Government*, Cheshire, Melbourne.

Chamber of Manufactures of New South Wales (1985) *The Crusaders: The Story of the Beginning of the Chamber of Manufactures of New South Wales*, CMNSW, Sydney.

Chan, K. (1971) 'The Origins of Compulsion in Australia: The Case of Victoria', *The Journal of Industrial Relations*, 13(2).

Clark, V.S. (1905) 'Labor Conditions in Australia', *Bulletin of the Bureau of Labor*, vol. 10, Government Printer, Washington.

Coghlan, T.A. (1918) *Labour and Industry in Australia*, Macmillan, London.

Coleman, D. and Mills, J. (1969) *A Richness of People*, South Australian Chamber of Manufactures, Adelaide.

Collicoat, S. (1972) 'Tensions That Keep Employers Apart', *Rydges*, December.

Commonwealth Arbitration Reports (CARs), various issues.

Commonwealth Law Reports (CLRs), various issues.

Copland, D.B. (1930) 'The Restoration of Economic Equilibrium', *Economic Record*, vol. 6.

Copland, D. B. (1934) *Australia in the World Crisis*, Cambridge University Press, Cambridge.

Cowan, Z. (1967) *Isaac Isaacs*, Oxford University Press, Melbourne.

D'Alpuget, B. (1975) *Mediator: A Biography of Sir Richard Kirby*, Melbourne University Press, Melbourne.

Department of Labour and National Service (DL and NS) (1953) 'High Level

Industrial Relations Council', paper prepared for formation of MLAC, Melbourne, mimeograph.

Department of Labour and National Service (1959) 'Sanctions', paper prepared for *ad hoc* meeting of Ministry of Labour Advisory Council, 27/2/59, Melbourne, mimeograph.

De Vyver, F. (1972) 'Employer Organizations in the Australian Industrial Relations System', *The Journal of Industrial Relations*, 15(1).

Dobson, W.T. (1979) 'The Associated Chambers of Manufactures of Australia 1904 – 1977', Unpublished M. A. thesis, Melbourne University.

Dobson, W. T. (1982) 'Employer Matters in 1981', *The Journal of Industrial Relations*, 24(1), pp 108–18.

Dufty, N. (1986) 'The Genesis of Arbitration in Western Australia', *The Journal of Industrial Relations*, 28(4).

Evatt, H. V. (1942) *Australian Labour Leader: The Story of W. A. Holman and the Labour Movement*, Angus and Robertson, Sydney.

Fitzpatrick, B. (1940) *The British Empire in Australia 1834–1939*, Macmillan, Melbourne.

Foenander, O. de R. (1937) *Towards Industrial Peace in Australia*, Melbourne University Press, Melbourne.

Foenander, O. de R. (1943) *Wartime Labour Developments in Australia*, Melbourne University Press, Melbourne.

Foenander, O. de R. (1947) *Industrial Regulation in Australia*, Melbourne University Press, Melbourne.

Foenander, O. de R. (1952) *Studies in Australian Labour Law and Relations*, Melbourne University Press, Melbourne.

Ford, G. W., Plowman, D. H. and Lansbury, R. D. (1980) 'Employer Associations: An Introduction' in G. W. Ford, J. M. Hearne and R. D. Lansbury (eds) *Australian Labour Relations: Readings*, 3rd ed., Macmillan, Melbourne.

Garran, R. (1958) *Prosper the Commonwealth*, Angus and Robertson, Sydney.

Gollan, R. (1963) *The Coalminers of New South Wales: A History of the Union 1860 – 1960*, Melbourne University Press, Melbourne.

Groom, J. (ed.), (1941) *Nation Building in Australia, The Life and Work of Sir Littleton Ernest Groom*, Angus and Robertson, Sydney.

Hagan, J. (1981) *The History of the A.C.T.U.*, Longman Cheshire, Melbourne.

Hainesworth, D. R. (1971) *The Sydney Traders*, Sydney.

Hall, C. R. (1971) *The Manufacturers: Australian Manufacturing Achievements to 1960* Angus and Robertson, Sydney.

Hammond, M. B. (1914) 'Wages Boards in Australia: Victoria', *The Quarterly Journal of Economics*, vol. 29, pp. 98-148.

Hancock, K. J. (1979) 'The First Half Century of Australian Wage Policy: Part 1', *The Journal of Industrial Relations* 21(1).

Hancock, W. K. (1930) *Australia*, Ernest Benn, London.

Higgins, H. B. (1921) *A New Province for Law and Order*, Dawsons, London.

Hutson, J. (1972) *Six Wage Concepts*, A.E.U., Sydney.

Lee M. (1980) 'The Industrial Peace Act, 1920: A Study of Political Interference in Compulsory Arbitration', M. Econ. thesis, Sydney University.

Matthews, T. (1971) 'Business Associations and Politics', Ph.D. thesis, Sydney University.

McCarthy, P. G. (1968) 'Wage Determination in New South Wales 1890–1921', *The Journal of Industrial Relations*, 10(3).

Ministry of Labour Advisory Council (1956a) *Productivity*, Australian Government Printer, Canberra.

Ministry of Labour Advisory Council (1956b) *Automation*, Australian Government Printer, Canberra.

Murray, R. (1970) *The Split: Australian Labor in the Fifties*, Cheshire, Melbourne.

National Secretariat for Catholic Action (NSCA) (1943) *Pattern for Peace*, Catholic Truth Society, Sydney.

New South Wales Employers' Union (1890) *The Labor Crisis*, W. E. Smith, Sydney.

Norton, J. (1888) *A History of Capital and Labour*, Melbourne.

Palmer, N. (1931) *Henry Bournes Higgins: A Memoir*, George Harrap, London.

Parnaby, J. E. (1951) 'The Economic and Political Development of Victoria 1877–1881', Ph.D. thesis, University of Melbourne.

Parsons, T. G. (1972) 'An Outline of Employer Organisations in the Victorian Manufacturing Industries 1879–1890', *The Journal of Industrial Relations*, 14(1).

Pember Reeves, W. (1902/1969) *State Experiments in Australia and New Zealand*, Macmillan, Melbourne.

Plowman, D. H. (1978) 'Wage Indexation — The Australian Experience', *New Zealand Journal of Industrial Relations*, 3(3).

Plowman, D. H. (1982) 'Employers and Compulsory Arbitration: The Case of the Employers' Federation of New South Wales 1903–1940', Department of Industrial Relations Working Papers, University of New South Wales.

Plowman, D. H. (1985) 'Industrial Legislation and the Rise of Employer Associations , *The Journal of Industrial Relations*, 27(3).

Plowman, D. H. (1986) 'Compulsory Arbitration and National Employer Co-Ordination 1890–1980', Ph.D. thesis, Flinders University.

Plowman, D. H. (1987) 'Economic Forces and the New Right: Employer Matters in 1986', *The Journal of Industrial Relations*, 29(1).

Plowman, D. H. and Smith, G. F. (1986) 'Moulding Federal Arbitration: The Employers and the High Court', *Australian Journal of Management*, 12(2).

Polites, G. (1963) 'Some Observations on the "Total Wage Concept" and "Work Value"', paper prepared for discussion by National Employers' Policy Committee and National Employers' Industrial Committee, ACEF, mimeograph.

Rawson, D. W. (1967) 'The ALP Industrial Groups', in J. E. Isaac and G. W. Ford (eds) *Australian Labour Relations: Readings*, Sun Books, Melbourne.

Report of Royal Commission on Strikes (1891), New South Wales Government Printer, Sydney.

Ross, E. (1970) *A History of the Miners' Federation of Australia*, A.C.S.E.F., Sydney.

Sawer, G. (1956) *Australian Federal Politics and the Law 1901–1929*, Melbourne University Press, Melbourne.

Sawer, G. (1963) *Australian Federal Politics and the Law 1929–1949*, Melbourne University Press, Melbourne.

Sells, J. (1924) 'Industrial Arbitration', *NSW Industrial Gazette*, May.

Shann, E. (1930) *An Economic History of Australia*, Georgian House, Melbourne.

Smith, B. (1885), *Trade Unionism in Victoria or Who Shall Be Master? A Note of Warning to Employers*, Victorian Employers' Union, Melbourne.

Somerville, W. (1926) *Twenty-One Years of Arbitration Court Work*, Western Worker Print, Perth.

Spence, W. G. (1909) *Australia's Awakening: Thirty Years in the Life of an Australian Agitator*, Worker Trustee, Sydney.

Sykes, E. I. and Glasbeek, H. J. (1972) *Labour Law in Australia*, Butterworths, Sydney.

Victorian Chamber of Manufactures (1979) *Enterprise: 100 Years of the V. C. M.*, V.C.M., Melbourne.

Ward, R. (1977) *A Nation for a Continent*, Heinemann, Melbourne.

Wise, B. R. (1909) *The Commonwealth of Australia*, Pitmans, London.

Wright M. (1981) 'Wage Policy and Wage Determination in 1980', *The Journal of Industrial Relations* 23(1).

RECORDS OF ORGANISATIONS

Australian Council of Employers' Federations

ACEF Economic Newsletter 1962–1972

ACEF Circulars 1950–1977

Agenda, Background and Supplementary Papers for Meetings of Executive Council 1960–1977

Agenda, Background and Supplementary Papers for Meetings of Secretaries/Executive Officers 1960–1975

Annual Report 1942–1977

Minutes of ACEF Industrial Committee 1953–1956

Minutes of Annual General Meetings 1942–1977

Minutes of Special General Meeting 28/10/77

Minutes of ACCA–ACMA–ACEF Conference 12/6/43

Minutes of Joint Meeting with ACCA Council of Management 29/4/48

Minutes of Meetings of Executive Committee/Council 1942–1977

Minutes of Meetings of Executive Officers 1966–1973

Minutes of Meetings of General Council

Minutes of Meeting of Secretariat Sub-Committee 17/6/59

Minutes of Meetings of Secretaries 1949–1965

Minutes of Meeting of Special Conference of Representatives of Employers' Federations 15/8/19

Minutes of Special Meeting of Presidents of Federations 12/5/53

Notes of Proceedings of National Tripartite Meeting on the Review of the Commonwealth System of Conciliation and Arbitration

President's Report 1942–1977

Treasurer's Report 1942–1977

Associated Chambers of Manufactures of Australia

Minutes of Industrial Relations Panel 1961–1965

Reports of Industrial Panel to Executive 1961–1965

ACMA Canberra Newsletter 1941–1975

Basic Wage Working Party
Minutes of Meetings 1958–1961

Chamber of Manufactures of New South Wales
Annual Reports 1910–1980
Manufacturers' Bulletin 1932–1948, 1950–1980

Central Council of Employers of Australia
Minutes of Annual Conferences/Conventions 1905–1930
Minutes of Special General Conference 14/11/34
Minutes of Executive Committee 1905–1942
Minutes of Meetings of Secretaries 1923–1926
Minutes of Meeting of Special General Conference 27–29/6/32
Proceedings of Annual Conferences/Conventions 1905–1930, 1934

Central Industrial Secretariat
Agenda, Background and Supplementary Papers to Central Council Meetings 1972–1977
Agenda, Background and Supplementary Papers to Meetings of Executive Officers 1973–1977
Annual Reports 1972–1977
Chairman's Report 1972–1977
CIS Economic Newsletter
Minutes of Central Council Meetings 1972–1977
Minutes of Meetings of Executive Officers 1972–1977
Minutes of Meetings of ACEF/ACMA Working Party 10/5/71
Minutes of Professional Engineers Case Working Party 3/6/73, 23/7/73
Notes of Proceedings of Industrial Peace Conference 11–12/12/71

Committee of Control re Basic Wage and Working Hours
Minutes of Meeting of Representatives of Federated Employers Organisations 11/8/24
Minutes of Meetings of Employers' Committee of Control re Basic Wage case 8/9/24
Minutes of Meeting of Contributors of Employers' Committee of Control re Basic Wage and Working Hours 29/9/26, 16/2/27, 10/8/27

Confederation of Australian Industry
Agenda, Background and Supplementary Papers for Meetings of NEIC Council 1978–1980
Agenda, Background and Supplementary Papers for Meetings of NEIC Officers 1978-1980

Agenda Papers for Meetings of Board of Directors
Auditor's Report 1978–1980
CAI Memoranda and Circulars 1978–1980
Minutes of Annual General Meetings 1978–1980
Minutes of Combined Meeting of NEA and CAI-NEIC 30/6/78
Minutes of Meetings of Board of Directors 1978–1980
Minutes of Meetings of Foundation Members 17/5/78, 2/8/78
Minutes of Meetings of Inaugural/Ordinary Members 30/10/80
Minutes of Meetings of NEIC Council 1978–1980
Minutes of Meetings of NEIC Officers 1978–1980
Minutes of Meetings of Presidents of Foundation Members 26/9/78
Minutes of Pro Tem Office Bearers 1977
NEIC Reports 1978–1980
NETIC Reports 1978–1980

Confederation of Western Australian Industry
Confederation Reports 1978–1980

Federated Employers' Assurance of Western Australia
Directors' Report 1913–1936

Employers' Federation of New South Wales
Annual Reports 1903–1906, 1907–1980
Employers' Review 1928–1980
Industrial Bulletin 1921–1928
Minutes of Meetings of Council 1934–1980
Minutes of Meetings of Executive Committee 1942–1980
Minutes of Annual General Meetings 1942–1980
President's Address 1903–1906, 1907–1980
Reports of Annual Meetings 1903–1906, 1908–1921

Federated Employers' Council of South Australia
Minutes of Council Meetings 1892–1906
Minutes of Meetings of Executive Committee 1892–1906

Interstate Conference of Employers
Minutes of Conference of Representatives of Employer Organisations 30/9/30, 29/9/31, 4/11/31
Minutes of Executive Committee of ICE 18/6/31

Ministry of Labour Advisory Council

Notes on Meeting of Sub-Committee of MLAC and Co-Opted Representatives of Employer and Union Organizations 16/6/55
Notes on MLAC ad hoc meetings 10/2/59 and 29/2/60 (AMIA)
Reports of Meetings of MLAC 1955-1958 (ACEF and AMIA)

National Employers' Associations

Annual Report 1961-1977
Minutes of Annual General Meetings 1961-1977
Minutes of Meetings of National Employers' Associations 1961-1977
Minutes of NEA Officers' Meetings 1961-1977

National Employers' Consultative Committee

Minutes of Meetings 1970

National Employers' Industrial Committee

Minutes of Meetings 1961-1977
National Industrial Arbitration Reports 1961-1977

National Employers' Policy Committee

Agenda, Background and Supplementary Papers for NEPC Meetings 1961-1977
Annual Report 1961-1977
Chairman's Report 1961-1977
Circulars to NEA Contributing Associations
Minutes of Meetings 1961-1977
National Arbitration Reports 1961-1977

South Australian Employers' Federation

Minutes of Annual General Meetings 1907-1952
Minutes of Meetings of Council 1907-1952
Minutes of Meetings of Executive Committee 1907-1952

Sydney Chamber of Commerce

Reports of Annual General Meetings 1890-1907

Victorian Chamber of Manufactures

Minutes of Council Meetings 1884-1975
Minutes of Executive Committee Meetings 1884-1975
Minutes of Industrial Committee 1953-1980
Minutes of Special Meeting of Engineering and Allied Trades Division 20/11/63

Victorian Employers' Federation

Minutes of Annual General Meetings 1903-1950

Minutes of Meetings of Executive Committee 1903-1950

Minutes of Meetings of General Council 1903-1950

Victorian Employers' Union

Minutes of Meeting of Executive Committee 1886-1903

Minutes of General Council 1889-1903

Western Australian Chamber of Manufactures

The Manufacturers' Journal 1933-1936

Industry 1936-1942

The W.A. Manufacturer 1943-1971

Inside Industry 1961-1971

Your Chamber Reporting 1971-1975

Western Australian Employers' Federation

Annual Report 1914-1980

Industrial News 1927-1930, 1950-1978

The Employers' Industrial Digest 1942-1943, 1947-1948

President's Report 1914-1980

Report of Executive Council to Quarterly General Meeting of Employers' Federation 1915-1928

Report of Executive Council to Half-Yearly General Meeting of Employers' Federation 1929-1950

INTERVIEWS

Mr E. Cole, former Industrial Director, Australian Woolgrowers' and Graziers' Council, 15/12/85

Mr J. Dickson, National Secretary-Treasurer, Metal Trades Industry Association, 19/12/85

Mr J. Doohan MLC, former member of AWGC Executive Committee and former President, General Council of Graziers' Association of NSW, 29/10/85

Mr A. Evans, National Director, Metal Trades Industry Association, 17/12/85

Mr R. Fry, former National Director, Metal Trades Industry Association, 24/1/86

Mr M. Grieg, formerly Industrial Director, South Australian Employers' Federation, 28/7/78

Mr A. Howard, former Research/Industrial Officer, CAI, 15/7/80

Mr B Purvis, Executive Director, Australian Wool Selling Brokers' Employers' Federation, 29/1/86

INDEX

Index

Index

Index

Index